DOING FIELDWORK

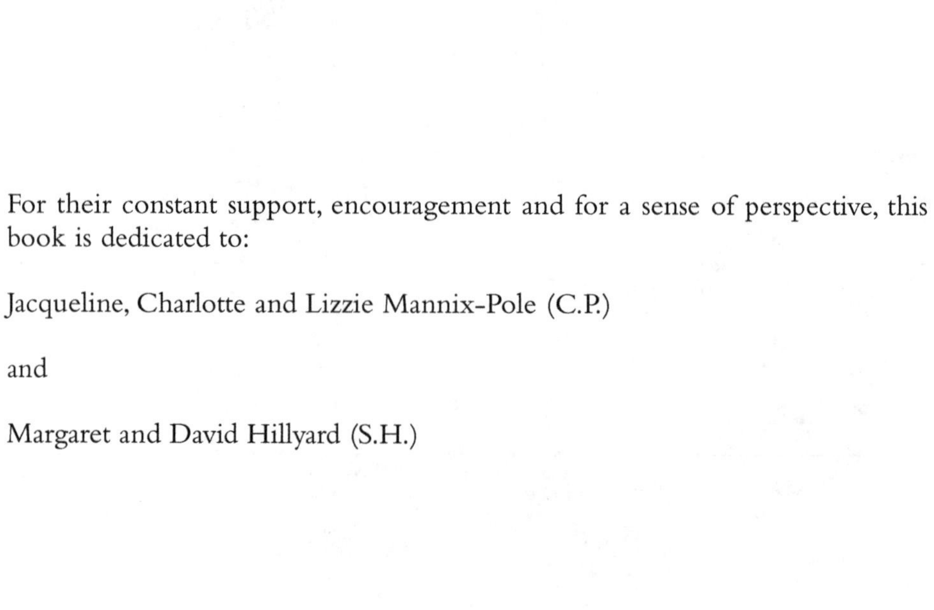

For their constant support, encouragement and for a sense of perspective, this book is dedicated to:

Jacqueline, Charlotte and Lizzie Mannix-Pole (C.P.)

and

Margaret and David Hillyard (S.H.)

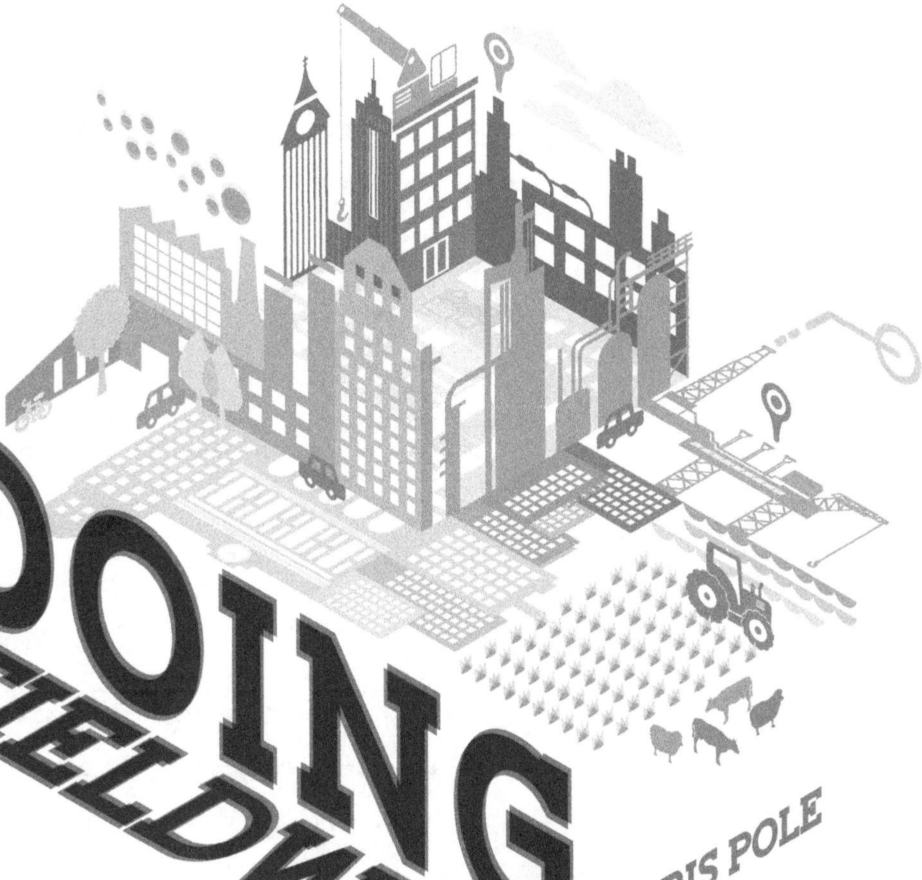

DOING FIELDWORK

CHRIS POLE
SAM HILLYARD

Los Angeles | London | New Delhi
Singapore | Washington DC

Los Angeles | London | New Delhi
Singapore | Washington DC

SAGE Publications Ltd
1 Oliver's Yard
55 City Road
London EC1Y 1SP

SAGE Publications Inc.
2455 Teller Road
Thousand Oaks, California 91320

SAGE Publications India Pvt Ltd
B 1/I 1 Mohan Cooperative Industrial Area
Mathura Road
New Delhi 110 044

SAGE Publications Asia-Pacific Pte Ltd
3 Church Street
#10-04 Samsung Hub
Singapore 049483

Editor: Chris Rojek
Assistant editor: Gemma Shields
Production editor: Katherine Haw
Copyeditor: Bryan Campbell
Proofreader: Rebecca Storr
Indexer: Judith Lavender
Marketing manager: Michael Ainsley
Cover design: Shaun Mercier
Typeset by: C&M Digitals (P) Ltd, Chennai, India

First published 2016

Library of Congress Control Number: 2015939819

British Library Cataloguing in Publication data

A catalogue record for this book is available from the British Library

ISBN 978-0-7619-5963-2
ISBN 978-0-7619-5964-9 (pbk)

CONTENTS

ABOUT THE AUTHORS

Professor Chris Pole is Deputy Vice-Chancellor at the University of Brighton. His long-standing research interests are in social research methodology, especially Ethnography and in the Sociology of Education and Childhood. Previous books in these areas include *Fieldwork* (Four Volumes. Sage Benchmarks in Social Research Methods), *Ethnography for Education* (with Marlene Morrison) and *Young People in Transition. Becoming Citizens?* (with Jane Pilcher and John Williams).

Dr Sam Hillyard is a Reader in Sociology at Durham University, UK. Her research interests are in qualitative research methods, interactionist social theory and rural studies. She is the series editor of *Studies in Qualitative Methodology*, and has published in the area of social research methodology in the journals *Qualitative Research*, *Journal of Contemporary Ethnography* and the *Oxford Review of Education*.

1

WHAT IS FIELDWORK?

Chapter overview

- Fieldwork is an intellectually and technically challenging total experience aimed at capturing meaning.
- Being there first-hand is important.
- Fieldwork is also curiosity-driven – to gain insight and understanding or verstehen.
- In this book we are against methodological fundamentalism, but rather advocate an inclusive approach to fieldwork.

This is a book about doing research. Not any research in general, but a specific kind of research which is as much about the role of the researcher as it is about the focus of the research. The intention is to provide an open and frank account of what it is like to do research: where you, the researcher, are the reason(s) why it will succeed or fail; where you are the main influence on what the research will discover and; how it will be received and evaluated by those who read or use its findings. The idea is that by the end of the book you will have a good idea of the ethos surrounding doing fieldwork – what it's all about and what knowledge it can yield. This includes what this kind of research entails, but also what it's like to do it. We will talk about the excitement of research, the challenges and frustrations, the rewards, the tedium and the sheer hard slog that all research projects involve in different proportions, at one time or another.

The kind of research this book is about is that which is based on *fieldwork*. The idea behind fieldwork is that *it is about getting involved with what and who you are researching*. It is about doing research in a practical, applied, 'hands on' sense. The essence of it is what Robert Park, when he was director of the Chicago School of Sociology, instructed his Chicago undergraduates to do, 'go get the seats of your pants dirty in real research' (Park in Prus 1996: 119). In this sense, fieldwork is about getting out there, wherever there is, and becoming part of what is going on and what you are researching. It is about what Geertz (1988: 1) called 'being there'. But, furthermore, in our digital age, understanding that this may also take place in a virtual research environment where no-face-to-face contact is made but nevertheless co-presence occurs.

However, this is not the full story. By emphasizing 'doing' research in this active (or participatory) sense, we are not suggesting that it is only about running around collecting data. To suggest that is all there is to it would be to reduce research to a set of technical operations. We are not doing what Mills (1959: 74) called 'fetishism of the Concept' and getting stuck with over-elaborations of method (Mills 1959: 74–75). This book is about making sense of, or analysing the data that are collected, about writing and representing the research findings and conclusions. In this sense, it is about the whole package. It is about the research process – from initial ideas and thinking about research, to designing, executing, analysing, writing and finishing research. We also want to emphasize that research based on fieldwork is real research – serious, scholarly and powerful. It can begin to tell us a great deal about things that are strange to us and also encourage us to question and re-examine things that are familiar. Indeed, perhaps the latter is trickier than the former.

In some ways, this is a book which is a celebration of fieldwork. We do not apologize for this, as the reason for writing it is that we believe it is central to social science and has an important role to play in the way in which we try to understand and make sense of the world. However, we are not saying that research based on fieldwork is the only way of doing research or that it should be the only way. Underpinning the approach we take is a belief in the need to fit the research question or problem with the right kind of research methods. Sometimes it will not be obvious which is the right method, but finding out which is, forms part of the research process and can, itself, tell us something about the subject we are researching and the things we value exploring.

WHAT IS FIELDWORK?

So far we have only talked in general terms about fieldwork. Before going any further it is necessary to define it in order that we know what we are concerned with throughout the book. However, as with many things in social science there will be disagreement over the definition of what we argue counts as fieldwork.

To some extent disagreement and debate is positive as it encourages us to think about the thing being defined and to come to an understanding of whatever it is we are concerned with. What we are presenting is our definition of fieldwork and we invite you to consider your own definition against it. If you can't do that now, it may be possible after you have read more of the book or after you have had a go at something you would like to call fieldwork. Having encouraged you to do this, we are not suggesting that anybody's definition of fieldwork is as good as anybody else's. To do this would be to suggest that anything goes, that fieldwork could be both everything and nothing. Whilst we would accept a fairly broad definition, we nevertheless, see it as a specific approach to research, which can be differentiated from approaches which are not fieldwork approaches. Therefore, it is possible to say what fieldwork is and what it is not. So here goes:

What it is: Fieldwork is a way of doing research where the emphasis is placed on the collection of data at first hand by a researcher. It relies on personal interaction or engagement between the researcher and those being researched in the research setting, during which the researcher(s) will use one or a combination of particular methods to collect data over a prolonged period of time.

What it is not: Fieldwork is not the kind of research that relies on a 'scientific' distance between researcher and research subject or object. Through its emphasis upon emersion, it is not research which can be conducted quickly. As a richness of data flows from emersion in the field, neither does fieldwork necessarily look to produce generalizations which cover large populations or groups of people.

The problem of providing definitions, either in terms of what things are or what they are not, is that there are always exceptions and grey areas. By offering these two definitions some of you will now be saying, 'But what about this situation' or 'Does that rule out that method?' Some of you will disagree with our definitions and, implicitly or explicitly, suggest your own. In turn, other people will take issue with your definitions and suggest that they too are ambiguous, exclusionary, too broad and confused. And so it goes on. The best we can hope for in offering these definitions is to identify some general principles, which underpin fieldwork, and to use these in our following discussions. In doing this, we may, ourselves, come to challenge the definitions and so push back the boundaries of what fieldwork is and what it is not. Importantly, we do not see the traditional as static or rooted in the past. So, these debates keep it fresh and better able to engage with changes in society.

RESEARCHING IN THE FIELD AND DOING FIELDWORK

From the definitions it is possible to draw an important distinction between doing fieldwork and working in the field. Whilst fieldwork takes place in the field – albeit a field that is broadly defined – it does not follow that all research which occurs there is fieldwork. In drawing this distinction we are separating location and activity. For example, there are many hundreds of books which describe the use of many different kinds of methods which might be used in the field. Many of these are, in our opinion excellent books that we have both used in teaching research methods (e.g. Berg 2004, Bryman 2012, Greener 2011, Mason 1996, Neuman 2011, Robson 2002, etc.) and doubtless have helped many researchers over the years. In most cases, however, these and many others, remain books about a range of methods, rather than books about fieldwork *per se*. By way of contrast, Burgess (1982, 1984), Delamont (2002), Hammersley and Atkinson (2007), Shaffir and Stebbins (1991) and Wolcott (2005) again to name just a few, address fieldwork as a distinctive approach to research. Whilst such texts may very well draw on a similar range of methods as those outlined in the more general books, it is possible to draw an important distinction between them. Whilst the former are concerned with research tools or techniques, the latter are concerned with a holistic approach *to a particular kind or style of doing research*. It is not the intention to suggest that one of these types of books is qualitatively better than the other, nor to dismiss any out-of-hand. Both approaches have their strengths and weaknesses. The intention is, however, to draw attention to the difference between research methods and research methodology. This merits further explanation. In short, research methods refer to *the range of tools* that the researcher has at his/her disposal. Methodology, meanwhile, is about the way in which the researcher *uses these tools*, the relationship between the tools, the data which they can yield and the knowledge which follows from those data. Applying this distinction to our discussion of fieldwork, we are purporting that fieldwork is a methodology rather than a method. It is simply more than the sum of its parts.

FIELDWORK AS METHODOLOGY

Having made what some might see as lofty claims for fieldwork as a distinctive methodology, we should say more about what it seeks to achieve and what distinguishes it from other approaches to research. This in itself is not easy. As with discussions about what makes ethnography a distinctive approach to research (Atkinson 1990, Brewer 2000, Hammersley 1990, 1992, Hammersley and Atkinson 2007, Pole and Morrison 2003, Walford 2009, Willis and Trondman 2000), the term fieldwork is often used interchangeably with a number of other phrases, which are seen, if not as direct synonyms, then as phrases that describe broadly similar activities. For example, ethnography, case study and qualitative research are all terms used to convey a picture of research that seeks to collect primary data at source, usually on a face-to-face basis. Therefore, in discussing and seeking to define fieldwork, it may be that we are also discussing other forms of research or certain aspects of it.

However, we want to adopt an inclusive approach. That is, our argument is that fieldwork may incorporate these synonyms, for example, an ethnographic approach may be taken to fieldwork, similarly, a case study may be conducted as part of fieldwork and fieldwork is usually based on qualitative research. Consequently, using these terms in place of fieldwork fails to convey all that this might involve. Whilst we would not wish to diminish ethnography or case study research, we would argue that there remains something which sets fieldwork apart from these approaches. In short, this is the capacity of fieldwork to embrace the entire research process and to incorporate research design, method and methodology, field relations, politics and ethics of research, analysis, dissemination and subsequent impact. It is then, a total experience. When we say we are engaging in fieldwork we are by implication taking on all of the above as integral to our research. Moreover, to return to a point made at the very start of this chapter, they are all processes which are mediated at first hand through the researcher.[1]

THE TOTAL EXPERIENCE

It is not our intention to build fieldwork into something which is unattainable or remote from all but the largest, generously-funded research projects. In defining fieldwork as a total experience we would see it as applicable or relevant to research of large and small scale, available to experienced researchers and to students who may be coming to research for the first time as part of their undergraduate studies.

In using the term 'total experience' we are doing two things. Firstly, we are attempting to convey a sense in which doing fieldwork is an absorbing activity by virtue of the involvement that it demands of the researcher, technically in terms of the deployment of particular methods and intellectually in thinking about and planning research strategies. In many respects, fieldwork may be seen as a form of living research. Secondly and closely allied to this, the term total experience relates to the theoretical underpinnings of fieldwork where the intention is to seek to understand whatever is being studied from the perspective of those who are being studied. In order to do this, it will be necessary for the researcher to immerse him/herself in the research setting and to deploy research methods which provide, as far as possible, an insider's view.

Whilst there are many modern commentators who base their work on such a position (e.g. Allan 2012, Atkinson 2005, Delamont and Stephens 2006, Sparkes et al. 2012, to name but a few), the approach may be traced back to that of late nineteenth- and early twentieth-century anthropologists like Powdermaker, Rivers and in particular Malinowski. These pioneers of modern anthropology sought not to rely on the second-hand reports of faraway places from missionaries and travellers, but to see and experience things for themselves. They talked directly to the 'natives'; they lived with them and took part in their everyday lives as well as the festivals, feasts and other less ordinary activities.

FIGURE 1.1

Source: Malinowski (1922) *Argonauts of the Western Pacific*. Plate I The ethnographer's tent on the beach of the Nu'agasi, demonstrating 'life among the natives'.

The intention was that by taking part in the everyday life of the research setting and by participating alongside members of the indigenous population, the researcher(s) would, as far as possible, become members of the social setting which they were studying. In an original anthropological sense, therefore, the notion of fieldwork could be taken quite literally, that it was work (research) conducted in a field (rural location).

The idea of sailing away to uncharted, faraway lands to study unknown or little-known people, lends to fieldwork a degree of exoticism in which the anthropologist (fieldworker) may be cast as explorer, swashbuckler or pioneer. This may have been the case at the turn of the twentieth century when foreign travel was rare and many parts of the planet remained inaccessible to Westerners. It is now, in a globalized context, little more than a caricature perpetuated largely by Hollywood heroes like Indiana Jones! Few of today's fieldworkers would see themselves in such a role.

The advent of relatively cheap and easy international travel has meant that few places in the world – physically or culturally – remain inaccessible to the tourist, let alone the intrepid anthropologist or researcher. In addition, a rethink about the ethical and political relationship between the 'visiting' anthropologist or fieldworker and the indigenous population, has led to a greater emphasis on researchers in what might previously have been seen as faraway places, researching their own societies. The world has, in effect, become a much smaller place. This more local approach to fieldwork was typified by the work of the Chicago School of Sociology, who produced many studies of everyday events in Chicago during the early decades of the twentieth century (e.g. Anderson 1923, Polsky 1967, Shaw 2013 [1930], Thrasher 1927). Their approach was to treat the relatively new phenomenon of the city of Chicago, with which they were familiar, in the same way as the anthropologist would treat the faraway locations. In doing this, the Chicago sociologists were instrumental in encouraging an approach that challenged the familiar and looked beyond what was often taken for granted within their own society.

In the words of Burgess (1982) as the twentieth century progressed, anthropology came home. By this, he refers to the fact that although traditional 'faraway' anthropology has declined, ironically, the research methods and the general approach are now more common than ever. Researchers may no longer travel to the islands of the South Pacific to gather data and try to understand 'exotic' and remote communities in the way that they did at the start of the twentieth century, but they are now more likely to be found 'at home' in their own communities practising fieldwork. For some modern day fieldworkers, the homecoming meant that they studied whole communities. Classic examples being Stacey's (1960) study and restudy (Stacey et al. 1975) of Banbury, or Frankenberg's (1957) study of a north Wales village. Here, the approach to what became known as the community study was, and in many respects remains (Payne 1996), very similar to that taken by the anthropologists working in the islands of New Guinea. The principles of working (and living) alongside the 'natives' did not vary with the location, be it Banbury or the South Pacific. The objective of understanding the location (the field) at first hand, from the inside remained the same.

Transporting the principles of anthropological fieldwork a little further, the approach did not always have to be applied to a field in a rural or geographical sense. The 'coming home' of anthropology meant that research based on fieldwork became common in what in some sense, were much smaller or more tightly defined fields. For example, the definitions of a school or a factory, a football stadium or a family as a field, meant that researchers could apply anthropological techniques to situations with which they were often very familiar. In this respect, it could be argued that the late-twentieth-century emphasis on the ordinary or the familiar research setting, as opposed to the exotic or the unfamiliar, limited the scope of fieldwork. However, such an argument emphasizes technical issues of geography and location over methodological and theoretical issues. Although fieldwork is now more commonly found in the researcher's own 'back yard', the principles which underpin its use remain largely unaltered. The concern is to understand the field and those who 'inhabit' it from the inside. So even in 'ordinary' surroundings, exploring the total experience remains the objective.

FAMILIAR AND STRANGE

The fieldworker born and bred in Birmingham, UK would doubtless regard an opportunity to conduct research in a village located within the Amazon Rain forests as an opportunity to observe and experience the 'exotic' and the unfamiliar. Similarly, a researcher from the Amazon Rain Forest is also likely to regard the prospect of conducting research in Mosely or Solihull in the same way. The concept of the exotic or the strange is of course relative. The fieldworker can also find themselves responding differently to the field, Atkinson (2012), for example, recounted 'doing fieldwork in the opera company':

> I went on tour with them. I spent a great deal of time observing rehearsals and a few performances watching from the stage wings and observing backstage activity. I hung out in the offices of some of the administrative staff. I got in the way in the props department. It was one of the best possible periods of field research [...] a rare opportunity to study performances at first hand (Atkinson 2012: 44).

Even sustained fieldwork in Birmingham is personal and emotive, as Moore (1977) recounted of his seminal study with Rex on race relations in the Sparkbrook:

> For a year I ate, breathed and slept Sparkbrook. I made new friends, made and dissolved relationships, took sides in conflicts, had problems with my landlady and went to parties [...] [The] demands on emotions are certainly felt very acutely when one is working in the field of race relations [...] The most beguiling interview was with a dim and amiable young prostitute who said as we parted that if I wanted to know any more about her work I should call at her place 'anytime' (Moore 1977: 87, 88).

The definition of what is exotic or strange depends on the particular circumstances of whoever is defining the situation. In the same way, the definition of familiar is contingent upon the same things. However, the concepts of strangeness and familiarity are central to an understanding of fieldwork and what it attempts to achieve. So it becomes important to think about what these concepts mean and how they work in fieldwork practice.

The researcher from Birmingham perceives the rainforest village as strange because it is unfamiliar. He/she does not have to try very hard to think of questions to ask about what he/she sees, hears and experiences because they are different and unfamiliar. Similarly, the researcher from the village in an Amazon rainforest is likely to find Birmingham strange and will, therefore, have many questions to ask of what he/she sees and experiences. This is part of our everyday thinking – what interactionists see as our making-sense of the world around us. However, to suggest that our capacity to ask questions about a particular location or institution or process depends on how well we know it, is to oversimplify things. For example, we have all been to school, but how many of us can say that we understand fully the way in which a school works? Or perhaps even more basic than that, most of us will live with, or have lived with, other people at some stage of our lives, as part of a family – in the many forms they can appear – but who can claim to fully understand the role of the family in all its different forms in the twenty-first century? We may all have personal experience of a school or family, but that does not mean that we know everything there is to know about them. Moreover, it is likely that we know about those situations from a particular vantage point, say as a pupil or a youngest son or daughter. How different does a primary school seem from the position of the head teacher or the caretaker? Similarly, how does the family seem from the perspective of a great grandmother, a father, a stepmother or an adopted brother?

These examples of where we may find the present-day researcher, studying a family or a school, suggest that fieldwork can be *as much about situations which are familiar to us as it can about those which are strange*. This is an important point, given the sheer scale and pace at which contemporary life is moving and working. We would argue, therefore, that the essence of fieldwork relates to the capacity of the fieldworker to pose questions about whatever situation or location he/she finds him/herself in. In some cases this may appear easy because everything is new and unfamiliar or strange. In others it may appear very difficult because everything is all-too familiar. In both situations there are problems and challenges, the fieldworker's job remains the same – *to attempt to get to the essence of what is happening.* This may mean making familiar situations strange by asking questions about everyday activities and situations. For example, in the context of the school we may wish to pose questions, which on the face of it seem a little strange, but actually succeed in getting to the heart of what happens everyday and which we take for granted. This is taking things apart in order to get a better picture of how they work together. For example:

- Why does the head teacher have their own office when other teachers do not?
- Why are the children grouped by age for lessons?
- Who decided that it would be a good idea to read the plays of Shakespeare?
- Why do we have prefects or houses?

Or in the context of the family:

- Why do I live with my brother and sister and not with my cousins?
- Why does dad pay towards the upkeep of the house although he doesn't live here anymore?
- Why does mum do most of the cooking and the housework?
- Why do my teenage daughters argue so much?

At first glance we may think that we know the answers to these questions, that they are obvious and not worth serious consideration. However, if we stop to think about our everyday lives – about what we do almost automatically, every day and why we do it – our familiar world starts to become less familiar.

We start to 'exoticize' or problematize everyday occurrences and to treat as strange those things we may have always regarded as so familiar. For many present day fieldworkers, the research task rests on their capacity to ask challenging questions, not to take things for granted and to look beneath what we may have always regarded as ordinary. Given that we are part of the social world we want to study, that is neither easy nor straightforward.

There are, of course, many anthropologists who continue to conduct fieldwork in faraway places, where most things are unfamiliar to them. Essentially, however, we would argue that wherever fieldwork is conducted, it is seeking to achieve the same things:

- To observe and experience at first-hand what is happening
- To examine the significance of events and activities, beliefs and rituals (including the mundane and the ordinary) to people involved
- To examine the ways in which activities and events, beliefs and rituals relate to each other and to the participants in the location
- To look for the significance and meaning of social behaviour
- To look below the surface of events and activities, beliefs and rituals for patterns and theories which can begin to explain social life in ways which go beyond the particular fieldwork location

As with the early and the present-day anthropologist, the fieldworker is driven by curiosity, by a desire to understand, to be there, as things happen and to use what he/she sees, hears and experiences to begin to explain social behaviour. Whilst this broad remit for fieldwork may be traced back to anthropology, the process by which anthropology 'came home' means that fieldwork is now a research process which is applicable to many disciplines. The fieldworker may be an anthropologist, a sociologist, an economist, a geographer or a member of one of many more disciplines which have primary research as their core. Whichever label the fieldworker attaches to his/her intellectual identity, we would argue the basic tenets of fieldwork remain the same. We should also add that fieldwork is defined here as an approach to doing research, whereas ethnography, for example, uses fieldwork. In this sense, it is the activity, the research process, the total experience which defines fieldwork rather than the discipline to which it is applied.

DOING FIELDWORK

In attempting to define fieldwork as a particular approach to research by identifying characteristics and objectives which distinguish it from approaches to social research which are not based on fieldwork, we have pointed to particular forms of research practice. Underpinning this research practice is the intention to understand at first hand what is happening in the particular field of study – to encounter that climate or environment. To do this the field-worker uses a range of different methods which allow him/her access to the interior world of those who populate that particular setting or field. For example, Sarah Pink's work on both visual and sensory ethnography (Pink 2012, 2013) has continued and extended moves by ethnographers to appreciate the embodied and emotional characteristics of fieldwork (cf. Coffey 1999, Madison 2011). Pink (2012) is clear in her own use of visual techniques as well as in her reflections upon their use that they are tools helping to achieve a rich and detailed understanding of a fieldwork site. Therefore, it remains important to reflect upon who took (or, to use Becker's term, made) any visual images that make up a portfolio of fieldwork data and contributed to an understanding of a research site. So, in a 'tour' of a locale in Wales using visual data, Pink (2008: 193) outlined how she sought to share the 'emplaced' feel of that environment and how visual techniques were instrumental to that process:

> the tour can be understood as an ethnographic pathway which, through its entanglements with the pathways of others, gathered memories, imaginings and the immediate present though multiple modes and media (Pink 2008: 193).

Pink (2008) used visual and sensory ethnography here to capture the sense of belonging and space in the locality of Mold, Flintshire, UK but we would argue they can be applied to a wide range of settings, including virtual settings. Again, the work of the early anthropologists and particularly Malinowski is relevant here in offering guidance on the principled use of fieldwork techniques. This is important because photographs and visual data are only artefacts that facilitate fieldwork, they are not fieldwork in themselves.

In 1922, in the introduction to his most celebrated work *Argonauts of the Western Pacific* and in a chapter entitled 'How an anthropologist works in the field', Malinowski outlined the preconditions for effective ethnography. For Malinowski, fieldwork and ethnography were synonymous. Whilst we may now wish to argue the differences between the two, and we would personally suggest that rather than being synonymous they are in fact facilitative, as fieldwork is the research approach used in the conduct of ethnography. Therefore, Malinowski's (1922: 6) three preconditions for effective ethnography offer a useful guide for our consideration of fieldwork:

- The student must possess real scientific aims and know the values and criteria of modern ethnography.
- He ought to put himself [sic] in good conditions of work, that is, in the main to live without white men, right among the natives.
- He [sic] has to apply a number of special methods of collecting, manipulating and fixing his evidence.

If we translate these preconditions into their present-day equivalents then we can see that Malinowski's concern was to facilitate access for the fieldworker to as much of the life of the research setting (the field) as possible. The conditions he identified centred largely around the researcher him/herself adopting appropriate behaviour, having particular abilities like languages and the capacity to blend in with the situation by spending time with the subjects[2] of the research. In addition, his preconditions highlight the need for a genuine and legitimate reason for conducting the research. His reference to possessing real scientific aims can be seen as a warning against research which is perhaps more voyeuristic than scientific. Moreover, some technical pre-requisites are identified to facilitate the effective collection of data. Like Malinowski, we need good access to key informants; we would need to be able to speak the language of those we are studying. For Malinowski this meant quite literally learning a new language in order to communicate directly with informants and not having to rely on translators. For present-day fieldworkers there may well be the need to speak additional languages, particularly where cross-cultural fieldwork (Pole and Burgess 2000) is conducted, but alternatively language may refer to a particular kind of speech or argot. For example, Hockey (1986) conducted intensive fieldwork with new recruits to the British Army. In order to understand much of the argot which passed between the squaddies, Hockey had to 'tune in' to a form of language often constituted by slang, sexual innuendo, swearing and mickey-taking. In short, he learned the language of the young soldier.

Similarly, we can see in Delamont's (in Atkinson et al. 2008) fieldwork the unravelling of not only the terms used to capture the Brazilian martial art form of capoeira, but the nuances in the teaching of capoeira across instructors. For Delamont, a highly experienced fieldworker, unlocking the complexities of this social form and its political context was deeply challenging (Delamont 2009). In the case of fieldwork conducted in single locations, the researcher would not necessarily be pulled into political debates, but Delamont's immersion and the knowledge that her fieldwork yielded led her to understand that the very status of capoeira in the UK was shot-through with wider concerns (see 2009). In addition, fieldworkers also need to be able to observe and experience the everyday activities and social rhythms of the field in which they are researching (indeed, why capoeira classes always start late). This means that they are not just interested in the spectacular or the unusual (though as Delamont notes, this can be useful in getting to know a research field) but in the ordinary and the mundane. For Malinowski, as for the fieldworker a century later, this emphasizes the need to spend prolonged periods of time in the field, to witness at first-hand the range of activities which shape the life of the community. For an opera house, it may be the rehearsals and intense background preparations before a new performance is staged (Atkinson 2005). For a gamekeeper, it would have to be the habitat, predation control and feeding routines that underpin preparations for the game-shooting season (Hillyard and Burridge 2012). Above all, Malinowski's preconditions are about enabling fieldworkers to get close to what they are researching, to see for themselves what is going on and to understand as far as possible from the perspective of an insider. To achieve these same things, the modern fieldworker uses a range of research methods that traditionally have involved face-to-face contact. In particular, these techniques include: observation and participant observation, interviews and conversational techniques, life histories, documentary analysis and the use of various sources of visual data including photographs, works of art and artefacts. Each of these is an active method in which the fieldworker is central to the data collection process. Unlike research which is based on questionnaire or survey techniques, fieldwork methods facilitate direct interface between the researcher and the researched. We also need to acknowledge here Savage and Burrows' (2007, 2009) call for empirical sociology to engage more seriously with what they term 'social transactional data' (Savage and Burrows 2007: 885). Their call is for sociologists to take more seriously the kind of digital data that capitalism now yields (such as new social media; archives not presently available to the academic and; the 'scraping' of unrestricted data from sources such as Facebook). They call for sociologists 'to get their hands "dirty" by exploring the potential of such methods and issues posed by their use' (Savage and Burrows 2009: 766–7). These new forms of media are important because they are new means by which people associate and construct their social worlds (Lawler 2013). But, we would also reiterate that pictures and artefacts facilitate fieldwork but they are not fieldwork in themselves. So, for example, Smith's (2012) use of CCTV footage of Aberdeen city and the working environment of the operators of that city's cameras is not fieldwork although it offers an insight into social action in the city, both malignant and benign. The proliferation of social data is a resource that can be used by fieldworkers and we attach great importance to it, as have many social scientists in their analyses in the past,[3] where new inroads were made into understanding the 'politics of [such] methods' (Savage and Burrows 2007: 885). Yet with fieldwork, you cannot hide behind the white coat of a laboratory scientist, the software of the social statistician and distanced manipulation of digital datasets.

Fieldwork is a human method dependent to a great extent on the social and interpersonal skills of the researcher. In this respect, this very human character of fieldwork makes it an unpredictable approach to research. The journey or apprenticeship involved in becoming a good fieldworker has been discussed elsewhere (Delamont 2002, 2009). Whilst it is important for fieldwork to be carefully planned in advance of entering the field, there are limits to which this is possible. Social life is difficult to predict and the fieldworker must maintain a degree of flexibility in his/her work. Unlike the experimental scientist, he/she needs to react and adapt to situations as they occur rather than stick rigidly to a set research procedure in the interests of uniformity and a notion of scientific replication and reliability. For the fieldworker, the intention is not to impose a restrictive framework on the research which must be adhered to, come what may. This is one of fieldwork's strengths, in that it has – at its very core – the capacity to be flexible and move to explore something unanticipated.

Given the aim of understanding social processes from the inside, the field-worker seeks not to influence the situations or the behaviour that he/she is researching. In this simplistic sense, it is a naturalistic approach to collecting data which attempt, as far as possible, to capture the reality of the situation from the perspective of those being researched. So, rather than a concern with objectivity, we might claim that fieldwork is concerned with subjectivity. This statement may seem to run counter to those in many 'general methods' text-books, which advocate the centrality of objectivity to social research (see Cooper et al. 2012, for a very clear introduction and overview by Hammersley). However, by referring to subjectivity in this context we are not suggesting or advocating that the fieldworker provides an account of events merely to suit his/her own prejudices or ideas about the situation being researched. By using the term subjectivity, we refer to one of the key reasons for conducting field-work, that is *to capture the significance and meaning of a situation, a set of events or whatever is being researched for the people (social actors) who are taking part in those events.* In this sense it is subjective insofar as it seeks to capture and portray the internal reality of the situation being researched. The fieldworker will unavoidably influence the field setting at some level, wittingly or otherwise. The issue then is to account for this in their analysis and reflexive discussion. Returning to our earlier example of the school-based research may help to clarify the point.

In seeking to understand the way in which a primary school operated by identifying some everyday activities, we may wish to examine or observe these activities from a number of different perspectives. For example, if we wished to understand the significance of the assembly to the life of the school we may see it as important to not only observe and take part in the assembly but also to talk to different participants about their experience of it. On doing so, we might collect a range of views. For example, the head teacher may see it as important in bringing the whole school together, providing a sense of collective identity for the pupils and teachers and at the same time an opportunity to recognize and celebrate the achievements of the school (this might be to reward individual pupils, say goodbye to school-leavers or to congratulate the school on displays arranged for the village flower festival or suchlike). From the perspective of the new arrivals in a small, rural primary school, this might be an exciting experience where they use the biggest room in the school and when the whole school (and bigger children) and even their mum and dad might attend. From the perspective of the caretaker, the assembly may simply be a nuisance. All the chairs and benches for teachers and parents have to be put out and then collected in, the floor to be re-polished after the children have walked on it in muddy shoes and the room re-organized for lunch-time.

The task of the fieldworker, therefore, is to collect these different experiences in the round (all of which represent a particular subjective view based on the different positions of the different actors) and then to analyse them in accordance with the context within which they were collected and the perspective from which they were expressed. In this situation, there may be no single objectivity possible. All the different views are subjective, based on the position of those expressing them, *but all are valid and important.* It is the role of the fieldworker, therefore, to collect and portray these different perspectives in the understanding of the school which he/she seeks to convey. In addition, as the fieldworker will have witnessed the school assembly at first hand, he/she will also be able to add his/her own perspective on the event. This will be useful not only in adding another perspective on the assembly, but also in providing something against which the other perspectives can be compared. In some respects, the fieldworker's view may be seen as one which is not shaped by vested interest or by him/her having a specific position in the school such as head teacher, pupil or caretaker. However, it will remain subjective in that it is the fieldworker's interpretation of events that he/she has observed and participated in. By being there, the fieldworker also, of course, becomes part of the social action being researched. Although he/she may take steps to minimize any direct impact or interference on the setting, the very fact of his/her presence means the situation has changed and it is therefore vital that the fieldworker adopt a reflexive stance throughout their fieldwork (see Atkinson 1990: 2 for an excellent definition of reflexivity).

It is worth reiterating at this point that fieldwork is an approach to research which requires the fieldworker, if not to take part, then to be there – or rather to immerse themselves in what action is taking place. Consequently, who the researcher is may have an impact on the interpretation he/she brings to the events witnessed and also on the extent to which and in what capacity it is possible to participate in events. For example, characteristics such as gender, ethnicity, age and social class may affect the role a fieldworker might play in any given situation. In Dunning et al.'s (1986) research into football hooliganism, John Williams as the principal fieldworker, needed to be there when violence occurred. He needed to blend in with the 'hooligans', to run with them and to experience, as far as possible, their emotions as the violence ensued. In order to do this, Williams needed to be male, young and fit. In addition he needed other attributes which enabled him to blend into a male, largely working-class group of football supporters. Things like accent (Williams has an identifiable Liverpudlian accent), knowledge of football and the right kinds of clothes, all went to help Williams in his quest to be there.

There are many more examples of attempts to blend in and be acceptable, some of which we will draw on in Chapter 4 where we discuss participant observation. The point to be made here is that in doing fieldwork, the field-worker's role is both facilitated and constrained by his/her own social, physical and emotional characteristics. In short, it is his/her identity that is fundamental to the whole fieldwork experience.

FIELDWORK AND THEORY

By now we hope to have established that fieldwork, in the way that we have defined and portrayed it, rests upon the capacity to understand situations as defined from the perspective of the insider. This in itself is a theoretical position based on Weber's (1949) notion of *verstehen* (by which we mean empathy or understanding). In addition, we have also discussed issues of objectivity and subjectivity in relation to the accounts of particular events that the fieldworker gathers and the interpretations brought to them. We have asserted that field-work is about *finding ways to portray the subjective reality of social action in terms of its meaning for the social actors.* Putting these two conceptual issues together we move towards a broad theoretical position for fieldwork research which is based upon interpretivism. By this we mean that fieldwork facilitates an approach to understanding the social world, which is based upon the interpretation of social action from the position of the social actors who create or construct that action. Whilst interpretivism is a broad church (which we like), fieldwork is not an approach to research which will facilitate large generalizations or social trends and behaviour across large populations. Rather, the way we see it, fieldwork is an approach which says: let's see how people shape the situations which con-stitute their lives; let's see what things mean and how they work out for the people involved in a particular social situation. It is curiosity-driven in the sense that it is exploratory, but it values people's own accounts of their everyday lives and their own actions and words.

This characterization of fieldwork is an approach which emphasizes inter-pretation, social construction and meaning. Together with the idea of subjectivity (in the way that we discussed it earlier) this locates fieldwork within a micro-sociology framework of social research. By this we wish to infer that for the fieldworker, the concern is with discrete social behaviour rather than large-scale social structures. This is not to say that the fieldworker ignores structure, far from it. It is, however, fair to say that fieldwork focuses on the ways in which structures are constructed, interpreted and made meaningful to the lives of those who live within them or who construct them. It is the performance of structures in the everyday realm which is of interest. In terms of its general theoretical orientation, therefore, we see fieldwork emphasizing social action and individual agency. This is important as it directly links the kinds of research methods upon which the fieldworker may draw and the desire to understand social behaviour from the inside. For us, the two flow into one another. The use of participant observation, observation, conversation techniques and documentary analysis, in short, the fact of placing a value on being there and seeing/experiencing at first hand is what defines the theoretical orientation of fieldwork.

SUMMARY

Our characterization of fieldwork in this opening chapter has attempted to raise a number of issues which will help to facilitate an understanding not only of how fieldwork is done, but also to begin to understand what it can achieve in terms of producing knowledge and understanding of the social world. We are not arguing that fieldwork is in itself a theoretical position – it is too broad for that. What we are saying, however, is that fieldwork lends itself to a particular way of attempting to understand the social world, how it is constructed and what it means to those who construct it. By this we are not rejecting the importance of large-scale macro theories of the social world, we see these as having an important role to play in explaining social structures and organizations of a different scope. Indeed, some large-scale trends demand exploration at the local level. Our view is that fieldwork is an approach best applied to facilitate an understanding of the ways in which people experience social systems and structures and how they, in turn, may influence them. It recognizes the structural limitations and constraints which are placed on free will and individual action, but rather than seeing these as the sole determinants of the ways in which individuals or groups live their lives, it seeks to recognize – even celebrate – the importance of human interaction.

Research based on fieldwork is, therefore, attempting to understand the significance of social structure from the perspective of the individual social actor. It is about being there, wherever the social action is, at home or faraway. Fieldwork is about doing and being. It can be tremendously rewarding, frustrating, fun, dull, exciting and ordinary. It can be all of these things because it is about life – the way people make it and how it is experienced.

NOTES

1 Although this mediation can also take place in virtual environments.
2 We discuss scales of participation and the importance of power in Chapter 3.
3 For example, Dingwall (1977), Travers (2007).

FURTHER READING

Hammersley H and Atkinson P (2007, 3rd edition) *Ethnography*. London: Routledge. (Chapter 1 and prologue to the third edition.)

Any text or article from the shortlist for the BBC/BSA Ethnography Award.

Sampson H (2013) *International Seafarers and Transnationalism in the Twenty-first Century*. Manchester: Manchester University Press. (2014 award winner.)

2

FINDING THE FIELD

Chapter overview

- Finding the field is both a conceptual and locational ambition.
- Gaining an insider's view is a key objective.
- Fieldwork 'at home' can be harder than fieldwork conducted in strange or exotic settings.
- Immersion is a key principle, as is the importance of finding a research role to build – and maintain – a strong rapport.
- Flexibility and adaptability are essential fieldwork skills.

Having established what is meant by fieldwork and before moving on to examine some of the principal research methods which it utilizes it is important to spend some time reflecting on the ways in which fieldworkers define their field of enquiry and how they secure access to it.

Looking back to the work of the early anthropologists once more we might surmise that for them the question of how to define the field was not so difficult. The general lack of information about far away locations, the unavailability of long-distance travel to all but the very intrepid or the foolhardy, meant that anthropology had a role not only in satisfying scientific curiosities but also in a more general desire to know about faraway lands. For the present-day anthropologist, as we have already said, the situation is very different and that in Burgess' (1984) words, anthropology has now come home. Whilst there is much evidence to corroborate this view, given the wealth of studies having been conducted in recent years into all manner of seemingly ordinary or everyday situations, this does not take us very far in understanding how the present-day fieldworker comes to identify the field in which they might work.

RESEARCHING THE FAMILIAR

For some researchers, the identification of an appropriate field for research is straightforward. Much of present-day research based on fieldwork has been conducted in settings with which the researcher has some familiarity for one reason or another. For example, studies located within a particular institution or which focus on a specific occupation may reflect the past experience of the researcher. Heley (2011) was a 'local boy' who returned to the village in which his family had resided for centuries to conduct fieldwork in that same community. Walford (2004) used his adoption of the role of University Procter as an opportunity to conduct an autoethnography. Roderick (2006) used his background as a former professional footballer as a means to explore professional football in his sociology of work monograph.

There are many other examples upon which we could draw where the researcher chooses to revisit situations with which he/she is very familiar, but then seeks a different view of what may previously have been taken for granted. In these situations one might surmise that the identification of the field was based upon the previous experience of the researcher – a desire to look at familiar situations differently and to pose the kinds of questions which they were perhaps unable to pose when they were living and/or working in that environment.

For many other researchers, however, there was not such a direct link between themselves and the area in which they chose to conduct their fieldwork. For example, Foster's (1990) *Villains*, which examined petty crime and general low life in south London, was conducted without any first-hand experience either of the geographical area or of petty crime on the part of Foster. Similarly, Barker's (1984) study of a religious cult, the Moonies, was conducted at the invitation of that church and did not draw on any first-hand experience of the Moonies which Barker had prior to starting the research. Distinctly, US-based sociologist Loïc Wacquant immersed himself in the boxing world – within which he was considered an unlikely member – to conduct a rich, longitudinal ethnography (Wacquant 2003). Delamont's research on capoeira, alongside Stephens, required collaborative and extended field observations. This was essential in order to not only engage with the language and terminology surrounding the Brazilian dance and martial art, but also its form, practice and the nuances between its performance (Stephens and Delamont 2010). There are many more examples of this kind, where researchers do not have first-hand experience and, consequently, may be regarded as strangers to the field.

Whether the researcher has first-hand experience of the field or not, the objective remains the same. The fieldwork is conducted with the intention of collecting information which provides a detailed insider's view of whatever occurs within the field. In the broadest sense it is this curiosity that drives the research and it is not dependent on prior experience. In order for there to be a curiosity, however, it is likely that the researcher will have some familiarity with the field. As we have seen, this may not be familiarity at first hand, but may be based on a range of things which have originally ignited the imagination; for example, reading accounts of previous research in the area, attending lectures or talking with researchers who have previously conducted research that was of interest. Whatever the reason, there is usually something, let's call it a spark, which acts as the catalyst for the research. In this sense, we would argue that the researcher always has a degree of familiarity with the field. Moreover, we would go so far as to say that without that familiarity, then fieldwork would be difficult and perhaps impossible. The familiarity, whether gained from reading and studying accounts of previous research or from first-hand acquaintance with the field, is important in guiding the fieldwork in terms of identifying a focus and identifying strategies for the most effective means of collecting data. As we noted in the opening chapter in our discussion of Malinowski's principles, the ability to ask good questions in fieldwork is important. In addition, a degree of familiarity may be particularly useful when seeking to gain access to the field.

WHAT AND WHERE IS THE FIELD?

In order to conduct fieldwork, the researcher has to gain access to the field. The importance of being there and experiencing the field – as near as possible as a participant – places great emphasis not on merely gaining access but also gaining the right kind of access. By this, we mean the kind of access that allows the fieldworker to take part, to question and to observe at close quarters, the range of activities, structures and interactions that constitute the field. Expressed another way, to immerse themselves in the field.

In emphasizing the importance of gaining access to the field we refer not merely to the field as a location (for example, a school, a police station or a specific geographical area), but also in terms of the focus of the research. Any specific setting such as a school or a police station is likely to present the researcher with a wide range of issues and topics upon which to focus his/her research. It would be impossible to study all of them in detail. However, the research process is such that it is unlikely and in most cases we would say unwise, for the researcher to identify the location and then begin searching for a focus within it. As we have already argued, all research requires the foundation of a clear rationale, and as part of this is a need for a clear focus. In identifying and seeking access to the field, therefore, we are concerned not merely with the physical location in which the research is to be based, but also with a conceptual notion of field. By this we mean the way in which the focus of the research is identified and defined. Returning to an example may be useful in elaborating this point.

Whilst we might identify a particular school as an appropriate location for fieldwork this in itself does not take us very far. A school is a complex organization, which presents an opportunity to study many issues. In identifying the field, therefore, our concern is to identify a specific topic or set of themes within the location. For example, Bagley and Hillyard (2011) in their research in two rural villages focused upon the role of the school in fostering a sense of community (or not) as a means to refine their explorations. Other ethnographers, when conducting research in schools, have focused upon a particular group within that setting. Hillyard (2003) for example shadowed one form-group in their first year at secondary school. Allan (2009, 2012) forged a close fieldwork relationship with girls at an elite school in their senior years, including spending time with them outside of the school environment. Clifton (2007) was looking specifically at a sample of the school population – army kids – and hence drew in themes about school provision and policy, but also the wider framework of the institution of the Army. Similarly, other educational researchers have been focused upon particular aspects of school work, such as homework. So, the fieldwork and data collection may not always, nor necessarily, take place in the institution within which the focus was initially provided.

In each case, the field was identified in terms of the substantive focus of the research and also the physical location, in these cases, the schools. Whilst there is a close relationship between location (the schools) and substantive focus, in each of these examples the field is defined primarily in terms of the substantive focus. The location is central to the way in which the research is conducted, to the collection of data and to the conclusions drawn from it, but in each case, it is fair to say that other locations could have been chosen whilst the substantive focus was maintained.

In finding the field and gaining access, therefore, the researcher is concerned with the interplay of locational, technical and conceptual issues. Only when an acceptable fit between these three concerns has been achieved can a field for the research be said to have been identified.

LOOKING FOR A WAY IN

Identifying the conceptual field in which to locate your research will mean engaging with the literature in your chosen field. For example, making use of libraries and archives to find out what previous research has been conducted in your area of interest and what has been written. In this way you will become familiar with current debates and also the way in which what is known about your topic has changed and developed over time. As Atkinson and Housely (2003) remind us, it's really important to avoid reinventing the wheel because you have not conducted sufficient reading before undertaking your field research. This process of familiarization and focusing may take a long time.

Whilst it may be something you set out to do as a distinct part of the research process, it may also be something that develops as your interest in an area develops. The idea is that by engaging with literature and ideas that inform your area you begin to identify a substantive or conceptual focus for your research. It is likely, however, that the focus will continue to be defined as the research progresses: that it shifts or that additional foci may also emerge. This is all part of the uncertainty of social research and also part of its richness. Nevertheless, we would argue that before fieldwork can be said to have commenced in any formal sense, you are already thinking about and refining your ideas. This may even be before a specific location is identified, because it is important to have a good idea of what you intend to focus upon. It is at this stage – when considerable thought has already been invested – that fieldwork, in both a locational and conceptual sense, may proceed.

Identifying the conceptual field and gaining access to the locational field involve quite different research skills. However, as we have seen, they are both integral to the conduct of fieldwork. Where identifying the conceptual field relies on traditional study skills based on library research, identifying the locational field often depends on the researcher's capacity to negotiate, to appear convincing and to be persuasive towards those who may grant access to the location. It is also important that we flag up here that access is a long and on-going process in fieldwork, because it is about establishing and maintaining a rapport. We say more about this later.

IDENTIFYING THE CONCEPTUAL FIELD

As we have said, identifying the conceptual field involves engaging with ideas, theories and previous research conducted in a particular area of interest. The objective is to come gradually to a clear idea of what to focus your fieldwork on. In this context, Glaser and Strauss (1967) introduce the idea of progressive focusing. By this, they refer to a process in which the researcher(s) starts with an idea of the general area in which he/she wishes to work and then by a process of interrogating the literature, conducting preliminary data collection, posing questions about the data and what is already known about the area, it is possible to arrive at a focus.

In identifying the conceptual field, the intention is to highlight the area in which we intend our research should make a contribution to knowledge. In this sense, the process by which this is achieved relates back to our discussions in Chapter 1 about identifying the rationale for the research. At this early stage, the focus is not cast in stone and may be refined as the research progresses. Moreover, identifying the conceptual field is of direct relevance to the locational field. Only when the researcher has a good idea of what the research is to be about, will it be possible to negotiate and gain access to the field location.

GAINING ACCESS TO THE FIELD

Each piece of fieldwork is different, which makes giving advice on negotiating and gaining access (in anything other than general terms) very difficult. Moreover, our discussion so far has assumed that it is always necessary to negotiate access. However, researchers may sometimes decide that this may not be the case. For example, there is considerable debate (see Hammersley and Atkinson 2007) on the necessity to negotiate access when fieldwork is to be conducted in public places or using publically accessible social media. If, for example, we decide to conduct fieldwork in the high street of a major town or city, which involves observing passers-by, or may require us to enter shops or car parks or any other public domain, we may decide that there is no necessity to seek formal consent from those who have an administrative or legal responsibility for those locations. Although we are conducting fieldwork, we are simply doing what other members of the public are doing: shopping/parking the car/walking the street – simply being in a town or city. We may decide, therefore, that we, like everyone else, have a right to be there. However, whilst this may be the case, our principal reason for 'being there' is quite different from other members of the public. As fieldworkers, we are there to observe others. Depending on the conceptual field of our research, it may be possible to conduct fieldwork in these public places without those who are the subjects of the research knowing about it. Consequently, there may be no practical reason to seek their consent as, on the face of it, our behaviour involves nothing out of the ordinary. However, practical concerns are not the only consideration facing the fieldworker.

In situations such as those above, the decision of whether to seek formal access to the subjects, or perhaps more accurately the objects of the research, will come down to the personal ethical code of the researcher. Whilst there are many important ethical codes and guides issued by professional and learned societies (e.g. British Educational Research Association 2011, British Sociological Association 2002) which advocate that wherever possible the consent of those being researched should be gained, fieldworkers are not bound in any legal sense to adhere to such guides and codes. The decision ultimately rests with the individual fieldworker, or in some cases, a research team may make such decisions collectively.

In coming to a decision, fieldworkers have to make a number of judgements. For example, about the extent to which the fieldwork and the research have the potential to harm or to embarrass or in any way adversely affect those who are its subjects. Scholarly opinion seems to fall into three general camps on this issue. In the first place there are those like Erikson (1967) who argue from an absolutist position that researchers should always get permission from those who are being researched. The basic argument is that not to do so is a violation of individual rights and a belief that the researcher can never fully appreciate the range of possible affects that the research may have on the life of the researched. At the other end of the spectrum are those libertarian scholars represented by people like Douglas (1976), for whom anything goes. They operate a kind of 'smash and grab' approach where anything and anybody are regarded as 'fair game' for the researcher. Their logic is that the ends justify the means. Consequently, the rights and the interests of the individual are sacrificed at the expense of the benefit that the research may bring to society in general and the contribution that it will make to knowledge about a given social phenomenon. Between these two extremes is the relativist position where the majority of researchers operate. This compromise position holds that the researcher should evaluate each case, weighing the costs to the individual against the benefits to wider society of conducting research on people without their knowledge. The trouble with this is that we can never be sure either about the costs or the benefits, nor any unintended outcomes that may be beyond our control.

Ultimately, decisions about whether to gain explicit consent to research or not come down to the ethical and moral code of the individual researcher. Learned societies can provide guidelines and advice, but ultimately they are toothless tigers. They have no authority over researchers. Membership of a society is not a requirement for researchers, who do not require a practising certificate in order to conduct their work. We would also add that universities usually have their own internal ethics committees, from which approval must be sought before any research conducted through the university begins. In the great majority of cases, however, whilst there will always be debates about what is ethical and what is unethical social research, our feeling is that very little research currently conducted makes serious breaches of ethical codes and guidelines. The problem with this statement is that it is only our belief, and who is to say whether something is serious or not?

In addition to ethical and moral concerns around gaining consent, there remains the question of whether it is physically possible to gain consent from people in public places when seeking access. For example, let us consider the research conducted over several years by John Williams and colleagues at the University of Leicester into football hooliganism and crowd behaviour. As we have reported earlier in this volume, much of this involved John Williams participating in the crowd behaviour. His intention was to observe and experience at first hand the same things as football supporters. On one occasion this even involved him being arrested by Spanish police and held in jail! Given his intention of 'blending in', not wishing to affect or change the behaviour of the supporters, he did not seek their consent for the research and, therefore, he carried out his work covertly. However, leaving aside the ethical questions, let us consider how Williams could have negotiated access in such a way as to gain consent.

Prior to entering the football ground he did not know exactly which people he would focus on or even what kind of activities they would become involved in for sure. Could he have issued a general statement to all members of the crowd as potential subjects of the research that they may be the focus of his observations, perhaps over the public address system in the stadium or in the match programme? This would have been a possibility but what would it have achieved? What if some people had objected? Would Williams have been able to omit them from his observations and concentrate on others? Or, if he was truly seeking consent rather than merely informing people that they were being researched should he have left the stadium and abandoned the research?

Another example is a longitudinal study by Gavin Smith and the closed circuit surveillance cameras in Aberdeen city. Smith (2012) was studying the operation of those cameras and centrally their management and was hence located in the CCTV control office. During his fieldwork, he became privy to the criminal and violent activities that those cameras recorded, including witnessing (albeit remotely) bystanders being savagely beaten whilst caught up in Aberdeen's night-time economy. Give his dual status as both observer and remotely via the city's CCTV system, he was personally unable to intervene. As in the case of Williams, above, would he have been allowed to observe if he had intervened in such instances? Could the occupants of the city centre at night have been informed that they were not only being watched by the council officers working the cameras, but also by a social scientist? Would those who were drunk and disorderly have been in a position to grant their own informed consent?!

Finally, there is the work of Erving Goffman, a Canadian sociologist who qualified as a black-jack dealer in order to study casinos and gambling. Given the vast size and scale of many casinos with card tables, should Goffman have sought to ask the permission of every gambler, or only those at the table? Or should passing spectators and casual on-lookers also be included? And would the casino's managers and owners welcome a roving fieldworker in their midst?! In relation to the latter, it proved not to be the case and Goffman was evicted! Whilst it is rare for a fieldworker to be effectively run out of town, it is a real possibility, as Colin Bell and Howard Newby found in a small community they visited in Australia and began to ask – as it turned out – unwelcome questions about major cotton-growing farms in New South Wales. Newby (2008) recounts they:

> rented a car, and went to a small rural town called Weewah, and started to look about. These were major multinational cotton companies, dreadfully exploiting aboriginal labour, who were living in corrugated tin structures, rather like you see for free-range pigs in this country. And we started to ask around, and we had the unnerving experience of being run out of town. We were told if we didn't get out, we would suffer the consequences (Newby 2008: 93–4).

These examples may be unusual and extreme but they do serve to illustrate the dilemmas facing the negotiation of access and consent. The practicalities are often difficult, and the definition of what is a public and what is a private space can be blurred. Neither is access straight-forward or guaranteed. For example, Williams may have taken the view that a football stadium is a public place and there was no reason to seek consent, as might Smith regarding CCTV camera surveillance. Ultimately, once again, the decision came down to their personal, ethical and moral code and whether they felt the research ends justified the means.

For many of us, however, working in private or restricted access locations, within institutions or with discrete groups of people, there is no decision to be made about whether or not to negotiate access. Much of our research, for example, has been based within educational institutions (cf. Bagley and Hillyard 2011, Deem at al. 2007, Edwards and Hillyard 2012, Pole 1993), where there is little alternative but to formally seek access to whatever it is you wish to research within that institution. Negotiating access and securing the consent of people in authority, within or over the location is, therefore, a pre-requisite of much – and probably most – social research. The decision the fieldworker faces therefore is not, shall I negotiate access, or, is it necessary to negotiate access? But rather how can we negotiate access in a way which will facilitate our participation and observation of as much of the life of the institution, the location or the group and for potentially as long a period of time as possible?

In many cases, the prospective fieldworker will face a formal hierarchy through which to negotiate access. In one case (Pole 1993), this started with officers of the Local Education Authority who said they would support an approach to any school within their area. Pole then approached the head teacher of Benton School and after various telephone conversations, a meeting and a written account of what he wanted to do, access to the school was secured. Or so he had originally thought.

Being granted access to an organization (whether it is a school, a factory, a shop or sports and social club) by someone in authority may guarantee your physical presence at the location, but it does not guarantee co-operation from everyone within it. We would argue that *without co-operation, access can be meaningless*. Moreover, where co-operation is coerced then this too can be meaningless. In effect, negotiating access must be seen as an on-going process rather than a singular, isolated task or moment. It occurs at all levels throughout the fieldwork site and with everyone who is a subject of the research. Even though the fieldworker may have the support of those in authority over the location, he/she would be naive to assume that all doors will be willingly opened as a result. On the contrary, some individuals may resent the researcher receiving support from those at the top. They may see him/her as a spy, an informer, or as someone to treat with caution, rather than to embrace and tell your secrets. In the case of Pole's study of Benton School, the Head granted him permission to be in the school whenever he wished and to have access to whatever classes, documents and most meetings held in the school. To realize this very generous gesture and to take full advantage of it, however, Pole also needed to secure the co-operation of teachers, administrators and pupils throughout the school. To do this meant developing and maintaining good field relations. We will discuss this issue in detail in the following chapter, but for now it is important to make the point that access is not a one-shot event and that access without co-operation may not be good access. Reluctant or enforced co-operation, perhaps more accurately seen as obligation, is unlikely to facilitate the collection of good data. In practice, access to the field is something that is negotiated and re-negotiated constantly, for example with different people, at different times with the same people and with the same people in different places. In the case of Hillyard's research, between 2009–11 in a Norfolk primary school, the head teacher changed three times during the fieldwork!

RESTRICTING ACCESS

A) STRUCTURAL

In some locations there will be an established procedure through which access has to be negotiated. For example, research in hospitals will usually require the consent of an ethics committee and research in schools will often require the consent of the school governors and parents. This may delay matters as it is unlikely that governing bodies and ethics committees will meet just to consider your proposed research. Knowing the likely access procedure in advance and building this into the research plan is, therefore, essential if the research is to adhere to its timetable.

It is also important to keep in mind that official bodies or committees which grant formal access can also refuse it outright or they can impose restrictions on it. For example, school governors may not allow access to pupils during the examination period or a medical ethics committee may allow a researcher access to the wards (cf. Atkinson 1995) but it may restrict access to patients' notes or other official or personal documents. Edwards also found that in his different case study school sites, he had different levels of access to lessons and pupils (Edwards and Hillyard, 2012). It is also worth keeping in mind that access to work with young people in any kind of institutional setting, will usually require the researcher undergoing a check from the Disclosure and Barring Service (DBS) (formerly Criminal Records Bureau (CRB)). Administratively, this can take some time to process, for example, approval of Hillyard's CRB clearance through Durham Constabulary took almost ten weeks. Simple logistics may act as a barrier to the field. For example, it may be that there is goodwill, but the school lacks the time and resource to participate fully. Similarly, Hillyard had negotiated access to a school in north Norfolk, but which proved impossible when their move into a new-build was delayed and clashed with the proposed fieldwork timetable. Where restrictions are imposed, the fieldworker may have to think carefully about their impact on his/her capacity to collect effective data. It may be possible to work within the restrictions by making changes to the research design or shifting the focus slightly. Alternatively, the restrictions may be so significant as to render the research impossible. If this is the case the researcher will need to think carefully about why the restrictions have been imposed, perhaps he/she was just asking for too much or perhaps those with whom he/she was negotiating were not convinced of the need for the research. It may be that access could be sought at a different location or alternatively, the research may be too ambitious and need to be re-designed. In this sense, ethical consideration may act as an indicator of the general efficacy of the proposed study, the salience of its design or even its very rationale.

In all research, there is a need for flexibility and compromise. Indeed, it is worth remembering that fieldwork's flexible character is one of its strengths. However, the extent to which it is possible to change either the focus or the research design will depend on the judgement of the researcher. Where the fieldwork is dependent on access to a particular institution, or where the focus of the research depends on access to a particular event at a particular time in the year, then compromise will not be possible. However, in many instances it will be possible for the researcher to seek access to an alternative fieldwork location which meets the identified selection criteria.

B) INTERACTIONAL

Access may also be restricted by the fieldworker him/herself. This may take a number of different forms. Given the desire to blend into the situation and to be accepted, as far as possible, by those who are the focus of the fieldwork, the researcher may just be the 'wrong' person. He/she may be 'wrong' because of a number of personal and/or social characteristics which make blending in and acceptance by the participants too difficult or even impossible. For example, the fieldworker may be the 'wrong' sex, the 'wrong' age, the 'wrong' size or shape, he/she may be the 'wrong' ethnicity or nationality or social class. The list could be longer or shorter depending on the specific focus of the research and the fieldwork location. The issue relates to the extent to which any one, or a combination of personal and/or social characteristics, preclude the participation of the fieldworker in the activities of the researched. They may mark him/her out as so different as to prevent acceptance by the research participants as someone who could understand and empathize with their situation. Issues of ethnicity (Beach and Lunneblad 2011, Pole 2010) and gender (Butler and Charles 2012, Cohen et al. 2011, Skeggs 2001) as well as age (Christensen et al. 2011, Hogan and Warren 2012) have been the focus of much debate in this respect. Not only in relation to gaining access, understanding and co-operation, but also in terms of the capacity of the researcher who is the 'wrong' gender or is of the 'wrong' ethnic origin, to do the research.

Whilst some of the literature in this area (Fonow and Cook 1991) sees difference as a problem which precludes effective fieldwork, others (e.g. Agar 1996) have made a virtue out of difference by suggesting that having the 'wrong' personal or social characteristics makes the fieldworker more likely to question what he/she sees and experiences and not to accept situations as ordinary, everyday, uninteresting events. Difference would be seen, therefore, as a positive characteristic which would assist the researcher in questioning and examining the field in great detail. Moreover, if we extend, to its ultimate conclusion, the model of research which stresses the importance of similarity in the quest for understanding and empathy, then we reach what Merton (1972) describes as a situation of methodological solipsism. In a similar vein, as Goffman said: 'Only a schmuck studies his own life' (Fine 2009). Where this occurs the only person the researcher can confidently research is him/herself! Ultimately, the fieldworker has to make a decision about how much difference is possible or desirable in the pursuit of rich and detailed data. It may be, however, that the decision is made for him/her as the participants either refuse access or fail to co-operate with the fieldwork.

When a researcher is in the field, a great deal may depend on the extent to which he/she presents a credible and acceptable face or self (Goffman 1959) to those being researched. Again, we will pick this up in the next chapter, but at this stage it is worth stating that effective fieldwork does not necessarily rest on levels of similarity or difference between researcher and researched. Much depends on the capacity of the fieldworker to gain the confidence of those he/she wishes to research. To metaphorically play the field!

C) EMOTIONAL

Issues of similarity and difference remind us, that social research is conducted by people and is about people (Coffey 1999). Unlike the white-coated natural scientist, the social scientist attempts to untangle the complexity of human social lives by seeking to get inside the social structures and interactions which construct them. In doing this the lives of the researcher and the researched become inevitably entwined.

Given this close relationship it is important for the researcher to think carefully about how he/she is likely to react to the research and what impact it is likely to have on his/her personal life. We all have prejudices, beliefs, issues which we find difficult, things that we feel strongly about and things that we find boring. In thinking about research and our capacity to conduct effective fieldwork, we need not only to be aware of who we are, in relation to such issues, but also to think about how they are likely to impact on and interact with the research that we wish to conduct. Could we, for example, cope with fieldwork in an abattoir as part of a community or local area study where the abattoir provided a significant proportion of the area's employment, if we were a committed vegetarian? Could we cope with the undoubted emotional stress of a hospital ward for terminally-ill children, as part of our ethnography of a children's hospital? Could we cope with participant observation in a study of a Conservative Party constituency office during a general election if we were a committed socialist?

Clearly, there are some topics which, because of our personal beliefs and biographies, we could not or should not research. In such cases it is our emotions that restrict access to a particular field. In going through the process of progressive focusing in order to identify both the substantive and the locational field, it is important to think not only of the research subjects but also of ourselves as the researchers. Much attention is given in methods texts to the likely impact of research on those who are being researched, but much less is paid to its impact on the researcher. In seeking to gain access it is important to recognize that research which is based on fieldwork relies on a productive relationship between researcher, researched, location and substantive focus of the study. As we will discuss in Chapter 3, without this synergistic relationship, fieldwork is unlikely to yield the empathy and insight which are its hallmark.

FIELDWORK AND FLEXIBILITY

The nature of fieldwork is in many ways fluid. The informality of being there, participating and doing whatever is being done, often makes rigid planning of fieldwork difficult. Ideally, the researcher needs knowledge of the locational and substantive field prior to starting the data collection. Whilst, to a certain extent this may be possible via accounts of previous research, it is likely that the specific detail and the peculiarities of the individual site will remain unknown until fieldwork has started. Consequently, unlike any other approach to research, fieldwork requires the researcher to think on his/her feet, to make and change plans as the social action unfolds before him/her. It demands on the spot judgement about the way data should be gathered, the way to approach research participants in what may be sensitive areas, the identification of actions and events which are important and those which are not. Fieldwork, like the social life it is attempting to capture, is underpinned by uncertainty (Thrift 2012). Its successful conduct depends, amongst other things, on the researcher's capacity to manage this uncertainty by remaining flexible. Again some examples will help to make the point.

John Hockey's (1986) study of new recruits to the British Army involved participant observation on exercises in Northern Ireland. In one poignant part of the study, Hockey describes an attack on his unit by a para-military group which resulted in one of the soldiers whom he had studied being seriously injured. Although Hockey, as an experienced ex-soldier himself, may have anticipated, even expected such an attack, there was no way in which he could have planned for it. The event is extreme but it highlights the need for flexibility in the field because Hockey needed to respond. In addition, it highlights a number of issues which question the very essence of fieldwork. For example, was Hockey to maintain the role of researcher whilst people were bleeding around him? What does research and fieldwork mean in this situation? Is the role of the fieldworker any different from that of the others present when faced with such extreme circumstances? Should Hockey have continued to collect data? Did he have a responsibility to collect data? If so, how should he do it? Was Hockey a *voyeur* rather than a researcher? These are just some of the questions which we can imagine that Hockey faced. Moreover, he probably wasn't even aware that he faced them until he started to think about the fieldwork after this particular event. The point to be made is that Hockey was there and the richness of his book is testimony to his skill as a fieldworker, his capacity to be flexible, to respect those whom he was studying and to his own personal strength to cope with the trauma which unfolded before him. There was no way he could have planned for the event, no series of questions prepared in advance or observation schedule prepared for such an event. The situation called on all Hockey's resources not just as a fieldworker but as a human being who had got to know the research participants extremely well over the course of the fieldwork.

Andy Sparkes' research on spinal injuries amongst sportsmen, where the scale and severity of their injuries make it unlikely they will walk again, let alone participate in high-level sport, is another instance where the research is delving into a physical mortification of self (after Goffman 1963) in which the individual is being asked to reflect upon their own ability to come to terms with the impact of injury upon the lives and futures of the research participants. Sparkes' work has therefore moved to utilize a series of representational techniques and scenarios in order to capture the intensity of emotion in these actors' lives and to be able to critically analyse their accounts. For it was the fieldworker who was able to literally walk away after conducting such in-depth interviewing, whilst the research participants, tragically, were not.

From the many examples of fieldwork-based studies which have found their way on to library shelves over the years there are countless examples of flexibility, on the spot decision making and compromise. Sometimes the need for flexibility and compromise means that access is denied to situations which would have been interesting and useful. Sometimes it means the opposite. For example, Hillyard (2010) doing research in a north Norfolk school, discovering the school records dating back to 1912 was a useful and unexpected additional source of data. In this case and with many others, flexibility meant making the most of the opportunities which presented themselves. It may mean that data are collected which do not fit neatly into the original research design, that there is much more data than was originally anticipated and the data are of different kinds. Again, all of this adds to the richness of fieldwork-based research and in so doing, adds to the richness of fieldwork. In many ways it also makes it a messy process. Never being sure what will happen in the field, how many data will be collected or even what constitutes data, means the researcher needs to be flexible not only in the field but also in methods of data analysis, a topic we consider in Chapter 7. Unlike the natural scientist or, for that matter the quantitative social scientist, the fieldworker is generally unable to apply controls to the data, to conduct experiments or to subject findings to statistical tests which establish degrees of accuracy for his/her results. We should not, however, spend too much time lamenting this. Such precision is not the objective of fieldwork, primarily because it does not reflect the pattern of social life.

Think for a moment about your own life. How much certainty is there in that? We may know generally what we intend to do each day, but our guess is that many unexpected events occur every day. Perhaps some of these things are minor, for example like bumping into someone in the street whom you haven't seen for some time or the onset of some serious weather cancelling a much-anticipated trip or visit. These are not major catastrophes, but they contribute to the uncertainty of life. They demand a different course of action to the one previously intended. In addition there are also big, more serious unknowns and unanticipated occurrences which punctuate life and demand flexibility and a change in behaviour. For example, the death of a relative, failing or passing an examination, falling in love, starting or ending a romantic relationship or being made redundant. All of these, potentially major occurrences, mean your life could be difficult for a time. In the face of such uncertainty, the problem is the same for the fieldworker as it is for whoever experiences the changes. How to cope with the uncertainty and how to locate the changes within the pattern of everyday life that we all live on a daily basis. In terms of methodology, the fieldworker needs to think about what counts as data, and how is it best collected? How do the changes and the uncertainty relate to other aspects of the life and lives being studied? To expect a neat and tidy approach to fieldwork and yet still expect it to convey the detail and richness of social life would be like expecting tomorrow to be exactly the same as today. The only certainty about this is that it won't be!

Recognizing that fieldwork needs to be flexible is important not only in terms of the time spent in the field, but also in terms of what we expect from the research as a whole. If, as we have said, fieldwork is about finding a way to contribute to knowledge, the fact of its flexibility has a bearing on the very kind of knowledge it produces. Again, this is a topic which will be addressed in greater detail in Chapter 7, but for now it is worth keeping in mind that fieldwork is in many respects, concerned more with uncertainty than with certainty. Its subject matter is social life, which we have seen is generally uncertain and the methods it uses to reflect this have to be accordingly flexible. Consequently, it would be unrealistic to expect the results of fieldwork to yield knowledge which imposes any kind of strait-jacket to our understanding of whatever is being studied. By this, we do not wish to imply that research based on fieldwork fails to yield knowledge in which we can have confidence. Far from it. We believe that knowledge from fieldwork is that which is grounded in the real life experiences of those who have been studied and in this respect it is real life knowledge. As we shall see in Chapter 7, it seeks to convey the richness and complexity of the field to which it relates. It is complex knowledge or knowledges which do not attempt to enumerate, assign findings to rigid categories or to establish macroscopic laws of human behaviour. Neither is it concerned merely with empirical description, though this is an important aspect of it, in order to convey the complexity of a social setting. It is, however, concerned with conceptualizing behaviour in ways which go beyond the specific situation from which data were collected. As Craib (1992) describes it, all forms of description are the beginnings of theorizing. In doing this it moves away from the kinds of inflexible knowledge that look for linear relationships between social phenomena and for explanations which reduce social behaviour to basic common denominators. The knowledge fieldwork seeks to access is richer and more complex. It is not necessarily easy to handle, but then neither is social life. But as Delamont et al. (2010) argue, when your focus and fieldwork come together, it can be magic.

CONCLUSION

This chapter has attempted to take us further into the field by thinking about ways in which researchers identify their field of study both substantively and locationally. It has stressed the importance of finding a focus for fieldwork – a foreshadowed problem – and in this sense it has been concerned with its limits and possibilities. These are important not only in assisting with the focus to the fieldwork, but also in the context of gaining access to the field and in the collection of data. The chapter has discussed the idea of flexibility in the field and has emphasized the uncertainty of social behaviour which fieldwork attempts to capture. Above all, the discussion has sought to stress that however fieldwork is defined and however fields of study are identified, it is still centrally about looking for ways of understanding and explaining social life. To this end, it needs: to identify boundaries; identify appropriate methods; and gain access to people's lives. Because fieldwork is about people and people are unpredictable, flexibility is its touchstone.

The chapter should also have conveyed something of the integral character of fieldwork (and fieldworker!). From initial ideas of a topic through the identification of substantive and locational fields, the gaining of access and managing the collection of data, fieldwork is concerned with a close and particular relationship between the researcher, those who are being researched and the knowledge that fieldwork produces. This highlights how key the fieldworker is to the fieldwork process. The relationship reaches across all aspects of the research, is central to its success and much of the strength of fieldwork as a methodology, rather than a method, can be attributed to it. It is this particular theme which will now be explored in-depth in the context of field relations in the following chapter.

FURTHER READING

Pettinger L (2005) Friends, relations and colleagues: The blurred boundaries of the workplace. *The Sociological Review*, 53(s2): 37–55.

Beaulieu A (2010) Research Note: From co-location to co-presence: Shifts in the use of ethnography for the study of knowledge. *Social Studies of Science*, 40(3): 453–70.

3

FIELD RELATIONS

Chapter overview

- Fieldwork enters into the everyday lives, routines or 'rounds' of a research site.
- Fieldwork relationships foster a rapport that is balanced between friendliness and formality.
- Ethical symmetry is an ideal type, rather than achievable in research practice.
- The fieldworker remains a professional stranger – an outsider trying to gain insider status.

Fieldwork is about people and a key element of successful fieldwork is the capacity of the researcher to manage relationships in the field. This may involve a critical relationship between the researcher and a gatekeeper or a key informant, relations between researchers and those being researched or relationships between members of a research team. In the course of doing fieldwork there are many relationships which will influence and in some cases determine its success. The management of these relationships usually involves the researcher playing-out a number of different roles or, in Goffman's (1959) terms, presenting a number of different selves to the people he/she comes into contact with. In most cases, researchers have no automatic right to enter a particular research field. Bell (1969: 417), for example, talks about the 'openness' of a research site. Allan (2012) similarly discusses problematic 'moments' in her research where she struggled to maintain certain levels of control in her project. Therefore researchers are present only with the permission and goodwill of those who do have a right to be in the location and only as long as they do not become troublesome to the day-to-day life of the field or its participants. Moreover, in many fieldwork situations, the researcher works with, if not the explicit, then the implicit knowledge that he/she could be told to leave the field at any time. By contrast, for Hutchinson (2014), it was one of her research participants who left the field, when they were deployed to Afghanistan. In this sense there is a degree of insecurity about field relations, as the researcher seeks to balance the need to collect data in a timely fashion against the need to maintain a good relationship with those who have granted permission for him/her to be there. One thing for sure is that the researcher will not be able to collect good data unless there are good field relations.

BEING THERE

In many ways, fieldwork is like being a guest in someone's house, someone who perhaps you don't know terribly well, but has been kind enough to offer you accommodation. It may be the kind of relationship that exists when a family plays host to a foreign visitor as part of an exchange scheme or a town twinning arrangement. The intention is usually that the house guest is treated like one of the family, is able to experience 'life in another land' and to appreciate the difference and similarities between his/her home and that of his/her host. Whilst there may be special events and visits arranged for the guest, which will demonstrate something of the local and national flavour, the intention is that he/she also experiences the everyday life of the home and those who live there. That is, the 'normal', everyday routine or round. The fact is, however, that the guest remains just that, a guest. For the guest to have a good time he/she needs to get on well with the host(s). He/she needs to like the hosts and to be liked by them. When this happens, the relationship can move away from some of the formality which surrounds the situation and people can start to relax and really get to know each other. Even if this means that the fieldworker's experiences include coping with the host's 'cat that rubbed incessantly against my leg' (James 2012: 571). Fieldwork involves wanting to become 'at home' in a setting. Seeking to become part of the field, to participate in what goes on, both the special and the everyday events and to facilitate all this, the fieldworker aims to be liked by those who have made their stay possible. From Goffman's (1989) point of view, they would also get to like the people in that field, too.

If we are liked by and if we like those with whom we are working, then the chances of not only getting rich data, but also of getting more data are increased. As we argued earlier in Chapter 2, a key goal of fieldwork is to get an insider's view. A good example to consider, which is very close to this analogy of the house guest, is the study of step-parents by Christina Hughes (1991). Over a period of several months, Hughes studied five different families in her attempt to understand relationships and family organization where stepchildren and parents were living together. Whilst Hughes did not actually live with the families, she spent large amounts of time with them, in their homes, on outings and generally doing what the family did. The research relied on a close relationship between Hughes and the families. She needed to be accepted and also to feel comfortable with them. Without this it was unlikely that Hughes would have been given access to the range of different data that she was. Christensen et al. (2011), in their research with children, talk about the time their research team spent with the children. Although it was not possible to observe children at home, the research team closely involved themselves in the children's school lives. The familiarity and rapport that they achieved was vital in the use and success of the Global Positioning System (GPS) devices they asked children to carry – and to tell them when they went wrong! Hillyard (2003) in her research with children of a similar age in their first year in a UK secondary school also became a familiar figure through the time spent with the form-group in and out of their lessons – akin to becoming their form-group 'mascot'.

However, the analogy with the house guest, visitor or school mascot can only be pushed so far. It is appropriate in the case of Hughes and for Hillyard, but even then, there was more to the relationship than that of guest and host. A crucial difference from the analogy of the house guest is that the researcher is present in the field for the specific purpose of collecting data which will be analysed and used to further the understanding of social phenomena. Moreover, it is unlikely that the researcher will have been invited into the field without first going through a process of negotiation during which he/she will have needed to reassure the host of the integrity of his/her work and have provided a convincing rationale for it. The fieldworker does not merely turn up and hope to be taken in with open arms. Furthermore, to speak of field relations between researcher and researched as friendship or as a question merely of being liked, is to fail to recognize many of the complexities of the relationship. Whilst it is important to be liked and friendship may occur as a result of the fieldwork, field relations are about much more than this. Moreover, field relations based on friendship may have the potential to hinder the research and in turn, the friendship may become challenged. We shall return to these specific issues later in the chapter.

RAPPORT

Rather than friendship, it is better to think of field relations as the process of establishing and maintaining rapport between the researcher(s) and those who are being researched. Rapport may lead to a friendship, but in using the term we are implying a relationship which is both more straightforward and more complex than friendship. Given the complexities of friendship, this is a 'big' statement to make about rapport. In doing so, we are stating that rapport refers to a relationship, in this case between researcher and researched, which is based on mutual understanding and respect, where the parties are able to communicate openly and honestly about their different roles in the field and the ways in which they interact. Rapport may be friendly, but equally it may be business-like and conducted more formally. Moreover, some qualitative researchers have sought to integrate participants into the research process itself for them to become the researchers. This has variously been termed participatory research (O'Neill 2012, Smith 2009), participatory action research (Kindon et al. 2008) and critical ethnography (Madison 2011). These emphasize that research is mutually-achieved, co-production of knowledge. Critical ethnography, particularly, suggests that this is a democratic process, in which researcher and researched have an equal input in the process. There are pros and cons to each of these positions. Above all, rapport is about facilitating a relationship which will allow the fieldworker to collect data in a way that is acceptable to the participants (rather than subjects) of the research. Furthermore, rapport is dynamic insofar as it is likely to develop and change as fieldwork itself develops and changes. It may get better, facilitating the collection of more and 'better' data, equally it may get worse resulting in obstruction for the researcher. Rapport involves what Goffman termed impression management and we would argue there is no perfect approach to rapport that guarantees success. Crucially, rapport that is established for the purposes of research relies on the parties understanding and accepting the relationship for what it is.

Relationships in research are not and cannot, in our view, be equal. Field relationships are based on the premise that the researcher will look for and gather information and that the researched will provide it or at least facilitate its collection, either consciously or unconsciously. Whilst the relationship has often been framed by other approaches which, quite laudably, have attempted to overcome the inequality of researcher/researched relationships, there remains in our view a structural barrier to equality based on one party giving and the other party taking. Certainly, some researchers give something back to those from whom they have taken and those who have provided or facilitated information may benefit from participation in the research process in many ways. Indeed, this is positioned as one of the central tenets of critical ethnography (Madison 2011). There are also important debates that discuss the possibility of including participants, such as children, in a more symmetrical relationship with researcher and the field (Christensen and Prout 2002, Uprichard 2008). However, it is usually the researcher(s) who derive the most benefit from the relationship and for whom the process proves most valuable. Publications, conference presentations, establishing a field of expertise and a successful career cannot, in many cases, be realized without good rapport and effective field relationships. Moreover, precisely because field relationships are not the same as friendship, these are things that the researcher needs to work at constantly. Researchers cannot make assumptions about the likely cooperation of those who are being researched, neither should they take liberties. They must be constantly aware that rapport is central to the success of fieldwork and that to abuse it is to risk losing the goodwill and cooperation of those who grant access and provide the data. Wolcott (2005) states: 'Maintaining rapport presents a continuing challenge through the very presence of an intrusive and inquiring observer forever wanting to know more and to understand better' (Wolcott 2005: 84). In this sense, rapport is a tool which the researcher uses to 'know more and to understand better'. If this is then the case, two important questions arise. In the first instance: *Can fieldworkers be taught how to develop and maintain effective rapport?* If the answer to this question is yes, then a follow up question would be: *If rapport can be taught and learnt can it be applied in every field and with all participants?*

In answer to these questions it is perhaps best to hedge our bets. In answering in the affirmative we might say that to some extent rapport can be taught and learnt. There are enough methods textbooks around which give pointers to establishing good rapport to suggest that many people think it is possible. And, if it is possible, then why shouldn't it be achieved with all, or at least the great majority of people? In a negative or more cautious answer we should not forget that we are talking about human relationships, as Madison (2011: 39) describes, these skills are both 'an art and a virtue'. Therefore, whilst there may well be pointers towards achieving good rapport, it ultimately comes down to something which is at the same time both quite simple and very complex. That is the way two or more people get on which each other. We cannot control for human nature or regulate human emotions.

A number of commentators have taken the time to reflect upon what has and has not gone well in their research and rapport has been an important aspect. For Scott (2004, 2011) this involved reflecting upon her own characteristics and tendency towards shyness and the impact this had upon her capacity to engage other, self-defined, shy people to explore that very issue. Allan (2012), 'studying up' had the problem of brokering a rapport with an elite group of young people. She reflected upon the 'dry remarks' she received from them during the course of the research, worried that her research approach (including visual techniques) had been hijacked and recalled the 'barrage of questions' she received whilst negotiating access (Allan 2012: 4.5, 4.2). This elite, Bourdieurian capital-rich subject group clearly differentiated themselves from Allan, whereas Scott felt shared characteristics. Hence our point here is: there is no assured or ideal route to good rapport.

PRESENTING OURSELVES

In his first book *The Presentation of Self in Everyday Life* (1959), Erving Goffman discusses the ways in which we present different impressions of ourselves to the world in different situations and at different times. In so doing, we emphasize different aspects of our personalities and play out different roles according to the context in which we find ourselves. The idea that we all present different selves to the world is central to the conduct of fieldwork and in particular to the management of field relations. As we have already discussed, fieldwork relies on effective rapport between the research participants and the researcher(s). The way we present ourselves to those with whom we wish to work is central to that rapport. Whilst we cannot change who we are, we can, to some extent, manage the way in which we present ourselves to the world. Moreover, as Goffman (1959) argues, this is something that we all do every day largely without realizing it and as researchers seeking to gain access to a particular field and to establish a rapport with those we wish to research, we present a version of our self which is probably quite different from that which we present in other situations. This may be a presentation or managed impression which is partly sub-conscious and partly deliberate. For example, as we have already seen in Chapter 2, although we cannot discard our personal biographical baggage, in the sense that we are who we are, we can, however, choose to emphasize certain things about ourselves and to downplay or disregard others. In doing this, we seek to make ourselves more acceptable to those we wish to study and more generally, produce a better fit between ourselves as the principal research tool, and the field. It may be useful to illustrate this process with reference to our own careers as fieldworkers conducting research in educational settings.

THE KNOWLEDGEABLE BUT NOT THE KNOW-IT-ALL SELF

Let us take the example of the 1993 study conducted in Benton School (Pole 1993). The plan was that I should spend three days a week in the school, keeping the same hours as the teachers, engaging in the rhythms of the school for a whole term, approximately four months. My intention was to get to know as much about the school, its routines, how it was run, its ethos as well as the actors within it, as possible, by being there, observing, participating and talking to teachers, pupils, secretaries, parents, virtually anyone who had a role in the school. The intention was to provide a context for the focus of the study which was concerned with the way in which the school assessed and recorded the performance, activities and abilities of its pupils. The research was about a particular process within the school which could have been reduced to a set of bureaucratic procedures, but it was also as much about the pupils and the staff who created and worked within those procedures.

As a field researcher I needed to appear friendly and approachable to the different people that I came into contact with. I wanted them to like me because if they did, I might be able to persuade them to give me information, or to provide avenues through which I could obtain it. More than this, however, I needed to appear credible as someone who not only knew about and understood schools and education but would also empathize with the pressures that teachers faced. However, although reluctant to admit it publicly, many educational researchers are aware of a degree of suspicion towards their work which exists amongst practising teachers. In my experience, this is based partly on a fear that research findings can be used as yet another tool with which to criticize their work and partly from a belief, which again in my view is mistaken, that no one can really know about schools and education unless they are a practising teacher. Against this background, seeking access to schools in which to conduct research can be difficult. In order to be accepted by the teachers, the researcher needs to demonstrate that he/she knows something about schools and is not, as some teachers might think, stuck in an ivory tower at university. At the same time, he/she does not want to appear too knowledgeable as this may seem threatening to some staff who may see him/her as someone else trying to tell them how to do their job. In addition, there is the problem of the pupils. A classic 'Whose side are you on?' (Becker 1967) dilemma existed in my case, which many educational researchers before me had faced (e.g. Benyon 1985, Corrigan 1979, Mac an Ghaill 1988, Willis 1977). My intention was to appear not as a teacher or as someone in authority over the children, but as an adult friend whom they could talk to openly and who would not report what he heard back to the teachers. This was a role which some children would find difficult to handle, based on the belief that everyone in a school, unless they are wearing overalls, is a teacher or someone like a teacher (Epstein 1998). Moreover, some staff would find it equally difficult to handle, expecting the allegiances of the researcher to rest automatically with the other adults in the school. My task was, therefore, to present a friendly, approachable self who, whilst knowing and understanding the stresses and strains faced by teachers, did not know more than the teachers about education. At the same time I was not to be an unworldly academic or someone who either the teachers or the pupils would mistrust. In addition, my credibility both with pupils and staff also rested on providing not only a convincing rationale for my research and the time spent in the school, but also one which suggested that the outcomes of the research would have some useful, tangible benefits for schools and education. Balanced against all of this were my own sociological interests in education and my role as a relatively young academic, anxious to contribute to the stock of knowledge of assessment of pupil performance. No problem!

The fieldwork required me to present several different selves at different times and with different people in order to maintain credibility throughout my time in the school. Above all, I tried to keep the situation simple by being as honest as I could with the different participants. With the teachers, I spoke of the research contributing to Local Education Authority practices on assessment and recording pupil achievement via reports and staff development sessions. With the pupils, I spoke of writing a book about the way Records of Achievement were used. Both accounts of why I was doing the research were true. However, they did not tell the whole story. The truth was that I didn't know the whole story. Few researchers can say for sure what the outcome of their work will be or how it will be used once it has been published and is, therefore, in the public domain.

This is regardless of how well formulated your 'foreshadowed problems or working-hypothesis might be (Delamont et al. 2010). I could not have foreseen, for example, that many years on I would be using my experiences in Benton School as examples in a book concerned with fieldwork.

THE SELF AND STATUS

The Benton situation presented a series of issues which most fieldworkers will have faced at one time or another. Whilst they are not unusual, in that fieldwork is often concerned with such issues of credibility, they serve to demonstrate the way in which a fieldwork situation needs to be carefully managed and monitored. As Delamont (2009: 61) argued: 'It is hard. It is physically tiring, intellectually taxing, demands a high level of engagement, and at every stage crises can arise.' The examples are concerned principally with the presentation of self in the context of establishing credibility for the research and the researcher and also for establishing and maintaining rapport. In many situations, however, the presentation of an acceptable self is crucial to the negotiation of access. Another example from a school-based study illustrates the point. On this occasion I was negotiating access to a prestigious boys' grammar school where, as with Benton School, I wished to spend a full academic term. Negotiations took the form of an interview with the Headmaster which I attended with the project director, a Professor of Sociology. We were shown to the Head's study and whilst awaiting his arrival we observed many items which depicted the school's academic reputation and prestige (Pole and Morrison 2003). The Head's gown hung on a coat peg, photographs of King's College, Cambridge on the wall, a bookcase holding many examples of 'great' literature. Prior to the Head's arrival, we were informed by his secretary that he (Dr Smart) would only have fifteen minutes to spend with us. Our conversation with Dr Smart did not go particularly well. He was not convinced of the rationale for our study or of the merits of our qualitative approach. However, the tenor of the meeting changed dramatically when we were joined by the Deputy Head. Dr Smart introduced us to his Deputy as Mr Barker and Mr Pole from Mercia Polytechnic. At this point Bob Barker interjected to correct Dr Smart informing him that we were in fact Professor Barker and Dr Pole form Mercia University.[1] The interjection changed the character of the meeting immediately. Barker had appealed to Dr Smart's concern for academic standards. Our personal academic status and that of our institution fitted very well with the ethos of the academic boys' grammar school. Rather than a burden on the institution, the research was now seen as interesting and worthwhile. Our negotiations were successful and we were granted open access to the school. Barker had not lied or embroidered the truth in any way. He had merely reflexively chosen to emphasize aspects of our biography which would appeal to the situation we faced. The selves which we presented were entirely in keeping with the school's academic ethos. As members of a respectable university, a Professor and a Doctor of Philosophy, we shared the status and structure of academia within which Dr Smart sought to locate his school. Similarly, in her fieldwork in primary school (Bagley and Hillyard 2011), in meetings with the head teacher of the school, Hillyard's affiliation with Durham University made good access to the school as the head teacher's son was a Durham graduate.

In using these examples, we are not suggesting that you should now adopt the title of Professor or that attending Durham University opens every door when seeking to gain access. Not only would this be unethical, but to do so in some situations would certainly do more harm than good. What we are suggesting, however, and what the examples illustrate, is the need to present a version of self in such a way as to appeal to those who you wish to work with and thus gain cooperation from. The examples are ones where the would-be researchers presented a high-status self, both personally and in terms of their institution and this appealed to the principal gatekeeper, in this case head teachers. There would be occasions, however, where presenting a lower status self is likely to be beneficial to rapport and field relations. For example, Roderick's (2006) research on professional footballers drew heavily upon his own background as an ex-professional. Roderick, in his preface, summarizes his own career pathway very carefully as a means to deconstruct the professional lives of footballers in which very few will enjoy highly lucrative careers. This allows him to reflect upon his many visits to footballers' homes and the forms of wealth on display there, such as the Lamborghinis and Ferraris displayed on the drive. He notes that, at that time, he drove a Ford Fiesta but what was key for his fieldwork was his personal intimacy with the professional game. This enabled him to gain insight and informed his nuanced sociological analysis of footballers' work, beyond the front stage world of premiership footballers that dominates popular perception. Similarly, Cox's participation in the field trialling community facilitated his and his colleagues' access into the relatively closed world of game shooting and rural land use (Cox et al. 1996). In these examples, the researchers felt that rapport would not be best served by emphasizing a self constituted by academic experience and a desire to contribute to a sociological understanding of football or field sports.

On other occasions, researchers have sought to present a neutral self to the field. For example, Epstein (1998) in her research on gender roles in schools, sought to avoid the adult-in-school status as a means to get close to the everyday schooling lives of the girls there. This invited questions from the participants, who were used to pre-defined roles of 'pupil' or teacher', which institutions such as school re-enforce. Hey (1997) was similarly determined in her ethnography of girls' friendship patterns to resist associating herself with any form of production of hegemonic power, the workings of which she was seeking to expose and critique. Alternatively, fieldwork situations can invite the researcher to downplay the roles they are ascribed in school. Edwards, for example, in his fieldwork examining school-sport partnerships, went out of his way to play down that he was 'evaluating' pupils' sporting achievements (Edwards and Hillyard 2012). This was to the extent that he had to become dis-attentive during his observation of physical education lessons, when pupils behaved increasingly competitively.

THE WELL TURNED OUT SELF

Whilst some aspects of self relate to the role the researcher seeks to play or aspects of his/her life and experiences he/she wishes to emphasize, others are more material and relate to the way a person looks or even sounds. Again, the emphasis is on acceptability in the field. For example, Foster (1990) feared that her southern, middle-class accent would hinder a close rapport with the regulars of the Grafton Arms, the pub in the then undeveloped Docklands area of London, where much of her research into criminal behaviour was based. Rather than seek to alter her accent, Foster explained it in terms of coming from Bournemouth where 'everyone spoke like that'. Whilst Foster was unable to blend in with her research participants, her explanation sought to neutralize the social class difference between herself and her participants by explaining away one of its most obvious outward signs. Blending in was, however, essential in the demanding work of Hobbs et al.'s (2003) study of bouncers and the night-time economy. As Lister et al. (2001) explain, as the research was covert, it was essential for the researcher to take on the role of a bouncer in its entirety. Looking the part was essential in respect of clothes, body form, language, gesture and a capacity to use violence effectively and appropriately when called upon to do so. What the researchers refer to as 'body capital' was central to the role of the bouncer in the often violent field of the nightclub, the bar or the pub. It was, therefore, central to the conduct of successful fieldwork. Hillyard (2009) travelling across the country researching the impact of the 2001 foot-and-mouth disease epidemic amongst cattle in the UK, variously visited working farms, union regional headquarters and government offices, all of which required quite different transport and attire. Indeed, whilst waiting to meet one of the project's participants she was mistaken for a vet!

Many researchers have discussed the importance of appropriate clothing for the field. Hobbs (1988) bought a supply of Polo shirts which sported particular 'acceptable' motifs on the breast as these were the kind worn by the participants in his field. Patrick (1973) had to ensure his jacket was buttoned correctly in order to blend in with other gang members, and Corrigan (1979) gave considerable thought to the length of his hair in order to be acceptable to both teachers and pupils. In my case, the fieldwork in the boys' grammar school, described earlier (Pole 1993), necessitated that I, like members of staff and the sixth form, wore a suit when on school premises. In contrast in her doctoral fieldwork on pupil groups, Hillyard (2003) wore more casual, 'student' clothing of the same colour scheme as the school uniform.

It is difficult to offer firm guidelines about what to wear and when to wear it. This is particularly difficult when you don't necessarily know what the informal 'dress code' will be. For example, attending a Parish Council meeting in a small Norfolk village for the first time, Hillyard erred on the side of formality and wore a jacket – whilst several council members arrived in shorts! Often the best way of assessing the situation once in the field is to look at yourself and look at those you are researching. Assess the differences, and if it is important to look the same or to modify your appearance for the sake of rapport and good field relations, then our advice would be to do so, even if this does involve compromise on your part. Perhaps the final example on this topic should be drawn from Scott's (2010: 164) study of swimming pool etiquette and the fragility of those managed encounters whilst being 'near-naked'. Whilst obviously choosing what to wear was relatively straightforward, finding somewhere to keep her notebook was not!

RELATIONS AND RELATIONSHIPS

So far, we have talked about field relations, cooperation and rapport. Whilst these are important issues we may be in danger of adding a scientific gloss to something more fundamental than these labels would imply. In using these terms, we are referring to relationships that occur in the field between people who happen to be researcher(s) and researched. In some respects relationships in the field may be similar to relationships in many other situations. However, there is also a fundamental difference. The primary reason for field relationships is that they facilitate the research. Whilst they may be enjoyed and genuinely valued by all concerned, they remain a tool of the research. In this respect, there will always remain an element of field relations and relationships which could be seen as imbalanced and exploitative. For the researcher who needs access and data it is easy to see what he/she will get out of the relationship and what its real value is. For the research participant it may be more difficult. Furthermore, whilst the researcher may see the relationship as a means of facilitating data collection, and be happy with this, the research participant may not. Where this degree of ambiguity occurs, the researcher needs to exercise caution for fear not only of jeopardizing the research, but also on an interpersonal level by remaining mindful of their responsibilities towards the wellbeing of others.

GETTING TOO CLOSE

Although the researcher may be clear about the nature of a relationship that develops in the field and furthermore, he/she may be prepared to exploit it for the benefit of the data it might yield, there is no guarantee that the research participant will see things in the same way. In particular, those who act as gatekeepers, providing and facilitating access for the research or as key informants working closely with the researcher, may experience a particularly ambiguous situation.

In performing a role as gatekeeper or facilitator, participants may not see themselves as part of the research. They may be surprised, shocked or even feel betrayed on seeing themselves feature in a research report, a book or paper based on the research. For example, after spending a full academic year studying a further education college in the UK as part of a study funded by a Local Education Authority (LEA), during which I had received considerable support from a LEA adviser, I produced a report for policymakers (Pole 1990) as was required to under the conditions of the research contract. The report gave a detailed account of assessment methods used in a number of specified courses offered by the college. The report was critical of college policy and practice and inevitably of the role of the LEA adviser as she was central to the new assessment schemes. In particular, her role was discussed in terms of poor communication between the LEA and the college. On receiving the report, the adviser informed me that she was shocked to see herself feature so prominently in the report. She felt that I had failed to inform her that she was also part of the focus of the research as well as its facilitator. What had been a productive working friendship ended quite acrimoniously and perhaps she was correct. Perhaps I failed to impress upon her that she, or at least her role, was part of the research. Ultimately, on reflection, I felt that we had become too close. Our relationship had crossed the line from researcher and researched to one of collegial friendship which, furthermore, was understood differently by the parties involved. Whilst I was always clear that the role of the adviser was central to the research and consequently saw our relationship in this context, for her, the situation was more complex. As the study was funded by the LEA, of which she was a senior member, she saw it as something being conducted for her benefit. Consequently, she felt that her role, despite its centrality to the substance of the research, should not have been part of the study. It may have been that I failed to communicate my view of the research properly to her. Furthermore, she would be remaining in that professional role and environment long after I had concluded my fieldwork. Alternatively, it may have been that her view of the relationship was based on unfounded and unexpressed assumptions. Whatever the interpretation, the end of the research was messy (Pole 1995). The adviser tried to discredit my work and to prevent its publication. The relationship was too close and we obviously understood our roles in the study very differently. I did not ensure that the adviser realized that she was part of its focus.

Deem et al.'s (2007) research within their own professional community also generated its own dilemmas in terms of role and rapport, including within the research team. Deem (2014) reflected upon the informal and formal moments researching in situations and environments within which there is an insider's knowledge. Hillyard, as a junior member of that research team, has subsequently worked with several academics who were part of the original research sample – echoing Lodge's (1984) *Small World.* Therefore, tensions with the team (Deem 2002) or about maintaining good field relations are not merely concluded when the end-of-award report is submitted, but flow across settings which involve 'anthropology at home'. As Hillyard noted in her fieldwork in Norfolk, you may become privy to confidential and salacious information (Edwards and Hillyard 2012) and therefore discretion and diplomacy are key skills in managing field relations.

Managing research relationships is therefore a difficult business. On the one hand, the situation often demands a closeness and trust through which access to information is gained. At the same time, it will usually demand a professional distance which allows the researcher to stand back from the relationships in an attempt to preserve his/her independence and that of the research. In this respect, the researcher, whilst seeking a familiarity with those he/she is researching will also need to remain a stranger. Indeed, Agar (1996) goes so far as to characterize the role of fieldworker in the pursuit of ethnographic research, as the professional stranger. In his use of this term, Agar seeks to convey the notion of the fieldworker as an outsider attempting to gain insider status. As such, he/she must negotiate a way into the social action he/she wishes to research by means of various 'stranger-handlers' (Agar 1996: 85–7). In gaining their confidence, the fieldworker finds access to information much easier to acquire. However, it is important to remember that all field relationships are different. This makes the task of providing guidance for their management, in anything more than very general terms, difficult. Getting too close may be a problem in some circumstances, in others it may not. Whether it is or isn't depends on the specific focus and context of the research, together with the capacity of the researcher to handle the relationship. Fieldwork is people work and the competent fieldworker will need to be able to interact with many different kinds of people during the course of a study. Moreover, field relations, like any other social relations are by their very nature, dynamic. Relationships between individuals are constantly changing. This is true not only of relationships between those who are the focus of the research but also of relationships between researcher and researched. Relationships may change for the better or worse, or may simply develop into a familiarity as individuals come to know each other. Where this happens, there may be a danger of the researcher losing some of his/her researcher-identity as he/she begins to take things for granted. Moreover, the very presence of the researcher may contribute to the way in which relationships develop between individuals in the field. Researcher effect is a phenomenon which is often discussed in the research literature, but frequently the concern is with the impact that the presence of a researcher has on the social action which he/she is there to research. Intrinsic to this could be the impact which the presence of the researcher has on relationships between participants in the field. For example, to return to the example of Hughes' (1991) study of stepfamilies, one can quite easily imagine how the prolonged presence of a researcher in the home could affect relationships between family members. Stresses and tensions might easily develop to the extent that they begin to affect the nature of the family unit, the very thing that Hughes was studying.

Where it is clear that the presence of the researcher is adding to the strains of a particular relationship, or influencing the research setting in a particular way, the researcher may decide it is time to stop the fieldwork and to leave the field. In such circumstances, the decision to leave the field may reflect the researcher's personal ethical code which underpins the research. The decision of when to leave the field is unlikely to be something the researcher can decide in advance, beyond an awareness of what the research funding will permit. Leaving aside the constraints of time and money, only once the researcher has entered and become part of the field can he/she come to any real judgement about researcher effect, and whether or not it would be ethically and morally correct to withdraw.

The fact that relationships are dynamic, that research is often conducted in sensitive areas, that situations change and above all that people are unpredictable, makes the provision of guidelines for field relations very difficult. Fieldwork demands that the researcher gets close to those he/she is researching. Sometimes this is fine, sometimes it isn't. Only the researcher's judgement can be used to decide which of the two it is.

'WHOSE SIDE ARE WE ON?'

Becker's (1967) simple yet very searching question, posed more than forty years ago, remains central to any consideration of field relations. In asking the question in the context of fieldwork, we begin to challenge the notion that research can be regarded as a neutral activity. The question presumes that there are sides for the researcher to take and implies that these different sides have different, perhaps competing interests. The complexity of the relationships which constitute research and the research process mean that there can be many sides. For example, the source of funding for the research may mean the research is prescribed in a certain way and in some cases the researcher is little more than what Finch (1984) described as a hired hand. Here, the researcher is merely a functionary, carrying out particular tasks to provide particular kinds of information and, in some cases, particular kinds of analyses, for the research sponsor. Burgess (1993) characterizes such research in terms of contractors and customers. Where this happens, the researcher may have no option other than to be on the side of the sponsor. Pressures on higher education may mean that there is a financial imperative for researchers to accept such work. However, for many, the idea of conducting research which merely reflects or represents the interests of a particular sponsor may be unacceptable. If this is the case, then the researcher chooses only to seek work which offers freedom to pursue their own interests. In such cases, the researcher is clearly on nobody's side but that of scholarly endeavour.

Beyond issues of research funding, field relations and relationships may lead to particular assumptions about allegiances and whose side the researcher is perceived to be on. A concern to prevent the perception of any particular allegiance developing, may mean the researcher takes specific steps to avoid over-association with any individual or group of research participants. Furthermore, there have also been more recent moves to conduct fieldwork on ourselves – via auto-ethnography or utilizing fictional narratives and theatrical performances. For example, highly-experienced educational researcher Walford (2004) used this technique to explore the role and routine of a University Proctor when appointed to this role. Similarly, Bagley (2009) positioned himself – as a non-artist researcher – clearly within the production of a piece of arts-based educational research and the generation of a piece of performance art. More radically, Smith (2013) and Sparkes (2007) have blended fictional narratives, interview data and personal experiences as a means to explore the challenges of the academic profession in an audit-culture. There are those who have been critical of such moves (Delamont 2009, Hammersley 2008, Walford 2009).

In many studies, however, there is no clear demarcation of 'sides', but this does not mean there can be no allegiances. For example, where fieldwork is conducted within an institution, assumptions will be made about who the researcher is seen talking to, eating lunch with, sharing a joke with and generally spending time with. Similarly judgements will be made as to why the researcher is not spending time with other people. Although the reason may simply be that the people he/she spends time with are those who have shown friendship or interest in the research, assumptions are likely to be made not just about the researcher, but also about the nature of the research and whose 'side' the research represents. Whilst it may not be easy, the fieldworker needs to give careful thought to patterns of association in the field. It may be easy to spend time with particular people, whilst others may be more difficult and unwelcoming, but no one said fieldwork or field relations would be easy. To avoid the assumptions of allegiance to a particular 'side', the fieldworker may need to spread his/her attentions around. As Payne (1996) noted, researchers need to speak to both the nice and the nasty.

THE RESEARCHER AS A TOOL FOR LEGITIMATION

Access to information about individuals and institutions which fieldwork affords often means that the researcher can be seen to have a degree of 'power' or influence over those individuals and institutions. This 'power' is most frequently realized through the publication of material based on the research. Those who participated in the research could find that decisions are made about them by their managers, based on the findings of the research, or they may decide to change their own practices based on their reading of the research output or simply their participation in the research. However, after a research report is made public, or material from a study is published in journal or book form, the researcher loses control of the research, in as far as he/she cannot dictate or influence what interpretation the reader makes of it, or how it is used. Indeed, the research may be used in ways which are contrary to the objectives of the research and the wishes of the researcher. Deem's (Deem et al. 2007) work on new managerialism in higher education institutions in the UK attracted questions about the outcomes of the research and its application for achieving 'better management'. Hillyard, as the junior member of a very experienced team of academics, witnessed how this occurred at many stages of the research process: in negotiating access into universities; the arrangements for dissemination at the institutional level; and even during the negotiation of the subsequent book contract Deem's team were clear that the project would not produce a 'management manifesto', but this was not what all those interested in the project always wished to hear. In such a 'small world' (Lodge 1984) as the academic community, it was important that Deem reflected upon the impact of the research and its use-value. This was as important during a data collection process, that included highly informal moments in the field (Deem 2014), as for consistency across the fieldwork collected by an inter-disciplinary research team (Deem 2002).

A more direct and blatant use of the researcher as a tool, or in this case as legitimation for a particular course of action, can be seen from Pole's work based on the period of fieldwork conducted in Benton School (Pole 1990, 1993). Following the period of fieldwork, a report on the findings was prepared for the LEA, the head teacher and the staff. Although not part of the contract, I agreed to return to the school after the staff had been given a chance to read the report in order to discuss its findings at a full staff meeting. The organization of the meeting, by the head teacher (Mr Fox), cast me firmly in the role of his ally. The staffroom was organized in such a way that I was required to sit at the front of the room, behind a desk, next to him. Mr Fox introduced the meeting and did most of the talking, inviting me to comment on the report and to respond to his reading of it. As the meeting progressed he began to refer to specific instances in the report where individual members of staff had taken particular actions. Although all members of staff, pupils and the school itself were referred to only by pseudonym in the report and I was careful to maintain their use throughout the meeting, the head teacher, like many of his staff, had managed to identify the real identities of the pseudonyms and made no attempt to use them in their discussion of the report, preferring to refer to individuals involved by their real names. It soon became apparent to me and I suspect to the staff, that the head teacher intended to use my report as legitimation for his concerns about practices deployed by staff in the context of pupil assessment. On the basis of the critical comments made in the report and the data which supported them, Mr Fox proceeded to take up issues with individual staff members throughout the meeting, in front of me and their colleagues, using their real names. I found the situation unacceptable, as individual criticism of staff was not one of my intended outcomes of the research. However, having made the report available and agreeing to the meeting, I could do little to temper the actions of the head teacher. He was in control of the meeting and, furthermore, he had evidence (or perhaps more accurately, ammunition) by means of my detailed and carefully-conducted research to use against his staff. Whilst I made objections during the meeting to his insistence on using real names as opposed to the pseudonyms, I could not object to his references to the data used extensively in the report, or to its overall conclusions. To do so would have been to cast doubt on the findings of my research.

The examples from two cases illustrate that research may be used in a way which is unanticipated by the researcher. They show that the way in which the findings of the research were used, placed the researchers in difficult positions, which they found uncomfortable and potentially unacceptable. Their work and, by association, the researchers themselves, had been used in such a way as to legitimate certain actions and behaviour. Moreover, in the case of Pole, the research report was used to imply an allegiance between the head teacher and the researcher against the teachers. Both were also examples where both Pole and Hillyard were members of larger research teams where they also had obligations towards the success of wider projects. In terms of whose side are we on, in such contexts, the researcher can feel as though they have few options available to them and limited choice.

THE RESEARCHER AS COUNSELLOR OR CONFIDANTE

Whilst the previous two sections have addressed what might be seen as structural issues in the context of field relations and relationships, much of what occurs in the day-to-day experience of fieldwork is shaped by micro-level interpersonal relations. Like any relationship, this makes it difficult to fully understand how researcher–researched relationships work in any generalized way. What is also clear is that the relationship may be perceived differently by the researcher and the researched. Indeed, we have already seen that in situations where researcher and researched become close, the researched may fail to realize that they are actually part of the researcher's gaze. Where this happens there are clearly different interpretations and expectations of the field relationship amongst the actors involved.

Other instances of different interpretations and expectations of field relationships are evident in situations where the researcher is cast in the role of confidante or counsellor by those who are being researched. Researchers are often privy to large amounts of detailed and personal information. In particular, this tends to be the case where unstructured interviewing has been a principal method of data collection and especially in the context of life history, where researcher and researched spend many hours together over what might be a period of months or even years. For example, during research with black teachers, using a life history approach, Pole interviewed one young, black teacher with whom he shared many similarities in background (Pole 2010). This engendered a close rapport, where Pole was able to gain an insight into his respondent's early experiences of university life which were very different from those approved of by his parents (Pole et al. 1999). During her fieldwork on academics, Hillyard was told 'off-tape' on several occasions, of instances where academics had personally or knew of colleagues who had suffered breakdowns due to pressures at work. Pressures of work were particularly acute for academic women who lacked the domestic support they witnessed amongst their male colleagues. There are also instances where fieldworkers might become privy to wider circumstances or opinions that surround a research setting, for example, perhaps relating to its future. In her fieldwork in a Norfolk primary school, Hillyard knew the opinion of the school's head teacher as to its future viability as he approached retirement and a replacement was being sought. Fieldwork often involves listening to and balancing opposing views. Some of these can be very personal. Certainly, during her fieldwork in the wake of the foot-and-mouth disease epidemic in the UK, Hillyard (2009) collected a great deal of deeply personal information about the impact of the epidemic upon individuals, communities and professional groups, much of which was necessarily off-record.

On some occasions, the role of the researcher as confidante may develop a step further to become one of counsellor. Where those at the focus of the research share sensitive and/or personal information with a researcher, the relationship may, in some respects, be compared to that which exists between a counsellor and his/her client, or in some cases between a priest and a confessant. Not only does the researched trust the researcher with sensitive and confidential information but the researcher is also recognized as someone of intelligence and integrity who has an interest in the topic around which the fieldwork is based. As a consequence, it may be that the subject of the research seeks advice from the researcher about a particular situation or the course of action he/she might take. Again, an example from our own research may be useful here.

As part of a study of the socialization and supervision of doctoral students in the social sciences (Burgess et al. 1992), Pole was conducting a lengthy interview with a Business Studies student where the interviewee became tearful and very distressed not only about the lack of progress she had made during her first year of study but also about the nature of her relationship with her supervisor. In revealing a situation where she felt threatened and powerless in relation to the disciplinary and institutional status of her supervisor, she asked me, almost at a point of desperation, for advice about how she should deal with the situation and whether I felt she should abandon her studies. Aware that

I had interviewed many first year PhD students, she regarded me as having relevant knowledge which I could use to help her to, as she put it, 'escape from this man'. Had I seen myself merely as a receptacle for the collection of information, unable to interact with those I was researching beyond the posing of questions in an interview, I would have found her requests difficult. However, I saw this as a situation in which I could offer advice and support to the student and promptly did so. I also met her on several other occasions to talk more about her situation. On each occasion she thanked me for taking time with her and said she valued the opportunity to talk with me as someone knowledgeable about her particular situation but at the same time, distanced from it. In doing this I may be seen to have moved beyond my role of researcher to one of counsellor or friend, one that I was probably not qualified or properly positioned to perform. Nevertheless, the example is useful in illustrating that we react to situations that occur in fieldwork not as inanimate research tools, but as sensitive, concerned, emotive human beings.

Finally, there are instances where the researcher has blurred the distinction between confidante or even counsellor. Wolcott (2010), a hugely experienced fieldworker and methodological commentator, reflected upon his own relationship with one of his respondents (Delamont 2009: 58). Using life history techniques, he had become very close to one of his participants, to the extent that they entered into a sexual relationship even though Wolcott was then living with a long-term partner. The new relationship was not successful and there were extreme consequences. Their relationship had soured to the extent that the participant burnt Wolcott's house down! Here, clearly the personal and professional distance Wolcott could have maintained in his roles with the young man he termed 'Sneaky Kid' was compromised with dramatic consequences.

CONCLUSION

Discussion in this chapter has demonstrated that field relationships can be unpredictable and difficult to manage. Whilst books like this are, hopefully, useful in providing an insight into the process of fieldwork, their limitations lie in the extent to which they can offer hard and fast guidelines for the management of field relations. Perhaps the only guideline that can be offered with any confidence is best summarized by the cliché 'Expect the unexpected'.

Fieldwork and field relations are, in our experience, characterized by uncertainty. Moreover, they change and develop as the fieldwork progresses. In this respect, they are little different from the many other relations and relationships we experience in other areas of our lives. The crucial difference, however, is the reason or rationale that underpins them. In the great majority of cases, field relations are constructed for the duration of the fieldwork. There are of course exceptions where, for example, researchers and researched have kept in touch after the research has been completed and on very rare occasions field relations have developed into more permanent partnerships (e.g. Gearing 1995 (cited in Coffey 1999)). However, most field relations will come to a conclusion which usually coincides with the end of the research project. Nevertheless, we have also acknowledged how, on occasions, such relationships can endure far beyond such a point.

Whilst reading this chapter will not guarantee that you will now be able to forge and manage effective field relations, it will hopefully mean that you are more aware of the complexity and the sensitivity which they embody. It is also to be hoped that the chapter will promote a reflexive approach to field relations in which you, the researcher, take time to consider your role in their creation and management. In doing this, they become not merely a means of facilitating data collection, but a source of data in themselves.

NOTE

1 The names of Dr Smart, Professor Barker, Mercia Polytechnic and Mercia University are pseudonyms.

FURTHER READING

Parker A (2006) Lifelong learning to labour: Apprenticeship, masculinity and communities of practice. *British Educational Research Journal*, 32(5): 687–701.

Lofland L (1989) On fieldwork. Erving Goffman. *Journal of Contemporary Ethnography*, 18(2): 123–32.

Bell C (1977) Reflections on the Banbury restudy. In: Bell C and Newby H (eds) *Doing Sociological Research*. London: Free Press, pp. 47–62.

4

TOOLS FOR THE FIELD

Chapter overview

- Fieldwork is an inclusive approach that encompasses a wide array of research tools.
- Fieldwork can involve different scales of immersion – active to passive.
- Methods or tools are not chosen in isolation, but are part of the integrated nature of research as an activity aimed towards particular objectives.
- Fieldwork tools are not atheoretical and therefore have implications for the kinds of knowledge generated.
- Given the messy, unpredictable nature of research, it is likely that fieldwork will need to be flexible.

Having discussed processes by which researchers identify the field for their work and manage field relations, we now turn to the business of doing fieldwork by considering some of the principal tools which researchers use for collecting data in the field. However, it is not our intention to provide a step-by-step instruction manual to the key methods which are available to the fieldworker. There are many excellent methods books already in print which do this and we can see little point in merely adding to this stock. However, it is our intention to offer a critical account of how some of the key research tools are used in the field by drawing on actual examples of their use and in doing so, to acknowledge some of their strengths and limitations.

In many respects, doing fieldwork is like doing any other kind of job, insofar as to do it properly and effectively requires appropriate tools. However, in making this statement, we do not wish to suggest that fieldwork in particular, or research more generally, can be reduced to a collection of specific methods or tools. To do so would be to fail to understand the holistic nature of research and to appreciate the relationship between fieldwork, data and the kind of knowledge that it yields. In addition, it would also be to emphasize the importance of fieldwork, method and technique above other aspects of the research process. The intention of this chapter and the one that follows is to provide an appreciation of some of the key research tools available to the fieldworker and to locate them in the context of the overall research process. As with the discussion so far, the intention is to emphasize the integrated nature of the research process and to discuss the ways in which decisions about which research tools should be used cannot be separated from issues of knowledge and epistemology. Nevertheless, recognizing that tools are only part of the story we will begin our consideration of research tools with a simple analogy about plumbing!

TOOLS AND TOOL BAGS

Imagine you have a dripping tap in your bathroom. Having little inclination for DIY and a healthy bank balance, you decide to call out a plumber to change the tap washer and stop the drip. The plumber arrives with a large toolbox. He/she enters the bathroom, surveys the dripping tap and confirms your suspicion that a new washer will solve the problem. He/she opens his toolbox and selects a hammer. He/she takes the hammer and begins to hit the tap with some force in an effort to remove the worn out washer. Quite quickly it is apparent that his approach is not working. He/she has failed to remove the washer and what's more, the tap is seriously damaged. You look on in horror, speechless in the knowledge that the plumber clearly has little idea of what he is doing and has selected the wrong tool for the job.

Although exaggerated and over-simplified and like many such analogies, it is not difficult to see a connection with fieldwork and research methods. The plumber has a job to do, he assess what needs to be done and makes a decision about the tools required to do the job. He/she selects from a range of tools available and begins work. In this case it is clear that although his assessment of the task is correct, he has selected the wrong tool and as a consequence, is unable to do the job effectively. For the fieldworker the situation is similar. An assessment is made of the research task, usually through a research proposal and the research design. Some initial assessments are made about the nature of the job and the field and the research tools are selected from the range available. Like the plumber, sometimes researchers select the wrong tool and the job is either impossible or its outcome is very different from what was first envisaged.

The point to be made from this rather simplistic comparison is that like the plumber, the fieldworker has a choice of tools at his/her disposal and the task is to fit the most effective tool to the requirements of the job. For example, if the researcher needs to collect a fairly limited amount of factual information from a large number of people who are dispersed throughout Europe then the best way to do this seems likely to be via a survey. Alternatively, if a researcher requires detailed attitudinal information from a small number of people located within the same city, then some form of interview may be his/her best bet. There may, of course, be circumstances when what seems likely to be the most suitable tool proves not to be. For example, back with the plumber, if the tap has become corroded or has seized up in a way that does not allow the use of a wrench, then the hammer may be the best way to fix the problem, although as a result it will be necessary to fit a completely new tap. Considering a similar situation in the context of research we might say that if a researcher wishes to collect data which allows wide-scale generalizations to be drawn across a large population then it would be inappropriate to think of fieldwork based on participant observation as a means of doing this. Participant observation does not usually yield the kind of data that can be easily coded and quantified in such a way as to produce statistical generalizations and comparisons. In order to collect data which will allow him/her to do this, the researcher must choose another tool. Failure to find the most appropriate tool for the task, in plumbing and in research is likely to result in the task done poorly or not at all.

TOOLS AND THEORY

Continuing the analogy with the plumber may be stretching things a little here, but let's see how it plays out. When the plumber makes the decision to use the hammer in an effort to mend the tap, he/she makes it on the basis of a theory of what kind of action is required to remove the worn-out washer. He/she decides the best way to do this is to beat the tap into submission. We assume that he must have some idea of the likely outcome of these actions in respect of what the tap will look like after the beating and the chances of producing a flood in the bathroom. Despite this, he/she presses on and discovers quite quickly that he/she is not able to change the washer using a hammer and, moreover, that the tap is dented as a result. He/she reviews the situation, replaces the hammer in the toolbox and takes out a wrench. He/she proceeds to apply the wrench to the tap and succeeds in removing the worn washer and replacing it with a new one. Eventually, he/she achieves the desired end. His/her initial theory of brute force was seen, by experience, to be inappropriate. The plumber's evaluation of the experience led to a change of tool, based on a change in the theory and its replacement with one which was much more subtle, based on the principles of threads and screws. Whilst the plumber may not articulate the theories upon which his/her work is based in any explicit way, they are clearly what underpin the practice and inform the desired outcome.

Again, there are some similarities with the fieldworker. There are also some fundamental differences. As part of the research design process, the fieldworker will need to make a series of decisions about the tools he/she will use in order to collect the data. However, the situation may be more difficult than that faced by our plumber, not least because the desired outcome of the tasks may not be so obvious. Indeed there may be a number of different desired outcomes to choose from which compete with each other as the most appropriate for the task in hand. In the context of research, the desired outcome relates to the nature of the knowledge which it will yield. For example, the researcher may decide that the most appropriate kind of knowledge will be that which provides rich and detailed insights into whatever is being researched. Alternatively, he/she may decide that the most appropriate knowledge is that which yields generalizations and allows the identification of specific factors of cause and effect. Depending on what is regarded as the most appropriate outcome for the research, the researcher will choose one research tool over another. Alternatively, it may be decided that a combination of methods or tools should be used in an effort to produce different but complementary data and hence a different outcome again. The example serves to illustrate that the methods or tools of research are not chosen in isolation from the desired outcome. Just as the plumber discovered that his tool was inappropriate for the desired outcome, the researcher may also discover the same. For the researcher, however, it is not so easy to disregard one tool and pick up another. Therefore, before deciding on the most appropriate tool with which to collect the data, the researcher will need to answer the following questions:

- What do I want to be able to explore by conducting my research?
- What data are required?
- What is to count as data?
- Where are the data located?
- Is their collection feasible?
- How should the data be analysed?

The answers to the questions may not determine the methods of data collection which the researcher will use, but they should be influential in guiding that decision. For example, a researcher who wished to produce generalized representative findings as a result of his/her research would be ill-advised to opt for small-scale, highly qualitative methods such as life history or detailed documentary analysis. Alternatively, the researcher who discovered that his/her principal source of data was a series of confidential documents would not be able to get access to their contents using survey methods. Similarly the same researcher may discover that access to the documents to which he/she requires is highly restricted for matters of national security and consequently the original research design may not be feasible and an alternative method may be devised. The examples illustrate the integrated nature of research design and emphasize the inextricable links between research process and outcome. The desired outcome cannot be left to chance and successful research relies on carefully planned data collection in which the relationship between process and product is fully understood. However, given the unpredictable nature of the subject matter of social research this may not always be possible and the researcher, like the plumber, is forced to make changes to the research design and to the methods he/she wishes to deploy in the light of the research experience. Indeed, it is unlikely that a project involving fieldwork would not undergo some kind of change: whether a result of the researcher's actions or unforeseen issues.

TOOLS AND METHODS

There may be lots of tools at his/her disposal but as we have seen above, the researcher needs to choose in the context of the task that needs to be done, from the many and varied tools that are available. At this point it may be useful to remind ourselves of the overall aims and objectives of fieldwork which we identified in Chapter 1, as these will be instrumental in establishing the tools that might be used in an effort to achieve these aims and objectives. These are:

- To observe and experience at first hand what is happening (including virtually).
- To examine the significance of events and activities, beliefs and rituals (including the mundane and the ordinary) to people involved.
- To examine the ways in which activities and events, beliefs and rituals relate to each other and to the participants in the location.
- To look for the significance and meaning of social behaviour.
- To look below the surface of events and activities, beliefs and rituals for patterns and theories which can begin to explain social life in ways which go beyond the particular fieldwork location.

Whilst these aims may be seen as fairly general, the common thread which runs through them is their concern with the interior world, be this of people's beliefs, attitudes and experiences, the ways in which structures within organizations operate or the significance of individual or group action and interaction. The concern is not usually with merely describing static, isolated events or structures, but with explaining and understanding the social processes which construct them. Therefore, fieldwork is orientation towards an interactionist theoretical tradition that emphasizes the capacity of the individual agent (Atkinson and Housley 2003). In this sense, fieldwork tools need to be more than blunt instruments which capture data. Given the sensitivity of the task of fieldwork, therefore, it is probably more useful to speak of methods rather than tools. In doing this, we also seek to convey a sense in which the data collection in fieldwork involves a process, where sequential steps are taken in an attempt to find a way of capturing whatever is identified as the focus of the fieldwork. Fieldwork therefore also has a temporal dimension. Consequently it is useful to see method as more than a tool that one might use for a specific purpose and then return to the tool bag. Method is intended to reflect the relationship that exists between the data, the theory which underpins the nature of that data and the means by which it is collected. Certain kinds of method will, therefore, be used for certain kinds of data which in turn contribute to understandings of the field within which the research is based. In that sense, methods or tools are not atheoretical, rather they have implications for the kinds of knowledge that are generated, in so far as the resulting research findings will only be as good as the data upon which they are built; hence the tools you use will shape the knowledge created.

We have already characterized fieldwork as an approach to research which seeks to discover and understand the interior world of those who construct and inhabit the fieldwork site. If this is the case, then clearly appropriate data collection methods will be those which facilitate access to and enable the researcher to work within this interior world. At this stage it would be fairly straightforward to begin to outline such methods and to provide guidance as to how best they might be operated in the field. However, as we said at the beginning of this chapter there are already many research methods texts which do this admirably and there seems to us little point in adding to this stock of information. Moreover, it is not the purpose of this text to offer a step-by-step guide as to how to do fieldwork, but more to communicate the ethos of doing good fieldwork and how it might be done better. This is not to imply that this discussion of method, or the book more generally, has no practical application; this is clearly not the case. The intention is to encourage would be and practising fieldworkers to think critically about their work and to consider methods as more than a set of techniques or tools and to realize the integrative nature of fieldwork as an activity aimed towards particular objectives.

WHICH METHODS?

Given the fairly broad remit we are using to characterize fieldwork it would be tempting to say that any means of collecting information from a particular field would be appropriate and as long as it tells us something about the people, process or institutions that constitute the field, then the method is acceptable. However, to adopt such a position would be to ignore, in our view, what is the most important principle of fieldwork. That is *to observe and experience **at first hand*** what is happening in the field. It is this notion of first-hand experience which differentiates research that is based on fieldwork from other more distant kinds of research. What is important here is closeness to the field, whatever setting that might be. By closeness, we mean the ambition of fieldwork to generate an understanding of the location or setting where it is concluded. This means placing a value upon the interactions within that setting and the sense-making activities of the social actors inside it. The methods or tools you use are therefore strategically employed to 'get at' or achieve access to that meaningful action. This ambition to be close to the field therefore does not dictate what methods you use to proceed, but we would argue that it is rare that fieldwork relies upon only one form of qualitative method. Consequently, the methods that fieldworkers use must be those which facilitate this first-hand experience, that seek to achieve an intimacy between the fieldworker, the field and those who constitute the field. The general theoretical orientation that underpins fieldwork is one that emphasizes the importance of the lived experience of the social actors who are the subjects of the research rather than the objects. It conceptualizes the social actor as an agent with some capacity to reflect upon and change their social situation. It is an orientation which values the subjective experience of those social actors above attempts to capture the objectivity of their situation. It is not necessarily concerned with producing large-scale generalizations or tests for statistical significance. Fieldwork may form the basis for future, more wide-scale research. It is, however, concerned with rigorous efforts to understand the detail of given situations and their significance to the actors. There are many methods which facilitate such an approach and others which do not. We are concerned here with those that do. Therefore, it may be useful to identify those methods which do not allow this degree of intimacy and to exclude them from this discussion on the grounds that they are simply not appropriate for the task in hand by virtue of the fact that they relate more easily to a different theoretical orientation.

Having said this, there are not large numbers of specific methods that can be easily excluded on the grounds that they cannot tell us something about the subjective reality of the lives of social actors. Those it is possible to exclude operate at a physical and emotional distance from the field and its participants, where also there is no prolonged face-to-face contact either with those who inhabit the field. We would also add a caveat regarding the importance of place and context to our perception of the field. We feel this has been somewhat neglected within more technical debates about particular methods. What is key for us is the emphasis upon understanding the social setting of the field *sui generis*. That is, more than the sum of its parts. What is 'the field' will of course be shaped by its place and context, be it a school, a village or an online virtual world such as Second Life. In essence, this rules out self-completion questionnaires, highly structured market research style interviews, secondary analysis of statistics and other data sets and also official statistics. However, although none of these methods require the physical presence of the researcher in the field and as such are excluded from our characterization of fieldwork, it would be wrong to imply that they are never used by fieldworkers. As a means of supporting or adding to data collected by face-to-face methods they may make an important contribution to what is known about a particular field. For example, a researcher conducting fieldwork into school exclusion by means of detailed interviews and school-based observation, may find useful data with which to contextualize the picture emerging from the field by examining national trends and statistics in school exclusion. For example, Hillyard's research in Norfolk included an analysis of changing demographic patterns and the village population over the centuries, including maps and aerial records. Whilst this may not add to the picture of the interior world of the field or of the lived experience of the social actors therein, it would, nevertheless, offer the fieldworker a guide to whether observations in the field were in any obvious way unusual or special. They may act to suggest a different or additional set of issues to be pursued by the fieldworker, in the field. Similarly, fieldwork may form one part of a wider research programme which combines a range of different research strategies, something which Burgess (1982) terms multiple strategy research. For example, Christensen and her research team employed a wide array of methods to capture children's networks around a geographical area (Christensen et al. 2011). This crucially involved some members of the research team becoming familiar faces at the schools in their case study area and conducting interviews with the children, but it also involved using technology (in the form of mobile telephones and GPS devices). Therefore this was a complex, multi-faceted mixed-method approach which involved researchers in direct face-to-face contact with members of the community being studied (the children) but also drew in other techniques where necessary. The overall intention is to produce a detailed insight into the community or group which exists within the particular location or setting. The combination of different methods allows different kinds of data to be gathered and in turn different kinds of knowledge can be produced from it. The point to be made here is that although some methods can be excluded from what are regarded as fieldwork methods because they do not allow the researcher to get close enough to the field, they may nevertheless contribute to a more general research programme of which field-based research is a part.

Given there are not large numbers of research methods which are ruled out from fieldwork, it may be tempting to suggest that 'anything goes' as long as it brings the fieldworker into contact with the field and those who inhabit it. This has not been the intention of this discussion. To do so would be to place fieldwork closer to tabloid journalism than to social research. In that it would treat the fieldwork site and those who inhabit and construct it as mere objects of the research, subject to the fieldworker's gaze, rather like microbes in a biologist's Petri dish or mice in a psychologist's maze. Approaching fieldwork in such a way leaves the researcher open to claims not just of unethical work, but also of an insensitive or arrogant approach.

In seeking to collect information from the field, the fieldworker has numerous responsibilities which shape the process of data collection. There are responsibilities to those from whom data are collected and who construct and constitute the field, to the data themselves in that they should be detailed, comprehensive and provide a fair representation of the field. Fieldworkers also have a responsibility to social science more generally in that they should endeavour to leave the field with the reputation of social science research and indeed fieldwork intact. In many ways, the future of fieldwork will depend on the way it has been conducted in the past. In addition, there are also responsibilities that the fieldworker has to him/herself insofar as fieldwork is only part of the research process and is conducted in order to facilitate analysis, writing and publication (Delamont 2009). Unless fieldwork is conducted effectively and appropriate methods are selected and used, then the fieldworker will be unable to fulfil these other essential aspects of the research process. With this in mind it will be as well to remember the need for effective research design and for planning. For example, doing excellent fieldwork will be of little use unless there is effective data analysis and in turn, none of this will be worthwhile unless there is some kind of 'product' or output from the research, usually in the form of published work of one kind or another. Moreover, rightly or wrongly, research is usually judged on the quality and quantity of published work it yields.

The success of the fieldwork and of research project more generally depends on these two features. First, choosing the methods which allow the researcher access to the interior world of the field and second, giving due regard to ethical considerations and responsibilities referred to above. In making such choices the researcher will do well to find out as much as possible about the field and those who inhabit it before he/she enters it. However, this may be difficult. Unlike other forms of research such as that which utilizes the survey or the highly structured interview method, fieldwork cannot usually be piloted. In capturing the essence of the field, the fieldworker has to be present as and when things happen, to witness things at first hand, as far as possible in the natural setting. Fieldwork is, therefore, largely one-shot research. There is no possibility and no point in repeating or staging activities for the benefit of the fieldworker who may have missed them first time around. Consequently, this may present something of a dilemma for the fieldworker. Conducting effective fieldwork requires planning in advance of entry to the field but fieldwork itself does not permit detailed planning. We do not feel this is a negative for fieldwork, but rather that flexibility to respond to the demands of fieldwork is a strength of the approach. Once in the field, the researcher seeks to become part of what is happening around him/her, to observe, record and interpret activities and events within the field, but not in a way which influences, directs or shapes them. Once in the field, the researcher is necessarily reactive to the characteristics, events and the actions of those who constitute it. This requires the researcher to respond to situations as they emerge by adapting data collection methods to suit whatever situation he/she may face. Whilst the fieldworker may have formulated elaborate plans in advance of entering the field, once in there, circumstances may change and unanticipated events may occur. This may mean plans have to be abandoned or changed in ways which meet the demands of the unexpected situations. Whilst methods have to be clearly identified and thought through before entering the field, as we have discussed earlier in this volume, there needs to be flexibility in the way in which they are used and the researcher must understand that he/she has the latitude to abandon the use of planned methods and to substitute others which are more appropriate to the demands of the field. We need also to note that the social world is descriptively inexhaustible. More simply, the lone fieldworker cannot be everywhere and capture everything at once!

In highlighting the need for flexibility in the field it is not intended to suggest that fieldworkers' approach to their work should in any way be casual or that they should adopt an 'anything goes' approach. Coping with the changing demands of the field and not least with the need for flexibility makes fieldwork a particularly demanding form of research. Moreover, it is in part this flexibility and its changing demands which gives fieldwork its structure and contributes to its definition as a distinctive approach to research.

Characterizing fieldwork as an approach rather than a method leads us to think about fieldwork as an activity rather than as a set of activities. Whilst the methods that a fieldworker employs may be common to qualitative research in general, it is the fact that they are deployed in a fieldwork situation that is significant. For example, although a qualitative researcher may use forms of observation or conversation techniques as part of his/her data collection process, on their own these do not constitute fieldwork. In terms of our definition of fieldwork which we rehearsed earlier in this chapter, the methods deployed can only contribute to the conduct of fieldwork, they do not define it. On their own they remain techniques or tools rather than methods. In defining fieldwork in terms of first-hand experience and the capacity to 'be there' (Geertz 1988, Wolcott 2005) we have imbued it with a sort of holism or synergy which implies that it is something more than a collection of methods. In doing this we have at the same time, suggested that there is an element of the experience of fieldwork which is in some way intangible, or at least greater than the sum of its parts. Whilst we can examine its methods and talk about design and output from fieldwork, this does not necessarily mean we are able to convey a sense of the experience of fieldwork to those who have not 'been there' as it has been conducted. Wolcott (2005, 2010) talks of the art and opportunism of fieldwork in an attempt to convey a sense in which it is more than a mechanistic or formulaic assemblage of techniques. In discussing methods, therefore, we need most usefully to focus on how they facilitate the notion of 'being there' and in so doing contribute to this holistic experience of the field.

In very general terms, the methods which contribute to the conduct of fieldwork may be identified under two categories. However, the categories are not self-contained and some methods may be located in either or both categories. The categories may be identified as:

- Those that facilitate active participation.
- Those that facilitate passive participation.

The two broad categories are intended to help make the fieldwork process, which we have already described as somewhat intangible, become more tangible. Given that fieldwork is, as far as possible, concerned with the holistic experience of a particular field, the methods which it employs should seek to capture the total experience of the field. Characterizing fieldwork methods in this way avoids the temptation to identify neat and tidy sequential steps, a sort of cook-book approach, which would fail to capture the essence of the experience. Somewhat ironically, therefore, broad categorization of the methods seems both a more honest and a more accurate way to attempt to represent the fieldwork process. In addition, the two categories are also, in part, an admission that a precise representation of the experience of fieldwork may be beyond any written medium such as this. To fully understand the experience you need to do it. However, having recognized these shortcomings we do not wish to push them too far, as to do so would be to raise questions about the capacity of fieldwork itself to capture or represent the experience of the field. Without wishing to fall into a trap of methodological solipsism it is, nevertheless, important to recognize the limitations of any approach to social research which is being used as a means to understand human behaviour. Having drawn attention to these limitations let us proceed by looking in more detail at each of the categories.

METHODS THAT FACILITATE ACTIVE PARTICIPATION

The key word here, and in both categories, is participation. Wolcott (2005) argues that to understand what is happening in any given field, the fieldworker needs to do more than just be there. He/she must take part in the activities of the field. Participation is, therefore, the best way of experiencing the field and this has long been recognized not only by anthropologists (e.g. Malinowski 1922, Spindler 1970, Watson 1999) but also by sociologists (Atkinson 2005, Atkinson et al. 2008, Delamont and Stephens 2006, Duneier 1992, Scott 2009, Wacquant 2003). The lists could almost be endless. These few examples illustrate not only the enduring significance of participation in fieldwork but also its capacity to be deployed in a range of contrasting fields – from the boxing ring to the opera house. The features that all these studies have in common is that not only were their authors there in the field, but they actually took part in the principal activities of the field. In Scott's case, literal immersion in a swimming pool! All of these and many other studies like them are characterized by the fieldworker(s) engaging in the everyday activities of their particular field. As a method, it is not possible to say what active participation involves in any detailed or definitive sense, simply because it will vary according to the activity or activities in which the fieldworker is participating. Therefore, amongst the studies cited above, participation involved very different kinds of activities for the fieldworkers concerned. Stephens and Delamont adopted a division of labour during their research into capoeira, but one in which both were very closely involved in the atmosphere and culture of their research field. This extended into 'private' time and space and included attending political activities in support of capoeira communities. Scott (2009) discusses her 'regular' status as a swimmer and Atkinson (2005) begins his monograph by situating his interest in opera within his own autobiography – as an enduring passion. In many of these instances, the field is akin to a total institution (Goffman 1968), demanding a 'total experience' or commitment by the fieldworker. For example, Wacquant's (2003) study of boxing and gym membership took him into the ring after many months spent training and acquiring the skills of a boxer, despite his diminutive stature. In one bout, he broke his nose, but gained respect within the club for having reached a standard capable of participating in an amateur bout (Wacquant 2003).

In some instances it is possible to identify limits to participation in the field, both in terms of location and time. In Wacquant's case, the gym was effectively a workplace – it was not opening twenty-four hours a day and therefore participation was, in the main, limited by the physical gym setting and the hours Wacquant spent there. A similar situation was experienced by Scott, but we also note that her field notes were not restricted to observations made in the swimming pool itself, but include arrival, post-swim shower room and changing room conversation. Stephens and Delamont (2006) also interweave the action of capoeira with the lessons and also the atmosphere (the smell of sweat and rum) – and even poor time-keeping that collectively constituted their field. The structural demands of these locations meant participation was very different both in terms of the time it took and in respect of the kinds of activities that it involved. However, there are perhaps more similarities to these two different examples of participation than is first apparent.

In essence, they are both concerned with the same thing. That is, the experience of the interior world of the participants who constitute the field and of the social rhythms, constraints and demands presented by the particular field in which they were immersed. In taking part in the principal activities of the field, in essentially the same way as the social actors in the field, these authors were engaged in *active* participation. Not only were they *being* (there) but they were also *doing*. Something of which Wolcott (2005) would clearly approve as a means by which fieldwork is actually constituted. Similarly, Atkinson, Delamont and Housley (Atkinson et al. 2008) all stress the engaged and interactive nature of the three fields they had respectively researched. Although in each of these cases participation was overt and the subjects of the research knew that they were being researched, the researchers sought to blend in with them and, as far as possible, to become one of them by actively experiencing the field in the same way that they did. Clearly, there would be limits to the extent to which total immersion in the field would be possible. For example, Atkinson would make no claim to be a professional opera singer (Atkinson 2005, Atkinson et al. 2008)! Rather the intention of this kind of participation was to be active in the same way as the research subjects, in essence and in the context of the field, to be ordinary.

Beyond characterizing this form of participation as active and as perhaps the art of being ordinary, it is difficult to give more specific details as to what it entails or how it should be conducted as a method of collecting data. However, whilst every instance of active participation will be unique to the field in which it is located, there will nevertheless be a number of structural and interactional constraints by which it will be shaped and influenced. For example, at a very basic level what is done in terms of active participation will be determined largely by the activities of the field. The researcher will not wish to influence these in any way and will, therefore, seek to do only what those whom he/she is researching are doing. In addition, participation will be constrained by feasibility. In the same way that Delamont (2002) discusses feasibility in relation to access, effective participation generally relies upon the feasibility of adopting an acceptable and unobtrusive role in the field. Whilst this may depend on the specific characteristics of the field it will also depend on the individual characteristics of the fieldworker. For example, whilst fieldwork has been conducted in hospitals (Atkinson 1981, Becker et al. 1961) the fieldworkers concerned did not adopt an active role as practitioners of medicine. To do so would have been beyond their personal capabilities and not least, would seriously infringe the various responsibilities that fieldworkers have, of which we spoke earlier in this chapter. In short and quite obviously, participation must be within the bounds of the fieldworkers' competencies and whilst this may be determined by the nature of the field, as in the hospital example above, it may also be shaped by the personal characteristics of the fieldworker. Courtney (2008) for example, was a young British white man researching Englishness, but in his hometown where his own accent was discernibly from that region. Stephens was himself acquiring the 'insider knowledge' of capoeira during his fieldwork and making sense of and writing about that very acquisition (Stephens and Delamont 2009). Therefore, there are interpersonal and physical demands made by active participation upon the fieldworker. Not all researchers would have been able to cope or attune to them; if they were unable to swim for instance or had a dislike of opera. Hence, participation in these fields would not have been feasible for all. Other personal characteristics include gender, ethnicity and age. For example, whilst some researchers claim to have integrated with and been accepted as equals by groups of children as the basis of their fieldwork, examples of this are difficult to find and those there are, usually draw attention to their role as what

Corsaro and Molinari (2000) describe as a typical adult, rather than as child equivalent (e.g. Epstein 1998, Uprichard 2008). At the other end of the age spectrum, fieldwork with old people generates its own issues with access and appropriate method that demands special attention by would-be fieldworkers (Warren et al. 2010). Whilst we could go on considering other characteristics such as religion (Brewer 2000), or political beliefs (Fielding 1981) which either prevent or facilitate active participation in fieldwork, the point remains the same and has already been made. That is, feasibility has many guises, but remains central to the conduct of effective and active fieldwork.

Other constraints on active fieldwork will emerge from the way in which the researcher is perceived by those he/she is researching and the role which he/she may be attributed. Issues of gender, age, ethnicity, etc. may again play a significant part here. For example a female fieldworker may only be given access to stereotypical female roles within an organization, for instance, those of a secretary or administrative assistant rather than on the shop floor. There may also be a sense in which those granting access to the field may not see the fieldworker as having the necessary skills, abilities or experience for full active participation. This can be in respect of age, as well as gender (Edwards and Hillyard 2012). Consequently, although participation may be active, it may also be somewhat restricted and tokenistic. The fear of this may be what leads fieldworkers to undertake covert research, thus avoiding being cast in a particular role which would limit their access to certain parts of the field. Whilst there are many examples of successful covert participation, some of which we discuss in Chapter 5, we should not assume that a covert role automatically gets around problems of limited participation or access in the field. Covert participation may give initial access to a field which might otherwise be denied (e.g. Goffman, see Trevino 2003, also Holdaway 1983, Humphreys 1970, Patrick 1979) but does not give the fieldworker total freedom to roam. Indeed, in some circumstances, the covert researcher may be more constrained than the overt researcher by virtue of the fact that he/she will usually have a particular or expected role to perform within the field. In addition, other participants in the field will expect him/her to have a certain level of knowledge or degree of familiarity with the field from the outset, as this will have formed the basis of the access which has been gained. Depending on the circumstances of the particular field, to seek to move beyond the role which legitimates the researcher's participation, or to ask too many naïve questions about the central activities of the field, may result in questions being posed about the unusual behaviour of the fieldworker which could ultimately lead to him/her being exposed as a researcher. As a consequence, the research may have to be abandoned.

Active participation may also take the form of interviewing and conversational techniques. Again, it is not the intention to provide a 'how to do it guide' to these data collection methods, as there are many such guides that do this more than adequately. It is, however, appropriate to consider some of the issues surrounding the use of interviews and conversations in the context of active participation not least because they represent two of the most frequently used fieldwork methods.

Whereas active observation is largely about participating in whatever activities take place in the field, interviewing and conversations are about active talking and listening. This may also be seen as a form of *doing* rather than merely *being*, However, it would also be true to see it as a form of artificial *doing*. By this we refer to the fact that interviews that take place in the field are situations which are arranged, in the great majority of cases, by the researcher, as a vehicle for the collection of information from the researched. As such they are not naturally occurring events which would happen whether or not the fieldworker was present. They are established precisely because he/she is there. Nevertheless, given they are tools which interface directly with the field by seeking information, views and reflections from actors in the field, it is legitimate to consider them as a form of active fieldwork. Given the many different circumstances in which interviews are used as a means of data collection, for example in academic and market research, in selection for jobs and places at university, by the police and other agencies and even as a form of entertainment, the interview is, by and large, familiar to most people. It is likely, for example, that most people reading this book will at some time have been interviewed, even if only by a market researcher wishing to promote a particular product or service. As a form of fieldwork, therefore, despite being artificial, interviews are usually a familiar and generally acceptable way of gaining detailed insight into a particular field.

Having said that a range of different kinds of interview exist; those that are most frequently, and arguably most appropriately, used in the context of fieldwork, require the establishment of a good rapport between interviewer and interviewee. As part of this, they may also involve an exchange of information between the two (or more) parties. Whilst highly structured interviews which follow a precise and predetermined format may gather some information that is relevant to finding out about the field and so 'qualify' as fieldwork, the way in which fieldwork has been characterized in this text, as an holistic exercise which attempts to understand the interior world of the field, leans very clearly towards the use of less-structured or even unstructured interviews. Here, an exchange of views between researcher and researched is encouraged and the possibility to explore issues which arise during the course of the interview means discussion can be shaped to address the issues that are important to participants in the field, rather than just those which the fieldworker considers to be important. A semi-structured schedule may be used to guide such an interview or a much looser list of topics may be identified as a possible direction for the interview with the interviewer seeking to cover the topics on the list but not necessarily in any prescribed order.

As an alternative to exchanges of verbal information which are clearly identified as interviews, active fieldwork may also include what has become known as 'conversations with a purpose' (Burgess 1988, Cottle 1977). Here, the emphasis is on an exchange of information in a seemingly natural conversational style. However, for the fieldworker the 'conversation' is pursued for specific reasons with the intention of addressing particular issues commensurate with the focus of the research. Consequently it is deemed to have a purpose. Whilst in a very general sense all conversations may be regarded as having a purpose, in the context of fieldwork the researcher takes steps to steer the conversation, to ensure that the purpose is met. In some instances the person with whom the conversation is being conducted may be aware that there is a purpose to it and that it is not just a casual exchange. In other cases he/she may be unaware of this. Where this is the case, questions may be posed about the ethical integrity of the method, similar to those which surround the use of other forms of covert research.

An extreme or concentrated form of interviewing, which may combine structured and semi-structured approaches together with conversational techniques is the life history interview. This may be conducted over many weeks, months or even years with the intention of gaining as full a picture of the life of the individual as possible. The approach is demanding of the time and the concentration of both researcher and researched and in many ways can be seen as a concentration of many of the aspects of fieldwork discussed so far and some of which will come in later chapters of this book. For example, negotiating and gaining agreement of people to commit to participating in such research should not be underestimated. The management of field relations takes on a greater intensity in a prolonged one-to-one situation, as does the maintenance of good rapport. Furthermore, as Pole discovered in his life history study of black teachers (Pole 1999, 2001) the life history may unearth sensitive issues which can be challenging both for the interviewee and the researcher. The detail of the approach may involve the interviewee in a re-appraisal of his/her life as he/she constructs and reconstructs a personal narrative. In this sense, the life history is more than a life story as the reflection that the interviewer encourages the interviewee to engage in may be seen as part of an analytical reconstruction of the events of the interviewee's life. If this is the case then the life history may be seen as a means of active participation not only in a technical sense of data collection, but also in respect of the generation or construction of data. Of course, here we also need to note the limitations of such techniques. Delamont (2002), for example, reminds us that such interviews are 'rehearsed' accounts – the front stage of people's lives that they are prepared to show to interviewers.

The point to be made from this brief discussion of participation and oral techniques is that they are methods deployed in a strategic way with the intention of collecting data which will facilitate an holistic understanding of the field. Consequently, like the discussion of participation above, they may be regarded as active methods.

METHODS THAT FACILITATE PASSIVE PARTICIPATION

Whilst active participation and the concept of 'doing' is central to the conduct of effective fieldwork, other forms of participation, those we might call *passive* may also be useful and appropriate methods of data collection. Inevitably, being present in any given field, will result in exposure to data (Wolcott 2005). However, the participative fieldworker does not rely solely on absorbing data that may come his/her way, but must put him/herself in a position which ensures the possibility of collecting data from simply being there is maximized. In this way, the emphasis is still on participation but the fieldworker is engaged in a *passive* role in as far as he/she is not actively involved in the activities of the field. Typically or most frequently, *passive* participation involves observing and listening. For example, the fieldworker may negotiate access to a particular field on the understanding that he/she simply watches and records what happens (e.g. Hillyard (2003) during her observation of lessons in a secondary school). This may be done informally as the fieldworker tries to capture the essence of what he/she sees, in detailed qualitative field notes (Delamont 2002, or in a more structured way Croll 1986) where specific observation schedules are drawn up prior to activities identified as relevant for observation begin. Arguably, observation of this nature is still a form of participation as the researcher's physical presence in the field inevitably means that the field will be different from times when he/she is not present. In addition, there is likely to be a degree of direct interaction with the research subjects who, at the very least will be curious about the fieldworker's activities. It remains passive, however, as the fieldworker does not take part in the activities of the field. In the way that it has been described above, it also remains overt, although in some instances researchers have resorted to the use of covert observation methods, where the research subjects (or in these circumstances it is probably more accurate to refer to research objects) are unaware that they are being researched. The use of two-way mirrors and hidden cameras (CCTVs) offer the researcher access to a field, but from a distance (e.g. Smith 2012). To describe such instances of covert observation or surveillance as forms of participation would probably be inappropriate as the researcher may be engaged in a form of *doing*, but this does not involve physically *being* in the field. In addition, passive listening may involve the fieldworker in activities similar to covert observation where secret microphones record conversations of research subjects and similarly, it may not be seen to constitute participation. Alternatively, fieldworkers may seek to summarize conversations from the field as part of their field notes (Delamont 2009, Pole 1993, Scott 2010). In these instances, verbatim accounts of what was said will not be possible. The aim will be to convey enough detail from the spoken word in a way which not only provides an accurate account of its content but also a sense of the context in which it occurred.

Again, as the researcher is not taking part in these verbal exchanges in any direct sense, this form of participation is most appropriately classified as passive. However, as it requires the physical presence of the fieldworker in the field, by our definition, this does make it a form of fieldwork.

ACTIVELY PASSIVE PARTICIPATION

In addition to the methods discussed above, there are also a number of methods which incorporate both active and passive characteristics. Lee (2000) in his interesting book *Unobtrusive Methods in Social Research* draws on the work of Kellehear (1993), Sechrest (1979) and Webb et al. (1966) to outline a number of possibilities for collecting data from the field in ways which do not involve direct interaction with the participants of the field. These range from what he terms 'found' data which may include measurements of the frequency with which particular artefacts are used by participants in the field (the classic example being the one given by Webb et al. (1966) who observed the extent of wear on floor tiles surrounding exhibits in a museum). Such 'found' data have long had a place in the tradition of empirical research – for example Thomas' 'discovery' of a bundle of Polish immigrants' correspondence to their homeland (Thomas and Znaniecki 1918–20). More recently, we would add Savage and Burrows' (2009) call for digital and new social media resources to become part of our research apparatus. So, for example, recent research by the Culture Lab connected to Newcastle University has used technology to record the movement of everyday kitchen items (the fridge or kettle) in order to explore consumption patterns of older people. Similarly, Scott and a research team from Sussex University studied museum visitors' movement patterns with interactive art displays in contrasting museum environments (Scott 2011). Perhaps in a more orthodox manner, Lee (2000) also discusses unobtrusive observation in a range of different circumstances, the use of personal records and documents such as letters and diaries. What underpins the work which Lee (2000) draws on is a concern to capitalize on everyday objects, activities, situations, basically anything which may be considered to contribute to the field. A final example would be the use of photographs by children of their own labour, as a means to record their working lives (Mizen 2005). As they do not involve the researcher instigating the conditions necessary to produce data, they are essentially passive methods reliant on techniques of gathering. They do, nevertheless, rely on the researchers' capacity to see the possibilities of eliciting data from every day and perhaps unexpected situations and activities, using or drawing upon what might be termed a research imagination and in this sense we would regard them as active.

In addition to the active use of found data, there are also a number of other sources of data that the fieldworker might utilize. Whilst the unobtrusive methods discussed by Lee (2000) rely, in the main on 'found' sources of data, or devising methods to measure the level of human interaction with an object in the case of accretion and erosion techniques, these methods rely upon the researcher requesting that research participants engage in specific activities which will yield specific forms of data. In these situations, the research participants are required to be active but the fieldworker's role, after initiating the activity, remains largely passive. Data collection methods which fall into this category would include activities like diary-keeping where research participants are asked to keep a systematic diary of activities they have been involved in or even of their thoughts around a specific issue. Often, diary methods can be used to complement other methods used in the field such as participant observation or interviews. This was the case in a study by Mizen et al. (1999) into working children where research participants, seventy young people aged between 13–15, were asked to write diaries on specific issues which related to their experience of paid work. It is worth commenting here that although in this particular study the use of diaries was very successful, problems of attrition and poor completion are common. In the study of working children the research team managed to overcome problems of attrition by paying their research subjects for every completed diary they received (Pole et al., 1999). Similarly Hillyard encountered difficulties in the consistency across a form group of Year 7 (eleven year olds) pupil diaries that made collecting data equally from *all* pupils problematic (Hillyard 2003). However, paying participants raises other issues which relate to ethics and reliability of data which will be considered in Chapter 5. Leaving such issues aside for now, the essence of the specifically completed diary method is that the researcher asks the researched to write about and reflect upon particular events or activities in which he/she has been involved in some way or another. It is, therefore, a personal account that the researcher seeks and as such it allows access to the interior world of the social actors at the focus of the research, albeit at a spatial and temporal distance. The researcher plays a passive role, although he/she is responsible for setting up the diary process by giving instructions to the diarist(s), whilst the research subject(s) are in active mode.

In some ways, a similar approach underpins the use of photography and other visual imagery such as video and painting/drawing as a form of fieldwork. Here it is usually common for researchers to ask research participants to represent aspects of their lives using a specific visual medium. Harper (2002) used photographs as a means to prompt, for example, the memories of retired farmworkers in his interviews exploring working patterns amongst farmworkers during the 1950s in the United States. O'Neill and Hubbard (2010) used 'walking' video tours with participants as a means to explore the experiences of immigrants in a British city. Again, the study by Mizen et al. (1999) provides a useful example of this approach. The same seventy young people who were asked to complete diaries throughout the period of a full year, were also given disposable cameras and asked to take photographs of any aspects of their working lives that were significant to them. Bolton et al. (2001) argue that the resulting collection of photographs offered a different insight into the world of children's work and economic lives, often portraying detail not merely of work processes but also shedding light on methodological issues relating to the role of children in research (Pole et al., 1999). Again, there are ethical issues surrounding the use of photographic and other visual images which will be discussed in the following chapter, notably around privacy and confidentiality. However, leaving these issues aside for the time being, such approaches may offer insights into particular aspects of social life, unobtainable in other ways. Indeed, the growing literature on the use of visual methods (e.g. Grimshaw 2001, Pink 2012, 2013, Pole 2004) as a means of understanding the social, clearly identifies techniques such as photography and video as capable of contributing to fieldwork in ways which lead to a better understanding of the significance and meaning of social behaviour. Again, with such approaches it is the researched rather than the researchers who are in the active role. As the subheading to this section of the chapter indicates, these are methods in which the fieldworker's passivity facilitates the active generation of data (Mason 1996) by the research participants. Indeed, it is the passivity of the fieldworker and the privileging of the research participants, as the means of generating data, which may be seen as a means of democratizing the research process (Pole et al. 1999). Where such approaches are taken, it is the research participants who determine what is to be included in their accounts of the social action and hence, what is to count as data.

Other fieldwork tools which fall into this hybrid category of active passivity might include adopting a conscious awareness of the surroundings in which social action takes place. For example, some sociologists and social geographers have emphasized the significance of the use of space to understanding aspects of social life. This is particularly apparent in the context of childhood research; for example, Christensen and James (2008), James and James (2008), Uprichard (2008, 2010), have in their different ways taken account of the ways in which the use of different kinds of space is able to reveal something about the material and symbolic position of children in late modern society. Similar approaches could be taken in respect of researching other social actors such as elderly or disabled people. Moreover, we need not confine ourselves to space as a physical entity or as an organizing concept, we could, for example, extend our observations to the interface of specific groups of people with architecture or with a wide range of artefacts. The point to be made here is that fieldwork, in addition to collecting data from individual social actors is also about the development of a sensitivity to and significance of, the surroundings and objects that shape and contextualize social action. In this respect, the fieldworker needs to remain open to possibilities for the collection of field-based data as and when they occur. Returning to one of the themes identified in Chapter 1 of this text, the need for flexibility in fieldwork design and practice is evident, as we consider the data potential not just of the research participants but also of the physical and social context in which they are studied. In our own work, we have noted the impact spaces have upon the frequency of contact – or infrequency in rural areas also acknowledged by John Urry (Hillyard and Bagley 2014). Urry understands that space and nature possess a certain kind of agency that exerts an influence upon us. This is subtle, almost non-cognitive, in the sense that we become so familiar with our surroundings that in fulfilling some activities we are almost on 'automatic pilot'. Fieldwork, we would argue, needs to be aware and acknowledge Urry's argument. Most recently, the work of US scholar Katherine Hayles, takes this even further, exploring our pre-conscious cognition.

CONCLUSION

From this wide-ranging discussion of different types of data and the active and passive methods by which they may be collected, we may conclude that there are few limits to the methods or techniques used in fieldwork beyond the very general qualification that they should facilitate the collection of data which will help us to explain and understand the social processes that constitute the field. In addition, there are also limits imposed by the various responsibilities that we discussed earlier in this chapter, which the fieldworker has. It should also be obvious from our foregoing discussion that some fieldwork methods are instigated by the researcher and as such may be seen as the creation of artificial situations. For example, whilst interviews may be the prime and most common example of such manufacture, others such as requesting that research participants keep diaries (Morrison and Galloway 1996), take photographs (Bolton et al. 2001, Mizen 2005) or draw pictures (Christensen and James 2000) are also examples of fieldwork methods. With the production and collection of textual data, be it visual or written, the fieldworker is usually cast in a passive role as direct participation in events which are represented in the text is in these circumstances, limited. However, other methods which might be regarded as artificial or manufactured and are perhaps not commonly used by fieldworkers offer the possibility of more active participation. For example, the work by Sparkes (2007, 2009, Sparkes et al. 2012) combines a range of activities in which he is centrally involved in researching, in order to stimulate the collection of what many would regard as unconventional data and representational forms. For example, this may include forms of dance, storytelling and drama. Hutchinson (2014) involved interviewing as well as visiting sites and having a virtual presence in a virtual environment during her fieldwork exploring the online world of *Final Fantasy IV*. The intention behind the activities being the same as that which underpins more traditional fieldwork methods, namely access to the interior world of those who constitute the field.

Whilst the intention of this chapter has been to illustrate some of the principal approaches to doing fieldwork, it is also hoped that a sense of fieldwork as something dynamic and exciting has been conveyed. The rules of fieldwork are minimal and part of the task of the fieldworker is to actively look for new possibilities of gaining access to the interior world of the field and those who constitute it. The abiding principle of fieldwork must be to represent as fairly as possible the life of the field. Having said this, it is not the intention to suggest that fieldwork represents a possibility of objective, value-free research. The very presence of the researcher in the field rules this out. Moreover, the complexity of the field and the inevitability of multiple perspectives on it from those who constitute it, add not only to the impossibility of a value-free representation but also to the undesirability of it. The fields in which social research takes place are highly complex and fieldwork is an attempt to acknowledge and represent that complexity rather than reduce it to an incomplete notion of certainty. The messiness of fieldwork is merely a reflection of the messiness of the forms of social life which it is helping to understand.

FURTHER READING

Atkinson P (2013) Ethnography and craft knowledge. *Qualitative Sociology Review*, 9(2): 56–63.

Christensen P, Mikkelsen MR, Nielsen TAS and Harder H (2011) Children, mobility, and space: Using GPS and mobile phone technologies in ethnographic research. *Journal of Mixed Methods Research*, 5(3): 227–46.

Back L (2012) Tape recorder. In: Lury C and Wakeford N (eds) *Inventive Methods: The Happening of the Social.* Abingdon: Routledge, pp. 245–60.

Thurnell-Read T (2012) What happens on tour: The premarital stag tour, homosocial bonding, and male friendship. *Men and Masculinities*, 15(3): 249–70.

5

FIELDWORK: VALUES AND ETHICS

Chapter overview

- Implicit in fieldwork is a broad ethical position allied to an insider, interactionist research tradition.
- The fieldwork account is produced by the researcher on the basis of his/her judgements rather than something that occurs naturally – there is no escape from the values upon which it is constructed and conducted.
- Thinking carefully about two central aspects of the research process – method and knowledge – will contribute to a robust research design and be essential to the effective defence of the research.
- Access and informed consent require constant attention throughout the research process and entirely covert research can very rarely be justified.
- The fieldworker's task is to find his/her own perspective and to use this as a means of interpretation and representation of the social action in the on-going research process.

WHY DO FIELDWORK?

Implicit in the argument that researchers should be afforded access to other people's lives is a belief that there are good reasons for such access. This in itself is an ethical standpoint which rests upon a general belief in the value of research as a worthwhile activity. This leads us to attempt to unpack the reasons why research, which uses fieldwork to provide that view of the lives of others, should be seen in such a way. In short, what are the reasons for research and fieldwork?

There may be many reasons why people engage in research. For example, for reasons related to social policy or a need for information upon which to base action or intervention, for reasons related to evaluation of a particular set of activities or policies with a view to taking action for improvement or to put things right. Alternatively, it may be undertaken for more fundamental reasons which are about understanding social life not merely at a policy, practical or descriptive level, but at a more conceptual or theoretical level, which is more to do with understanding for understanding's sake, driven by curiosity, than for any practical concerns. Underpinning all of these reasons is a desire to know and to understand particular and more general aspects of social life. In the way that fieldwork is defined in this text (see Chapter 1), its role in collecting and generating data places it at the centre of research endeavour, as a means of facilitating this quest to know and to understand. Implicit in this portrayal of research and fieldwork as a means of knowing the social, is a belief that it represents not only an effective and reliable way of finding out about aspects of social life, but also that providing certain conditions are met, it is an acceptable way of acquiring knowledge. By this we mean that fieldwork as an activity directed towards certain aims and objectives, is seen as legitimate activity as a basis for finding things out. Indeed, we might argue that fieldwork has itself become an accepted and broadly understood aspect of global capitalism. How many of us, for example, have not been asked to co-operate in some kind of fieldwork, either randomly, perhaps being stopped by interviewers in the high street, or having been selected as part of a research design because our personal characteristics fit the profile required of the study that is being carried out? Who doesn't have some kind of record collating their social transactional data? Unlike other forms of research, for example experimental psychology, certain forms of medical research or research associated with say, theoretical physics, we would suggest that not only is there a broad acceptance of fieldwork amongst the general public as a worthwhile activity, but also a utilitarian understanding of what it might entail and what it intends to achieve. In short, we have become participants in and consumers of fieldwork to the extent that it now forms an unexceptional aspect of many people's lives. In this sense there is a general recognition of it as something that is worthwhile or at least has the potential to make a positive contribution to social life. This general, common sense perspective of fieldwork may, therefore, be seen as a broad ethical position, as although we may wish to add many caveats, fieldwork is not something that should automatically result in objection or rejection.

However, saying that, many members of the general population are now familiar with some aspects of fieldwork, having experience as the focus of it, is not to imply that they are themselves fieldworkers, but it is to suggest that they may have been part of the focus of someone else's fieldwork. As we have seen and shall see in later chapters, fieldwork is about much more than the collection or provision of data. Nevertheless, the fact that many are familiar with some aspects of it serves to demystify fieldwork and to make it understandable by those who are often at its focus. Again, in general terms this familiarity may be seen as an ethical issue as fieldwork may not only focus on 'ordinary' life or particular aspects of it, but is also accessible to 'ordinary' people. The fieldworker does not hide behind a white coat or a laboratory bench. The practice of fieldwork does not require special, experimental conditions or expensive equipment. For the most part, as we have already seen, fieldwork relies on the capacity of the researcher to be there (Geertz 1988, Wolcott 2005), to be aware and to record what happens, sometimes simultaneously, sometimes after the event. In this sense, we would argue, the fact that fieldwork is usually concerned with aspects of everyday social life gives it a sense of the ordinary, rather than the exotic. As such it is not attempting to deceive, to misrepresent or to appear esoteric. Its very purpose is to pursue understandings of social life by concentrating on the ways in which real people live their lives.

PERSPECTIVES AND POSITIONS

In broad terms, the approach which is outlined above, and in earlier chapters in this volume, may be seen as an ethical position in itself, as it attributes greater value to an interactionist perspective which is based upon attempts to understand human behaviour through an analysis of meaning, interaction and interpretation than it does to perspectives which privilege social structure. This is not to imply that it fails to recognize the importance of structure in shaping social action (Archer 1995, 2007, Giddens 1979, 1984). Archer (2007), for example, conceptualizes social agents within their situations via a three-stage model. The first includes the structural and cultural, the second the agent's own subjective reaction to order and finally, the third perceives a reflexive, subject deliberation upon both their subjective reflections and their objective circumstances (Archer 2007: 17). Archer's (2007) concern was to prioritize the third stage as in need of serious sociological attention. We might see 'traditional' ethnography (Atkinson 2012, Walford 2009) more attuned to the second stage. Like Archer (2007), we are concerned here with the lived experience of aspects of social life, the way in which individuals make sense of and encounter social structures as they go about their lives. To this end, we would suggest that there is an epistemological and technical fit between fieldwork and the methods employed in order that it may be conducted. Implicit here is a broad ethical position allied to an insider, interactionist research tradition, the antecedence of which has a tendency to be overlooked (Atkinson and Housley 2003, Maines 2001).

As we have seen so far, research based on fieldwork is not usually large scale, it is not concerned to produce generalizations as means of social explanation, or statistical analyses which can be tested for forms of reliability and significance. Fieldwork is usually concerned with discrete social settings which are time and space bound, within which the detail of social life is studied. Consequently, as we have seen in Chapter 4, the research tools used by those who engage in fieldwork are designed to provide rich and thick (Geertz 1986 [1973]) detailed descriptions of what occurs within those discrete locations. From this, however, it should not be inferred that fieldwork is concerned merely with accounts of observable events and phenomena in some kind of crude positivistic way. The methods deployed are also concerned with tapping into the ways in which individuals interpret and make sense of events. In this sense, they are concerned with the unobservable and the intangible aspects of social life alongside the observable and tangible. Characterizing fieldwork in this way, locates it within the broad spectrum of interpretivist and naturalistic research which:

> refers to social research which attempts to minimize the degree to which it interferes with the situations and processes being studied and which attempts to produce findings which are consistent with the view of social reality of respondents or people within the research setting (Pole and Lampard 2002: 290).

It is this view, therefore, which establishes the broad political and ethical parameters of fieldwork. From the outset, therefore, we can argue that research based on fieldwork is subjective research. It is subjective in that it seeks to reflect the experiences, values, beliefs, prejudices, hopes, fears, etc., not of the fieldworker, but of those at the heart of the fieldwork – the research participants. In this sense, fieldwork could be said to be partisan research merely by virtue of the fact that it identifies this insider perspective as interesting and important. By attaching value to this it inevitably privileges the perspective of the insider over any other. This starting point is, therefore, a value position. Having said this, it is important to add some notes of qualification here. By saying that fieldwork reflects the beliefs, values, prejudices, etc., of those being researched, this is by no means to imply that this is done uncritically or that such values are reflected as anything other than those of the researched. It is important to stress that the researcher is not, usually, in the business of espousing, promoting or necessarily rejecting them. From this we might conclude that the researcher is, therefore, no more than a conduit for whatever he/she sees, hears or experiences, that he/she has no role other than that of scribe or reporter. However, to do so would be to misunderstand the purpose of fieldwork and of the role of the fieldworker as we shall explain below.

VALUES

THE FIELDWORKER AS NEUTRAL OBSERVER

Whilst the foundation of fieldwork may be the collection and reporting of data, drawn from first-hand experience of the research location (the field), it is also about analysis and interpretation. As we have said above, the very reason for fieldwork is to explain and seek to understand aspects of social life. To provide explanations, the researcher must make a number of decisions about the data that have been collected, about how they have been collected and perhaps most importantly, what they say about the lives that they reflect. These decisions take us to the essence of concerns about the ethics and politics of fieldwork, for in making such decisions, the researcher is involved in a process of judgement. The judgements he/she makes about how to interpret the data, what to regard as significant and what not, what to include in the analysis and what to leave out, are central to the picture of social life that the researcher is able to construct from the research. The account of the social action that has been the focus of the fieldwork is something that is produced by the researcher on the basis of his/her judgements rather than something that occurs naturally. As this is a human process, it brings into question the basis upon which the researcher makes the judgements upon which the account is based. The fact that it is about judgements made by the fieldworker means that it has the potential to be highly problematic. The judgements made will, inevitably, be founded on the beliefs, ethic and moral codes, interests and experiences not only of those who are being researched, but also of the fieldworker. Consequently, it is the coincidence of the values of the researcher with those of the researched which is central to the outcomes of research based on fieldwork, in that the accounts of the field will, inevitably, be a product of both sets of values. As the social actors construct their social lives, so too does the researcher construct the accounts of them (Atkinson 1990). Whilst the researcher may not consciously seek to imbue the accounts with his/her own values the fact that fieldwork is a social process, as is the means by which it is represented, means inevitably that the accounts will be riven with the values that have underpinned the research process, its methodology and the epistemology upon which they are founded. It might be argued, therefore, that all research is subjective in that there is no escape from the values upon which it is constructed and conducted (Hammersley 2000, Weber 1948 [1919]).

To illustrate our own stance in relation to Weber, it might be useful to consider the fundamental purpose of fieldwork in which we characterize a process designed to produce knowledge of a given situation from an enlightenment perspective (Hammersley 2000). In choosing to engage in research we, *ipso facto*, believe it is a worthwhile activity which can help us to get to grips with or to the heart of the matter. Or, to put it more directly, we believe that research and the systematic process upon which it is based can take us towards the truth. Whilst eschewing crude positivistic notions of certainty, we agree with Hammersley (2000, 2010b) and his collaborators' (Cooper et al. 2012) suggestion that the reasons why social scientists invest time and considerable effort in careful and robust research design, ensuring that the method fits the focus of their research, must be because they believe they are able to achieve explanations and understanding of social behaviour which are conclusive. Their intention is to provide or perhaps discover (Glaser and Strauss 1967) knowledge which is robust and will withstand scrutiny from the scientific community. From an enlightenment perspective, therefore, research is founded on a belief that the research process is capable of producing conclusive knowledge. This belief is in itself a value position, as it assumes that such knowledge is attainable. Implicitly, such an assumption also demonstrates that research cannot be value-free. Moreover, if we add to this debate by considering, as Hammersley (2000, 2008) does, the challenge to research brought by post-enlightenment theories to the idea of conclusive knowledge, then the case for value-free research is further weakened. In short, such theories question the very notion of certainty or truth. They claim that all knowledge is partisan, in that it is reflective of a particular perspective. At best then, it is only ever possible for research to yield a version of the truth. Objective knowledge does not exist and, therefore, if this argument is taken to its logical conclusion, it would be pointless for researchers to strive towards it. If one were to accept this position, then the whole rationale for social research would be called into question and it would seem reasonable to pose the question; if there can be no certainty in the accuracy or truth of research findings, then why should anyone wish to conduct research at all?

If we choose to answer this question from a pessimistic position, which would be to agree that research knowledge is inevitably subjective knowledge and therefore of little use, then we would be accepting a relativist perspective on knowledge. This would be to argue that given there is no possibility of certainty in the knowledge to come from research, then research is little different from propaganda, conjecture, rhetoric, journalism or even fiction. Our position would be one that saw no distinction between research knowledge and any other kinds of knowledge, all of which would be of equal value and have similar claims to truth. Concerns about absolute relativism such as this have punctuated social science for many years (Atkinson 1990, Atkinson et al. 2001, Atkinson and Housley 2003) and may have led some researchers to lose faith in their work and in the integrity of research *per se*. Alternatively, a relativist position may lead us towards a postmodern perspective on research (Lather 2001, MacLure 2011, Stronach and MacLure 1997) which rather than seeing relativism as problematic, regards it as axiomatic and in which case it may not be something about which we should agonize unduly. However, for many researchers, positions of relativism or postmodernism are potentially ruinous because of their disintegrating character:

> In the case of constructionism, there is an important distinction to be drawn between, on the one hand, those versions that suspend assumptions about the reality of the constructed phenomena, or about the truth of the discursive claims being examined, in order to focus exclusively on how these phenomena

> were socially constructed, and, on the other, those that treat constructionism as a sceptical philosophical position throwing into doubt or uncertainty *all* claims to knowledge or judgements about existence and truth. The first is a reasonable strategy, though it may imply a disciplinary difference in focus from conventional social science. By contrast, the more radical position breaches the essential assumptions of any kind of inquiry. If we cannot take it that the phenomena investigated, and this includes discursive practices, exist independently of any account we give of them, and/or if we are barred from assuming that reasonable judgements are possible about which account is more likely to be true, then enquiry is impossible. Whatever the philosophical value of scepticism of this kind, it is not a position that a social scientist can adopt: it is incompatible with empirical research (Cooper et al. 2012: 10–11, original emphasis).

We therefore prefer to share MacLure's (2011) recognition that 'truths are always partial and provisional' rather than her metaphor of the enlightenment project as a 'crumbling edifice' (MacLure 2011: 997). Yet if the researcher is determined to hold on to the belief that research is worthwhile and that the knowledge to come from it has some value, he/she must have a means of coping with such challenges to research and its output. Furthermore, adopting a position which challenges the possibility of truth does not free the researcher from concerns about value positions. Asserting that truth is not possible is in itself a value position, as is a belief in the multiplicity of truth. If the search for truth is seen as a value position, then so must its antithesis which denies that truth is possible.

For many social researchers, debates about multiple truths or no truths at all may be a luxury, only afforded to those who write and think about research rather than those who do it. Rather than merely being a cheap jibe at the expense of social theorists or professional methodologists, there is a common sense logic to this statement in that presumably those who engage in research hold an implicit belief that it is worthwhile and that it has a capacity to produce something that is of value, be that useful or interesting. If this is not the case, then the researcher must be committed to wasting his/her time. Given that this seems unlikely, it is probably safe to conclude that although researchers are aware of the challenges brought to their work by post-modernist, post-enlightenment and relativist positions, they are, nevertheless, committed to research as a worthwhile activity.[1] Moreover, given this text is essentially about doing research, this is also the position which we take. However, this is not to espouse what might be seen as a kind of blind-faith approach to the conduct of research, or a belief that all research always and inevitably produces outcomes that are worthwhile. As researchers committed to conducting work which will further knowledge in our chosen field, we must surely be able and prepared to make judgements about research knowledge and the value that should be ascribed to it. In doing this we are, however, getting close to re-opening the debate about relativism, as coming to a conclusion about what is and what is not worthwhile will be as difficult as declaring what is the truth. Indeed, we might argue that research output can only be deemed to be worthwhile if it is the truth.

However, one important way in which researchers may come to a conclusion about the degree to which research outcomes are worthwhile, and in this context, we may take worthwhile to mean the contribution the research knowledge makes to the given discipline, is to look to the research rationale, design and its method. Here, the researcher should be able to point to a robust foundation for his/her work which will differentiate it from the likes of journalism, conjecture and fiction discussed above. He/she must be prepared to open the work to close scrutiny from his/her peers and from whatever user communities may be involved in the study in respect of the rationale for it and the way that it has been conducted and data analysed. The close reading not only of the findings of the research but also its methodology will help to establish its reliability, to locate it within the cannon of existing knowledge in its field and contribute to debates about the extent to which the research has moved the field on. Although peer scrutiny is an important aspect of all aspects of the research process and of its output, it should not however, be regarded as a panacea in respect of debates about truth and certainty. Indeed, if the degree to which research findings and output can be regarded as worthwhile is determined, to a large extent, by its interpretation, interrogation, acceptance or rejection by members of user and research communities, then the question of values remains central. The judgements made of the research and its conclusions at this stage, as at all others, are based on the values of social actors, in this case members of the academic and user communities to whom the research has relevance. In defence, we might argue here that those making judgements at this stage are outside of the immediate research process, may not have any vested interest in the research outcomes and have not been party to the micro-politics of the research setting which may affect any reading of the findings. Nevertheless, the judgements that are made of the research do not emerge from an intellectual and social vacuum. They are, inevitably, a product of those who make them and will, therefore, be imbued with their values. Scrutiny is, therefore, important but it does not remove the research process or findings from concerns about values or from charges of relativism. Indeed, it might be argued that it merely introduces more values to the process, those of the wider academic or research community and members of the various interest groups who may evaluate the research.

AVOIDING RELATIVISM

At this point a feeling of futility may be setting in. If the research process is riven with values from start to finish then we may, reluctantly, come to the conclusion that any contribution it makes to our knowledge of the social world will always be contingent on the values that underpin the research process. Ironically, this may be a truth or a fact that we have to accept. However, before we decide to abandon all ideas of research as pointless and decide to write a novel instead, there are a number of issues we should consider which may serve to temper the idea that research is mere opinion and conjecture on the part of the researcher.

Firstly, we should return to the question of research design and research method, as it is important to stress that decisions about methods of collecting, generating and analysing data are not made arbitrarily. Researchers have a wide array of research tools at their disposal and as we have seen in Chapter 4 of this text, the decision of which tools to use in the field is made on the basis of careful consideration of the nature of the research focus, limitations of the research site, research funding and its timescale. In addition, as Hammersley (2008) is clear, decisions about the type of method to use are made not solely on the basis of the technical issues such as cost and location but are also underpinned by epistemological considerations about the nature of the knowledge that the methods will yield. For example, a researcher wishing to produce wide-scale generalizations across large research populations will require different methods from those who are concerned to produce thick description (Geertz 1986 [1973]). The choice is not merely about tools but also about the nature of what can be said of the social world as a result of the research. Whilst we have already acknowledged that all decisions are based on values, the coincidence of technical and epistemological concerns at the research design stage necessitates careful consideration of the range of options open to the fieldworker. Whilst we would agree with Cooper et al.'s (2012) assertion that we are working at a time of paradigm wars, like Bryman (1984) we would find it unusual for any researcher to cleave, unquestioningly to the same set of methods or a theoretical position regardless of the particular characteristics of the specific study. Being attuned to the various possibilities and their consequences, therefore, is likely to temper any rush to research without thinking through the likely outcomes. Although this dual concern for method and knowledge will not remove the values from the study, they will nevertheless, be exercised within what might be seen as a rationale framework. Moreover, thinking through the way in which these two central aspects of the research process link together will contribute to a robust research design, which will be essential to the effective defence of the research.

The second point to note in this defence of research against accusations of futility, conjecture and absolute relativism relates to the standpoint of the researcher. In some instances, for example feminist research (Delamont 2003, Skeggs 2001, 2011), there may be a clear imperative on the part of the researcher to conduct research and present its findings in a way that advances a particular political or social cause. Both Delamont and Skeggs are very clear in that their approach is based upon their own feminist politics and intellectual autobiography. Hence 'it is impossible to have one water-tight definition, as ethnography is used to mean different things when it emerges in different disciplinary spaces' (Skeggs 2001: 426–7). But even Skeggs acknowledges, at heart, there remains the concern to unravel the process by which capitalism generates new sources of value – for example through the structure and organization of social classes. This then provides an impetus for fieldwork to explore this new source of value's affects upon our everyday lives (Skeggs 2011). Fieldwork becomes a means to investigate how we are doing value differently. Within ethnography there has been an emergent 'critical ethnography' that at its core seeks to make a difference to the social lives of those researched (Madison 2011, Thomas 1993). Similarly, there are many researchers who regard their work as central to bringing about change in a particular field and whose research may be funded by or operated in collaboration with organizations (e.g. charities, NGOs) who are committed to bringing about such change; for example, O'Neill's (2012) account of bringing together ethnographic practice, participatory arts and public scholarship. Alternatively, for some, their work might be motivated by the urge to highlight the needs and agency of excluded or marginalized groups, such as the elderly (Hogan and Warren 2012) or marginalized homosexual rural residents (Fenge and Jones 2012) by exposing the patterns of social exclusion they are forced to endure. Where this occurs, then the values of the researcher with respect to motivation for embarking on the particular study are clear from its outset. Moreover, the objectives of the research are usually spelled out explicitly in terms of what the intended impact of the research will be. In the case of Hogan and Warren (2012) this would be to redress the negative and pejorative body-image and social expectations associated with ageing in contemporary society and for Fenge and Jones (2012) to raise awareness and understanding of the presence of a gay community in the English countryside. Consequently, those who engage with the ensuing publications – both written, visual and in film – and evaluate the contribution of the research may do so against its clearly articulated aims. In such instances, the values of the researcher are integral to the social and political imperatives of the research.

For most researchers, however, their work is not underpinned by such a clearly defined catalyst. This is not to say that most researchers are disinterested in the issues that they research or in any policy and practice outcomes that might flow from their work. In fact the opposite is more likely the case, with interest and genuine curiosity providing the original impetus and motivation for engaging in the research. For many researchers, however, their intention is to understand the field and the lives of the social actors that constitute it and not necessarily to change it. This may be the role of practitioners and policy makers who make use of the research, but it is not necessarily the *raison d'etre* for the research. This is similar to the distinction made by the Economic and Social Research Council (ESRC) in its understanding of impact that distinguishes between impact upon social and economic wellbeing and contributions towards scientific knowledge. In this sense it is important to draw a distinction between researcher as advocate and researcher as inquisitor, where the former is concerned to effect change in social behaviour, beliefs or attitudes and the latter to understand it. However, to suggest that the two are mutually exclusive is patently erroneous as one would clearly need to understand a situation in order to be an effective advocate and understanding would only emerge via inquisition. The distinction does, however, suggest that for most researchers there is not automatically an explicit political or social position or cause they wish to champion through their work. It is not, however, intended to pass any judgement as to the worth of one over the other.

Clearly, though they may all be based on fieldwork, different kinds of research will be conducted for different reasons and it is the reasons which may hold particular relevance to questions of value. This takes us to the third issue in this defence of research against charges of relativism. Here, the work of Weber (1948) [1919] is helpful in its distinction between value neutrality and value relevance. For Weber, value neutrality or value freedom meant a freedom from all values. It was enshrined, therefore, in a search for the truth. However, given that truth itself is a value, value neutrality could only ever be an ideal at which to aim, rather than something that could be achieved. It is, therefore, Weber's concept of value relevance that is of greater use to our discussion thus far in this chapter. Here, Weber believed that research could and should have relevance to practical values and possibly to particular groups. If researchers are to embrace this distinction, then their research will be selected according to its relevance to particular values. The distinction is clever and useful in that it allows researchers to hold to an idea of value neutrality whilst at the same time recognizing that whilst this is associated with the concept of truth it remains unattainable. Nevertheless, it also allows for what might be seen as a control on values in that these are identified and recognized at the outset of the research and its findings must, therefore, be judged in accordance with those values. In the examples discussed above, the value relevance of Hogan and Warren 2012, Warren et al. 2010) and that of Fenge and Jones (2012) of their work was made explicit at the outset of their respective studies. Here, it was clear that the research was intended to highlight the creativity, productivity and authority of older people, particularly women (Hogan and Warren 2012) and the position, identity and engagement with a community of gay older people in rural areas (Fenge and Jones 2012).[2] In each case it was clear where the researchers stood on the issues being researched and there were a number of specific interest groups for whom the research held particular salience. In each case, therefore, the values of the researchers were apparent and the findings of their work could be judged in accordance with them. Similar claims could also be made for the feminist and critical ethnography standpoints mentioned earlier and for other examples within the research literature. For example, within the rural field, standpoints have included those advocating more generic, broader-sweep 'green environmentalism' (Halfacree 2007) or even jointly-authored articles where both sides of an argument are acknowledged in an advocacy of fieldwork to explore game shooting (Hillyard and Burridge 2012). In such cases, therefore, the research may be regarded as partisan research but its rationale and the position of the researcher is clearly articulated. In this context, for Weber (1948) [1919] whilst research must seek the truth it must simultaneously recognize that the truth remains an ideal. Any truth that is achieved, therefore, may only be regarded as such if it is value-relevant truth. It is here, also, that the influential work of Gouldner (1973) is relevant. Whilst he acknowledges that all positions are inevitably partisan, Gouldner believes that a degree of objectivity is possible by the researcher adopting an outsider's perspective (see also Hammersley 2000). By this he is not suggesting a methodological approach that is not commensurate with the methods of fieldwork, rather he advocates that the fieldworker should identify a standpoint that is different from the position of the research participants. In doing so, Gouldner believes the fieldworker is able to do justice to the perspective of the participants and thereby achieve a degree of objectivity. Clearly, Gouldner's notion of a standpoint is different from that discussed above in relation to the examples of age and feminism. Nevertheless, there are some similarities in approach. Although Gouldner is not advocating partisan research as feminist and participatory researchers engaged with praxis do, his position has similarities with theirs in that it enables the standpoint of the researcher to be acknowledged and taken account of. Consequently, readers and users of any such research are in effect, able to take account of at least some of the values of the researcher, in the accounts of the field that he/she produces.

WHOSE SIDE(S) ARE WE ON?

From the foregoing discussion and the examples of value relevant and standpoint research, we may come to the conclusion that although value neutrality may be an objective of research that is based on fieldwork, in reality it remains inevitably unattainable. This may be due to the social processes that underpin all fieldwork, the fact it is reliant on the perception and judgement of the researcher from conceptualization to conclusion. Alternatively it may be conducted to make a contribution to a specific cause or interest group. If we accept either of these positions then not only does value neutrality remain illusory but the researcher is inevitably cast as partisan. In short he/she may be seen to be taking sides in the research.

For Howard Becker (1967) the issue of researchers taking sides was the basis of the celebrated paper 'Whose side are we on?' This was followed some thirteen years later by an equally important paper by Barnes (1979) who asked the related question '*Who Should Know What?*' In posing these important questions Becker and Barnes drew attention to the significance of the researcher as a political actor in the research process, specifically in relation to the ways in which data are interpreted and analysed, and in turn to the uses to which the outcomes of research may be put. In considering the ethics and politics of fieldwork these two questions are important in simply acknowledging that there may be different sides to research and that the researcher will need to make decisions about where and how to focus his/her attentions, what weight to give to differing perspectives within the field and how to represent contrasting and perhaps conflicting positions. The situation for the fieldworker is, therefore, complex and riven with the need for judgement.

If we take Becker's question first, there are a number of dimensions that we should consider. In the first place, what is meant by sides? Becker makes it clear in his paper that any discussion as to whether the researcher should take sides or not is pointless. In short, he argues that as it is impossible to conduct social research that is 'uncontaminated by personal and political sympathies' then the question should not be about whether or not the researcher should take sides, as this is inevitable, but whose side should he/she take (Becker 1967: 239)? Becker discusses the relevance of hierarchies of credibility in social life and in accounts of research. One of the outcomes of social research is that, through the research process, power relations come to be exposed rather than any deliberate intention to explore them. Hence Becker's is an individualist, rather than collective, sociology rather than one focused purely upon the underdog (as Gouldner assumed). Therefore Becker argues, like Goffman (1983), that perspectives on the reality of any given situation espoused by those higher up the social hierarchy will usually be afforded greater credibility than those lower down. He states:

> In any system of ranked groups, participants take it as given that members of the highest group have the right to define the way things really are. In any organization, no matter what the rest of the organization chart shows, the arrows indicating the flow of information point up, thus demonstrating (at least formally) that those at the top have access to a more complete picture of what is going on than anyone else (Becker 1967: 241).

For Becker, this is problematic and the research task becomes one of giving opportunity or voice to those lower down the organization who may have an alternative and perhaps conflicting perspective on the reality of the given situation. In this respect, Becker argues that the researcher is (or should be) on the side of those who are not members of the highest group. Becker's position is not one of value neutrality but may be seen to accord to one of value relevance. The important contribution that he makes, however, is the contention that the debate should not be about whether or not researchers should take sides as this is inevitable. It is, however, about which or whose side they should take. This position is one very different from those who espouse a value-free research as the only or most desirable means of achieving knowledge of the social world.

Barnes (1979) also acknowledges that research is inevitably riven with the vested interests of the different participants, be they sponsors, those being researched (the citizens) and the researchers (the scientists). For him, however, the issue is not one of taking sides but of finding a way through these different and possibly conflicting positions. For Barnes, the scientist (researcher) has a key role in mediation here. He states:

> The research process is thus one in which several different parties are involved whose interests and obligations are partly parallel and partly divergent. In general it is the scientist who is the entrepreneur who takes the initiative in trying to get the parties to cooperate fruitfully, so that the new value, in the form of knowledge or action, emerges from the joint endeavour (Barnes 1979: 88).

Barnes' position, whilst acknowledging the inevitability of values also identifies what might be seen a compromise between the various interested parties, as a means of taking things forward. Although such a role may be a reality of the research process, Barnes does not acknowledge that achieving fruitful cooperation will also entail compromise on values. In addition, he fails to recognize that the idea of compromise is in itself a value position, neither is it clear whether Barnes ascribes sufficient recognition to the values that the scientist will inevitably bring to the process of reaching such a compromise. Nevertheless, the position is important in identifying the role of cooperation and compromise in the research process leading to the emergence of knowledge.

In acknowledging the inevitable existence of sides in research, both Becker (1967) and Barnes (1979) pose serious challenges to the notion of value neutrality and value freedom. Their work is important in acknowledging the centrality of values to the research process, and also in respect of the role of the researcher vis-à-vis those values. It purports that not only are values ever present but also that it is the role of the researcher to work with, make choices about and negotiate those values as part of the on-going research process. Indeed, if we were to adopt a value neutral perspective on research in which the researcher is merely the conduit for information, then the notion of there being any sides to consider, let alone to decide which one we are on, is surely anathema. If the role of the researcher were to be seen merely as one of gathering and relaying information, then we get close to Finch's (1984) notion of the researcher as technician or Burgess' (1994) idea of the researcher as hired hand. Here, the researcher has no responsibility beyond the collection of and reporting on the data.The approach may be one which underpins some policy-focused research in which the researcher is required merely to gather the data for interpretation and use by policy makers,[3] but as stated earlier, the fieldworker is central to the research process. As the principal instrument of the research, he/she is required to do much more than simply gather and report data. For most researchers it is the analysis and interpretation of the data together with the writing of accounts of social life based on that analysis that is central to their work. Moreover, it is the fact that research is about analysis, interpretation and presentation of findings, and not merely the collection of data, that provides the motivation for engaging in research based on fieldwork. It is also here that the notion of a side to the research is central. In analysing and writing, the researcher is usually faced with decisions that need to be made about selection, emphasis, inclusion and exclusion of different perspectives and experiences of the social action. In simplistic terms, the researcher has to decide whose version of events to represent in the analysis and writing. However, this is not merely a question of reporting in a way that attributes equal importance to the different perspectives represented. The issue is one which centres on different interpretations of reality about which the researcher has to make decisions. The researcher clearly has the capacity to be on one particular side rather than another, by choosing to represent one perspective rather than another, or to represent a perspective in a particular way. For the researcher the task is to find his/her own perspective and to use this as a means of interpretation and representation of the social action. This may mean that he/she emphasizes some aspects of the data over others and selects what is relevant and not relevant to the understanding of the situation. These decisions are inevitably influenced by his/her own values. However, this is the professional role of the researcher. It is not value free or value neutral, it cannot be. It may be value relevant in Weber's (1948) terms but above all it should be value sensitive. By this we refer to the need for the researcher to be aware, as far as possible, of the range of values and influences which come to bear on the research. Integral to this is a sensitivity to the value position of the researcher him/herself in respect of the research subject. As a form of value reflexivity, the intention is that as far as possible the researcher is able to at least account for the range of values present. He/she will not, however, be able to control them.

ETHICS IN PRACTICE

Whilst much of the discussion in this chapter so far can be seen to relate to issues of ethics in a broad sense, as yet we have not considered the more practical issues relating to the conduct of fieldwork in what might be termed an ethical manner. As with Chapter 4 which dealt with the tools of fieldwork, it is not our intention to provide a do's and don'ts guide to conducting ethical fieldwork. There are many guides to this which can be found in the ever-expanding number of conventional research methods text books in publishers' catalogues. Many of these are excellent in alerting the novice, and not-so-novice, researcher to the ethical pitfalls of fieldwork. It is not our intention, therefore, to seek to add to this resource in particular, as it is difficult to see what further contribution it needs or could be made to it and also because it has been our intention, throughout this volume, to encourage readers to come to their own conclusions and understandings of aspects of fieldwork through questioning and consideration of the issues that underpin practice. With this in mind, it is our intention to conclude this chapter by highlighting a number of ethical concerns which probably have a greater relevance to fieldwork than to other approaches to research. In some respects it is difficult to identify discrete topics or headings under which to discuss these issues, as the nature of fieldwork makes for a high degree of interconnection between different aspects of the fieldwork process. Having made this point, for the purposes of this discussion and for convenience, we do propose to consider five linked issues under specific headings: being there; negotiating access; protecting the innocents; exceptions; and ethical guides and codes.

BEING THERE

Although we have already established the significance of being there (Geertz 1988) to the conduct of fieldwork, specifically in Chapter 1 but also at other points throughout this volume, we have yet to consider its ethical implications. Specifically, the implications of fieldwork's ambition to either seek to become part of a community, organization, institution or a more informal group for the specific purposes of research, or of using already existing membership of such an organization or group for the same. There seem to be two principal issues to consider here. The first concerns the extent to which the fieldworker is prepared to negotiate access with the research participants and how far he/she intends to deceive them by not informing them of the extent of the study or even whether a study is being conducted at all. This will be dealt with under a separate heading in greater detail below. The second concerns the very presence of the fieldworker within the specified field.

NEGOTIATING ACCESS (OR NOT)

If fieldwork depends on being there and being a part of whatever is going on in wherever is defined as the field, it is important to consider the basis on which the fieldworker is actually there and how this fits with any notion of ethical research. In any absolute ethical sense, the fieldworker will be there with the knowledge and approval of those who are at the focus of the research and perhaps even at their invitation. However, to adopt the concept of knowledge and approval as a prerequisite for fieldwork would be most likely to result in the denial of access to many locations and fields of interaction for the field-worker. Moreover, whilst there may be a general moral stance to which, perhaps, most of us would subscribe, that is, we should know if we are being observed, monitored or researched in any way, to hold, unerringly, to such a position would mean that many of the studies within the social sciences which are now regarded as classics simply would not have been done. Therefore, their contributions and enlightenment about certain aspects of social behaviour would not have been possible and therefore not carried out. Probably the most cited example of fieldwork which falls into this category is that of Humphreys' (1970) *Tearoom Trade*. Here, Humphreys conducted participant observation amongst Boston's gay community by taking the part of the Watch Queen during sexual activity in public toilets. More recent examples can be taken from Hobbs et al.'s (2003) study of bouncers and door security which entailed a fieldworker taking a job as a bouncer in order to gain access to the aspects of the night-time economy in a major UK city which would have been otherwise unavailable to the research team. Although these examples are separated by more than thirty years, the studies have in common a concern to gain detailed and intimate access to interior worlds which the fieldworkers deemed to be impossible by other means. Many other examples could be cited here often relating to the worlds of criminality and deviance and the everyday and seemingly mundane in one way or another: O'Connell Davidson (2008) on researching sex tourism, Hammers' (2009) fieldwork in bathhouses and Palmer and Thompson's (2010) research into football fans' alcohol consumption; and Hutchinson (2014) entered into an online virtual environment to conduct aspects of her research. In all of these examples, to insist that permission to be there from all those who are the focus of the research would have been to exclude the possibility of these and many other studies. Is this, however, sufficient justification for conducting research covertly, without the permission of those whose lives constitute the field? O'Connell Davidson is clear that whilst:

> There are some (albeit limited) situations in which it may be both necessary and morally defensible for sociologists to act covertly in the sense of failing to actively seek the informed consent of research subjects, there are no circumstances in which it would be considered acceptable to bully, deceive or cajole someone into participating in a piece of research after she or he had explicitly refused to give consent to participate. If researchers are working in a context that requires them to secure the consent of research participants, then they are expected to understand that 'No' definitely means 'No' if they meet with refusal (O'Connell Davidson 2008: 51).

However, in contextualizing her own fieldwork, O'Connell Davidson then acknowledges such decisions are far from straightforward. For instance, 'if someone does give informed consent to a lengthy period of participation in research that closely interrogates and then publicly dissects the intimate details of her life, experience and emotions, should we accept that 'Yes' means 'Yes'?' (O'Connell Davidson 2008: 51). The period and type of immersion involved in fieldwork therefore makes the situation complex and messy and highly variable across fieldwork situations. O'Connell Davidson (2008) through her own ethnography of one prostitute, talks about the emotional intimacy involved in such fieldwork and how this would not always be clear to the fieldworker at the beginning of a project. Additionally, the field itself shapes what is and is not possible. For example, Hutchinson's (2014) presence and engagement in the field was intrinsic to the 'shared experience' of this world and the basis upon which she later conducted interviews with her sample. Yet it would have been impossible for her to negotiate access with all participants present or online in that virtual world when she entered it. On a physically more exposed level, Scott's (2010: 164) research settings of swimming baths were in 'near-naked' contexts. She was therefore interested in how these – potentially embarrassing circumstances – were neutralized and civilized. The very style of fieldwork, immersion in the pool or the showers, made negotiating access with the baths' clientele a practical impossibility. Hammers' (2009) fieldwork in bathhouses and the negotiation of sexual encounters in those settings was challenging, both for the demeanour of the fieldworker (she chose to remain clothed) but also regarding when and with whom to discuss the research. At the other end of the scale, Palmer and Thompson's (2010) fieldwork involved visiting football grounds on match days. As with that of Williams, discussed earlier, consent forms for crowds of people would have been unfeasible and impractical. Yet the study's focus upon fans' alcohol consumption patterns and behaviours at match events created its own pressures. Foremost, the team needed to be there but furthermore, to deflect accusations of being 'a corked up nun' or 'wowser', Palmer elected to overtly consume alcohol alongside the participants (Palmer and Thompson 2010: 427). Therefore, because sometimes individuals were engaged in nefarious activities on the one hand, and mundane activities on the other, is this any reason not to afford them similar rights as those we might study in more open and less contentious settings? To reach a definitive answer on this and similar questions is, in our view, neither possible nor useful. As we have indicated elsewhere in this text, fieldwork requires a great degree of flexibility on the part of the fieldwork in order to conduct successful, detailed and illuminating research. Fieldwork is concerned with unique sets of activities, relationships and interactions. It is this which, in part, attracts the researcher to a particular field in the first instance and sustains his/her interest once immersed within it. Seeming to legislate from the unique to the more general would be a difficult task and one which would become a meaningless catalogue of caveats and exceptions.

The general point to be made here is that, as with so many aspects of fieldwork, decisions as to whether the research is to be conducted overtly or covertly need to be made by the researcher in the context of the specific study. Blanket outlawing of particular approaches may serve to prevent research that ultimately does little or no harm to research participants and may actually do some good. In making this statement, however, it is not our intention to suggest that the researcher has *carte blanche* to blunder into any location on the off-chance that some good may eventually come of his/her work or that covert research may always be justified on the grounds of social scientific curiosity or interest. To do so would be to elevate the researcher to a position of moral superiority over those at the centre of his/her research. Consideration of the impact of the research on those at its focus must be the primary concern of the researcher when making a decision as to whether a study should be conducted covertly. Only after due consideration to the range and scale of anticipated outcomes can a decision be made as to whether the research can and should be conducted covertly.

In short, this discussion has attempted to convey a cautious perspective by arguing that whilst covert research should not be universally ruled out, it must only be used after careful, detailed and exhaustive consideration of the risk it poses to the research participants. In many ways this makes it little different from the decisions that have to be made about the conduct of overt research. In either case it is the risk to which research participants are exposed that is of principal significance. Although it is never possible to be absolutely certain in these matters, if the researcher can be as sure as possible that participants will not face adverse effects in any way from the research, then the study should proceed. Implicit in what has been said here is a concern that all decisions about access are taken only after serious consideration. That is, because the research is to be conducted overtly, it should not be assumed that the researcher is, therefore, absolved of all ethical considerations. Indeed, in several aspects, overt research has the capacity to be just as unethical as covert research. For example, although the research participants know they are being researched and consent has been given for the study, questions remain over how such consent was gained, who gave the consent, under what circumstances was it given and what were the opportunities for individuals to opt-out. Research within any organization that is structured hierarchically serves to illustrate these points. In a school, for example, the head teacher may give permission for fieldwork to be conducted, or similarly a Director may give consent for a study of a company. Were this to be the case, without reference to other members of the organization, those much lower down the hierarchy, say at the level of probationary teacher or junior clerical officer, although aware of the research, may not have been afforded any opportunity to object to the study. Furthermore, given it had received approval and hence, in some senses the sponsorship, of senior personnel within the organization, making any unilateral objection would be difficult. This could be construed as having something to hide or being obstructive to the plans of management. Either way not a good career move and, therefore, easier to go along with the decision made on their behalf by senior personnel. Whilst the researcher may not have been involved in any deliberate deception in such circumstances, access may not be seen to have been achieved in an open, transparent and fair way. On the face of it, decisions about overt or covert research may seem fairly clear cut. In practice, they are anything but.

PROTECTING THE INNOCENTS

Informed consent for fieldwork may to a large extent rest on the degree to which researchers are able to give assurances of confidentiality and anonymity to the researched. Moreover, in seeking informed consent it is sometimes assumed that researchers are able to give guarantees of confidentiality and anonymity to those upon whom the research is focused. Similarly, within some of the guides to ethical research or good professional conduct (see below) there is an implicit assumption that confidentiality and anonymity should be promised to research participants. In our experience of conducting fieldwork it is never possible to give an absolute guarantee of confidentiality and anonymity. To do so would be to fail to appreciate the realities of research based on fieldwork. As we have seen in Chapter 4 of this volume, fieldwork usually entails some degree of participation in a set of activities, or within an institution by the fieldworker. It relies on him/her being part of the social action as it occurs. Consequently, there is usually a high degree of social contact between the researcher and the researched. It is, therefore, this essentially social nature of fieldwork which in our experience makes it impossible to guarantee anonymity and confidentiality. For example, participants in any given location or institution that might be the focus of research will also interact with people who are not part of that location or institution. A good example here would be the many school ethnographies conducted on the basis of prolonged fieldwork (e.g. Allan 2009, Ball 1981, Burgess 1983, Delamont 1984, Pole 1993). Similarly so for research conducted in rural locales, such as small villages (Bagley and Hillyard 2011, Bell 1995, Heley 2010, Hillyard 2009). In such instances, staff or members of these organizations or communities will be inevitably aware of the research being conducted and will, most probably, have discussed the presence of researchers in their social world with friends, people in other schools, family and neighbours, etc. Despite the researcher's attempts to disguise the location of the fieldwork, for example, with the use of pseudonyms and perhaps changing other non-essential information about that locale and possibly its residents and members, the fact that people talk about the research renders any guarantee of confidentiality and anonymity deeply problematic. A few personal examples will illustrate this point further.

During the early 1990s, Pole was asked to provide some training in action research for a group of staff at a large comprehensive school. Whilst making final arrangements on the telephone for the visit to the school with one of the deputy heads, he asked whether Pole knew which school it was that he was to be visiting. Thinking this a strange question, he said yes of course and reminded him that they had met in his office at the school the week before. He replied with almost a repeat of his original question; *No. I mean do you know **which** school this is?* and he went on to reveal that this was in fact the school to which Bob Burgess (1983) had given the pseudonym 'Bishop MacGregor' in his book

Experiencing Comprehensive Education. Although it had been more than 10 years since the publication of that book and Pole had worked closely with Burgess for some five years, not until that moment had he known of the real identity of Bishop MacGregor school.

Similarly Hillyard, in selecting a site for her doctoral school field research was informally 'warned off' approaching certain schools, as university researchers had recently or were currently engaged in fieldwork there. In a later project, led by Deem in which Hillyard was involved (Deem et al. 2007), both the universities and individuals interviewed were anonymized. The research team had also been proactive during the sampling process and rejected some universities on the grounds that their very specific or unique characteristics would have made protecting their identity problematic in subsequent publications.

The point we wish to make here is that although the fieldworker can take elaborate measures to preserve the anonymity of those he/she is researching which (as in the case with Burgess) is very effective, it is not possible to place a gagging order on all of those involved in the study. The researcher has little control over his/her published work which may be discussed and represented in many different ways. Where there is salacious value to be gained from exposure, for example in the printed press, researchers have found their fieldwork sites exposed. At the risk of exacerbating its exposure, Heley's (2010) village pseudonym was uncovered by a UK national daily newspaper that then interviewed villagers about Heley's findings about its 'new squirearchy'. Given Heley's public profile as an academic and his decision to research and publish expressly upon his own village (Heley 2011), his assumption that it would be possible to preserve the anonymity of his village seems naïve in retrospect.

In our own fieldwork, we have been cautious in how we have revealed the characteristics and profiles of institutions or locales within which we have conducted research. More generally, the best the researcher can hope for is that those who do learn, or think they have learned, of the true identity of locations, institutions or individuals represented in accounts of fieldwork also respect the attempts made by the researcher to preserve their identity. Again, this reveals that anonymity cannot be guaranteed and therefore this should be made clear in any university ethics committee applications. In that light, fieldworkers must think very carefully about any promises made to participants who disclose private information during the course of the fieldwork. In Hillyard's research on the fair access agenda, the research team all work inside the university that they are researching. Therefore, the focus of interviews cannot help but be informed and framed by their front stage roles as university employees. The 'hidden curriculum' remains behind the scenes and best-discussed off-tap (Bowles and Gintis 1976).

However, there are examples from classic studies where individuals central to the research have wished to reveal their own identity after publication of the study.

Perhaps the two most well-known instances of this are the characters given the pseudonyms 'Doc' by Whyte (1993) [1943] in his celebrated study *Street Corner Society* and 'Stanley' by Shaw (2013) [1930] in his Chicago School study *The Jack-roller.* Both Doc and Stanley were absolutely central to these important early studies. For Shaw's life history, Stanley was the entire focus of his work. Shaw worked closely with him to produce the volume which was important not merely in offering an understanding of delinquency in the early twentieth-century USA, but was also central to establishing life history as a useful and legitimate research method. The book became, and remains, well known, selling many thousands of copies worldwide. Whilst Shaw does not reveal the identity of Stanley, at least to our knowledge, in any formal publication, it is Stanley who reveals his own identity, as Jon Snodgrass, in his own book published as he reached the age of 70 (Snodgrass 1983). As well as providing reflections on Shaw's original 1930 publication, Snodgrass updates his own story, thus revealing his identity and providing details of many aspects of his life. Meanwhile, Doc, who had been Whyte's gatekeeper and had facilitated so much of the fieldwork for *Street Corner Society*, enjoyed a modicum of celebrity after the publication of the book, appearing on talk shows and being featured in newspaper articles about the research. However, as Boelen (1992) shows, in her rather destructive appraisal and revisiting of *Cornerville*, Doc also attributed some of the difficulties he encountered in the area, long after Whyte had left, to his close association with the study. In both of these cases, despite the researchers' best efforts to preserve their anonymity, the principal contributors to the fieldwork chose to reveal their identities. Whilst we might argue that they had the right to choose to do this and the researchers were of course powerless to stop them, it is also worth noting that in revealing their own identities they were also likely to reveal those of others involved in the respective studies, along with the actual location of the fieldwork, not just in terms of its geography but also the particular institutions and organizations in which it was based.

Whilst these examples reveal the difficulties of promising anonymity and confidentiality, they should not be seen as attempts to deny the importance of protecting research participants, those with whom they associate and the institutions, both formal and informal, of which they are members. We are aware of researchers who have gone to considerable lengths, including the use of counterintuitive pseudonyms, to protect the identities of their research sites. What the examples do not reveal, are the consequences of exposing the identity of participants and places. The reason they do not do this is because these are not, for the most part, known. This takes us to a central issue relating to the protection not only of those upon whom the research might focus, but also of the researcher(s) themselves. Put very simply, this relates to the fact that we as researchers have no way of knowing, for certain, what the consequences of the research are likely to be for those on whom it focuses and those who conduct it. We cannot identify the unforeseen impact of how the research might be used and who may gain access to it. Because of this uncertainty it is essential that the researcher takes comprehensive measures to protect those who are the focus of the research. Such measures may include not only the use of pseudonyms for people and places but also ensuring secure storage of information collected in and about the field. This would also include limiting access to such information to members of the research team. In both of these instances it would also be necessary to ensure compliance with the Data Protection Act, which amongst many other things, requires information which relates to individuals to be kept only if there is good reason to do so. It would also include talking with research participants about anonymity and confidentiality and seeking their cooperation in trying to preserve this. In some instances where researchers have felt their research to be particularly sensitive, a considerable period of time has been allowed to elapse between the end of fieldwork and any publications to arise from it. Here, the assumption being that any adverse effects of the research would be mitigated by the passage of time. Deem (2014), for example, reflected upon how pervasive her various projects inside the academy had been, including work that had been conducted over ten years before. Whilst the immediate focus of some of those projects – upon senior academics – had meant some participants had subsequently retired, others had also moved to occupy more senior positions. Indeed, as had Deem herself. In the different setting of fieldwork in rural villages, families can remain embedded in their communities for generations, there is hence a need to be conscious of situated ethics not only during the fieldwork (Edwards and Hillyard 2012) but also after its conclusion. Hillyard, in seeking to protect the identity of three rural village research sites, has had to deflect persistent questions about the precise location of case villages during dissemination activities. This includes being clear with those working on the project, such as offering transcription services, that the identity of the village is confidential. In relation to her most recent work in Norfolk and following the advice of the ESRC's qualitative data archive team at Essex University, very little of the material could be successfully archived for fear of revealing the village's identification. This was unanticipated at the outset of the research, but became ethically necessary later. These examples demonstrate the need to be attuned to the temporal and ethical implications of the fieldwork site and the dataset that it yielded. Whilst we acknowledge the legitimacy of Delamont's (2009: 60) argument that there is an obligation to publish fieldwork findings, the timetable by which this might be ethically appropriate requires judgement and discretion. As Bell (1977) discovered, not all personal retrospectives of research are well received, nor permissible under the UK's libel laws.

Beyond these measures we have outlined above, it is difficult to identify strategies which will protect participants yet still allow the publication and dissemination of research findings. We should also note here that in addition to protecting the research participant, where research is very closely intertwined with the personal life of the fieldworker, it can prove necessary to disguise the very identity of the author (Congressi 2006, European 1920). What is crucial to this consideration of ethics is that fieldworkers need to be aware, as far as possible, of the potential ramifications of exposing their research participants and take whatever measures they can to avoid this. Seeking to protect their participants should be seen as an element of the respect that researchers must show to those who facilitate their work. In doing so, fieldworkers would do well to keep in mind that they have no absolute right, either legal, moral or of any other kind, to conduct a particular study. They are, however, usually allowed to do so at the discretion of those they wish to research and as such, they have a responsibility towards their wellbeing in respect of its conduct and any outcomes from it. Were research participants to feel that these responsibilities were not being met they could, of course, withdraw their cooperation and bring a halt to the study. Were this to happen, the consequences would only be felt by the researcher.

Other considerations to keep in mind here relate to the identification of the researcher. In particular, where covert fieldwork is being conducted, there may be sound reasons not to reveal the identity of the researcher. For example, fieldwork for Hobbs et al.'s (2003) fascinating study of bouncers and the night-time economy relied on one researcher working for a prolonged period of time as a bouncer. Not only was the researcher routinely exposed to violence in the nightclubs and on the street, but he also became privy to sensitive information. This related to gang culture and a range of illegal activities in which those with whom they worked and were employed by, participated. Therefore, to expose himself as a researcher who intended to publish material based on his undercover participation would have been to risk serious personal injury. In the more genteel field of rural village research, Hillyard heard cases of perceived fraud, suspicions of embezzlement and overheard racist opinions in the pub. When encountering 'subversive talk in the tap house' or inadvertently discovering personal information that a participant does not wish to become widely known, where this falls beyond the remit of the research, the fieldworker can remove themself from that situation to protect both themselves and the participants (Newby 1985: 162). There also can be instances where the fieldworker's presence may be an unnecessary intrusion and the best course of action may also be to leave, albeit for different reasons (Edwards and Hillyard 2012). In such situations, maintaining the anonymity of those being researched and of the locations and situations in which the fieldwork was conducted will be of great importance to those conducting the research.

EXCEPTIONS?

The discussion so far may be seen, in Becker's (1967) terms, to have been on the side of those being researched. The discussion has assumed that there is always a need to protect their identity and to afford them freedom and privacy to conduct their lives unhindered, as far as possible by the conduct of the research. Whilst in the great majority of cases this would seem entirely acceptable and an example of good research practice, there may, however, be occasions when the researcher feels a duty to expose the identity and activities of particular individuals or groups of people to relevant authorities. Such instances may be rare, relating to extreme circumstances and are not well documented in the research literature. However, a fictitious though not unrealistic example may serve to illustrate the point here. The example relates to research with children, who, in the context of social research, are often seen as relatively powerless individuals.

When researching aspects of children's lives, such as those central to Pole's own work on children as consumers (Pole 2007) or children and work (Pole et al. 1999), the researcher is likely to learn a great deal about the children's lives, most of which relates directly to the topic at the focus of the research, but also much that does not. The researcher seeks to establish a rapport with the child in order that he/she will feel comfortable and confident and willing to talk openly about a range of issues. Moreover, discussions may take place in relatively private or even intimate settings (Pole 2007) adding further to the sense of trust between researcher and the child. In such circumstances it would not be unthinkable for the child to reveal things that he/she had never revealed before. If, for example, the child revealed that he/she had been abused in some way, sexually, physically or a combination of the two, by a relative, a family friend or a teacher, yet begs the researcher not to report this to any authorities, what should the researcher do? There is a clear ethical, legal and personal dilemma for the researcher he/she may feel there is a responsibility not to expose and betray the trust of the child, fearing not least that to do so might be to bring greater harm to the child. At the same time, the researcher will also be aware of a legal responsibility to report the abuse to the police or children's services. Personally, there may be a dilemma about the likely impact of reporting the abuse on the study, as to do so may preclude any further research. Our guess is that as we consider this example and consider the circumstances, we come to a decision about the action we would take. Whilst we may seek to resolve the dilemma by looking to act according to the law, thus protecting the child, it is not entirely clear that this will be in the best interests of the child. Alternatively, we may decide to respect the confidentially of the child and do nothing, thus choosing to ignore the abuse and protect the abuser. This would also mean that we had chosen to continue our research, when the more ethical stance may have been to abandon it.

Whilst this is a fictitious example, it is not one without foundation and indeed is a scenario Pole and his team discussed at the start of their research into children and work (Mizen et al. 1999) which involved working closely with children aged 12–16. The conclusion they came to, should such a serious situation arise, was reached quite quickly. This was that they would report any case of abuse to the appropriate authorities, thus breaking the confidentiality of the child and exposing the abuser. Whilst some might see this as compromising their neutrality as researchers by intervening in the lives of those they were researching, to do so would be to assume that they would be able to place their decisions, experiences and consciences in a box marked 'Fieldwork' and assume they would and should stay there. To do this would, in their view, be to ignore the humanity of research.

A less serious example, but again drawn from our own fieldwork experiences, was encountered by Hillyard during the fieldwork for her doctoral research in a comprehensive school in the Midlands. It involved spending time with the form group she was shadowing during out-of-lesson times in more informal locations on the school site, such as the cafeteria, the playground and on the playing-fields. Many of the boys in the form were keen footballers and there was an intense rivalry between the form group she was shadowing and another in the school. The two forms often played football against each other at lunchtimes (this was a relatively large secondary school, with over one thousand pupils). One lunchtime on the playing field, the game spilled into a conflict between two boys from each form group. Of course, lunchtime games were not 'refereed' by adults as lesson-time or after-school games would have been and this meant Hillyard was the only adult in the immediate vicinity. As a fieldworker, she faced an unexpected but immediate decision as to whether to intervene to protect the boys from harm. Intervening would appeal to her authority as an adult-in-school (Epstein 1998), which she had sought to downplay during the fieldwork in order to generate a closer rapport and empathy with the group. Fortunately, the situation diffused by itself and the boys did not come to blows,[4] but Hillyard was clear that not to have stepped in would have been ethically unacceptable. In hindsight, this was on both a personal level and also the obligations a fieldworker has towards their university and their discipline.

As with so many of the issues relating to the ethics of fieldwork, it is difficult and probably unwise to attempt to give definitive guidelines on what to do and how to do it. Every situation that the fieldworker enters is unique and it is this uniqueness that may be part of the motivation for the study. It is also what challenges the authority of generalized, prescriptive advice. In our view, the best advice is that which recognizes the uniqueness of fieldwork and alerts the researcher to the possible consequences of his/her work. Moreover, we should also remember that as fieldworkers, we inevitably, become part of the situations that we research and as a consequence cannot abdicate responsibility for our actions or their consequences under the rubric of science. We can seek some degree of protection and defence for our work, however, by ensuring that we subject the way in which we conduct our research to the scrutiny of others, be they our academic peers, the users of our research and the wider public. We do so by publishing, not just the results of our work but also accounts of our methods and methodologies. These accounts are no longer buried in the appendices, but are as important as the findings presented. This is because by making details of the process and outcomes of our work public, we invite comment and criticism. This will help us not only in achieving the reflexivity which, as we have seen earlier in this volume, is central to the conduct of successful research, but also aid in avoiding practices that have not been carefully thought through. The fact that we know our work will be subject to scrutiny is in itself a useful check on conducting fieldwork and other aspects of the research process in ways that are less than honest and that cannot be supported by a convincing and appropriate rationale.

ETHICAL GUIDES AND CODES

In addition to what might be described as a sort of self-policing of fieldwork, there are of course, many codes and guides to the conduct of ethical research. These are produced by most learned societies[5] with the intention of supporting researchers through some of the difficult decisions they may need to take. Guides such as these have a difficult task in that they seek to alert researchers to the potential problems that they might encounter in their work and to provide guidance on how to avoid or get round them whilst at the same time lacking any real authority. If we take the British Sociological Association's Statement of Ethical Practice (2002) as an example, we can see that although it offers laudable advice on professional integrity, responsibilities to research participants, covert research and anonymity, privacy and confidentiality, it does so without any real authority. The British Sociological Association (BSA) is an organization established to represent the intellectual and sociological interests of its members and amongst other things, for the promotion and use of sociology and sociological research. However, there is no compulsion for those who regard themselves as sociologists or who conduct sociological research to become members of the association. Moreover, those who do choose to join the BSA cannot be subject to any meaningful sanctions by the association for the conduct of unethical or inappropriate research. The BSA is not their employer and does not issue a practising certificate or register of conduct. Indeed, it is the BSA that runs the risk of negative exposure to its own reputation as an organization, if a researcher's work showcased at BSA events comes under attack (Brewer 2012). In fact, the only sanctions that may be brought against a researcher for improper conduct are those which fall within the ambit of the law. In this sense, social researchers are treated no differently from members of the public. This may lead some to interpret the guidance issued by learned societies on the conduct of research in the social sciences as of no significance and therefore, to be ignored. To do so, however, would be to disregard the important role that this guidance undoubtedly plays in encouraging debate and sensitizing researchers to the range of ethical challenges they may face in the course of their work. Moreover, to expect these or any other organizations to provide definitive regulations on the conduct of ethical research would be to misunderstand the nature of social research by looking for certainty where there is none.

CONCLUSIONS

Perhaps the most honest conclusion to draw from the foregoing discussion is that there are no absolute conclusions. The uncertainty that surrounds the values and ethics of fieldwork makes definitive positions erroneous. What can be concluded is that the only thing for certain is that, from start to finish and beyond, fieldwork will present the researcher with often difficult challenges and decisions. Taking the right decision will depend as much on the values of the fieldworker as it will on the particular circumstances of the research. This is not, however, to be taken as an opportunity for researchers to reject any sense of responsibility for their work, assuming that no right answers mean that anything goes. On the contrary, it is to emphasize the importance of judging each decision that needs to be made and every difficult situation that has to be faced on its own merits and within its specific circumstances. It will demand discretion and sensitivity on the part of the researcher. The lack of certainty may, therefore, foster a closer attention to detail and hence a more ethically sensitive and informed approach to fieldwork.

NOTES

1 See Cooper et al. (2012: 5) for a useful overview of the evolving 'paradigm wars' between qualitative and quantitative approaches and amongst its own advocates. Clearly, there is a politics to method (Savage 2010).
2 It is also worth noting that both projects had methodological ambitions – to raise the profile of participatory research methods.
3 However, even if this were the case, questions would still need to be posed about the capacity of the researcher to remove him/herself from the decisions that structure all forms of fieldwork. To suggest that this could be the case would be to suggest that the researcher should adopt a role similar to that of a tape recorder or video camera which is able to merely record and play back. Clearly, this would not be possible.
4 Nor did she see fit to report the incident to staff.
5 For example, the British Sociological Association publishes several guides to the conduct of research. These relate to ethics, professional conduct and the use of language. The British Educational Research Association produces similar guides as does the Social Research Society. Equivalent bodies in the USA (American Sociological Association, American Educational Research Association) and in other countries throughout the world, produce similar codes and guides for researchers. These are available through the websites of the associations concerned and are an important resource.

FURTHER READING

Sanders C (2010) Ethnography as dangerous, sad, and dirty work. In: Hillyard S (ed.) *New Frontiers in Ethnography (Studies in Qualitative Methodology, Volume 11)*. Bingley: Emerald, pp. 101–24.

Deem R (2002) Talking to manager-academics: Methodological dilemmas and feminist research strategies. *Sociology*, 36(4): 835–55.

Newby H (1977) In the field: Reflections on the study of Suffolk farm workers. In: Bell C and Newby H (eds) *Doing Sociological Research*. London: Free Press, pp. 108–29.

6

WHEN IT'S TIME TO GO

Chapter overview

- Managing the end of fieldwork has similarities to managing its beginning – both require careful thought.
- Opportunities to conduct open-ended fieldwork, free from internal and external restrictions, are rare.
- Attuning to the internal rhythm of the research site can provide saturation markers.
- Leaving the field can take place in stages, such as primary and then secondary involvement.
- Storage, security and access to data remain issues long after the end of fieldwork.
- Whilst fieldwork is only as good as the data its account is based upon, more does not necessarily mean better.

LEAVING THE FIELD

Whilst many books and papers give attention to processes and procedures associated with gaining access to and entering the field, far fewer give attention to leaving it. But as Wolcott (2005: 118) argues, by striking a comparison with sexual liaisons, getting out of bed with someone often requires more grace than getting into bed with them. Therefore, we see this lack of attention to leaving the field as somewhat curious, as managing the leaving process and issues about the impact of research on research participants and research sites once the fieldwork is over are of just as much importance, and in some cases perhaps more, as those relating to the beginning of fieldwork.

This comparative absence in the literature may be for a number of reasons. Firstly because it is not always clear what is meant by leaving the field. Secondly, deciding precisely when is the best time to call a halt to fieldwork may not be clear. Thirdly, there may be important ethical issues that surround not only the immediate end to fieldwork but also its impact on and future implications for those who have participated in it. Indeed, the relative failure of researchers and those who write about research methods to attribute sufficient attention to the end of fieldwork may be seen as an ethical issue in itself. Moreover, there are many issues associated with the end of fieldwork which relate to its impact on research participants, the analysis of data, writing and publication of material based on the fieldwork and the possibility of contact with participants after its designated end, that are imbued with ethical and political significance. The decisions taken about what constitutes the end, when and how to achieve it, may also reflect the approach taken to fieldwork and the significance that has been attributed in the research process more generally. In this chapter we shall consider these issues and in so doing seek to establish that the end of fieldwork can be as significant to its success as the beginning.

IS THERE AN END?

There are a number of ways in which to define the end of fieldwork but none may be entirely satisfactory. Delamont (2002) for example uses the metaphor of a journey of discovery in her account of educational fieldwork which by implication has a sense of reaching a desired, final destination. But similarly, the 'for lust of knowing' or curiosity that comes with Delamont's selection of a metaphor derived from a poem hints at a much longer quest. We could, for example, say that fieldwork ends when the researcher stops making visits to the field or in the case of prolonged participant observation, when he/she moves away from the field, back to his/her life lived before embarking on the study. Bell, for example, reflected that it was the physical and habitual impact of years of immersed fieldwork and only when he relocated to Sussex and was sitting on a beach with his family, he felt he had left (Bell 1977). Lacey had also moved into his research field – living opposite the school he was studying (Lacey 1970), as did Newby who lived with a farmworker and their family during his doctoral fieldwork (Newby 1977). These examples refer to the physical presence of the researcher in the field and in this sense is clearly indicated by the absence of the researcher from the setting in which the study has been located. However, absence of physical presence does not necessarily mean the end of all contact with research participants – if, for example, after physically leaving the field or making a final visit a researcher may maintain contact with participants via some other means such as telephone,

Skype, email or by written correspondence, say in the form of a diary or text messaging. In such cases, data collection may continue, albeit in a different form from that collected in the field, but does this mean that fieldwork continues? The question goes to the heart of the definition of fieldwork. As we have seen earlier in this volume, some definitions are limited to the presence of the researcher in the research setting or field. For others this may be too narrow a definition as it would include only data collected at first hand by the researcher whilst in that field. If it is adopted, however, it makes the end of fieldwork easier to identify. If it isn't, on the grounds that it does not necessarily signify the end of data collection, then an alternative would be that fieldwork ceases and hence the researcher leaves the field when data collection finishes. However, this assumes a definition of fieldwork that is only concerned with the collection of data. Whilst this may seem a reasonable assumption to hold, as the capacity to collect data is, of course, the principal and perhaps only, rationale for entering a particular field, Shaffir and Stebbins (1991) draws a distinction between primary and secondary involvement in the field. Whilst primary involvement entails the direct interface with research participants within the designated setting of the field, for the purposes of collecting data, secondary involvement encompasses analysis and writing. Although secondary involvement is usually characterized by the physical removal of the researcher from the research setting, by continuing to work directly and in detail with material collected from the field, Stebbins believes the researcher remains in contact with the field and therefore does not leave it until after the analysis and writing is complete. Taken to an extreme it could be argued that researchers never or rarely leave the field, in that even though data are no longer being collected, analysis is complete and publications have been produced, the experience of the field remains part of the repository of experience upon which the researcher may draw throughout his/her career. Allan (2012) and Dovemark (2012) are fieldwork-based papers which have slightly different theoretical orientations to the ones that underpinned the original fieldwork conducted by both of these researchers and were published later. Crow and Takeda's (2011) summary of sociologist Ray Pahl's career, argues continuities in theory and method are sustained across a highly productive career spanning five decades, including single-site studies conducted over five year periods or more. Similarly, Atkinson (2005) at the very outset of his monograph discusses his enduring passion for opera, stemming from his teenage years. It is therefore highly unlikely that this interest or his engagement with his local opera house would conclude when he stopped collecting field data (indeed that engagement made good his access). Therefore, after spending a prolonged period of time in the field during which effective rapport, friendships and a feel for the setting may have developed, it seems unlikely that a researcher would ever cease to take an interest in that particular field and those who constitute it. For example, throughout this text we have drawn both explicitly and implicitly, on fieldwork experiences from the 1990s onwards, where both of us have spent prolonged periods of time in a variety of educational institutions, research settings and locales. These fieldwork experiences not only provide illustrative material for examples in this and other methods texts to which we have contributed, but have also informed our approach to more recent fieldwork and contributed to the maintenance of our interests in qualitative research methods over many years. As to some of the sites themselves, however, direct engagement with them is no longer possible as one school was demolished some ten years ago to make way for a housing development and another has been relocated to a new build on the outskirts of the village. The pupils of both schools, upon whom so much of the fieldwork focused, will now be out of education and making their way in different walks of life. Despite this, quite literal, physical end to the field, they remain a reality not merely in our stock of experience but also in the published work from it. If we accept this argument then one conclusion would be that the researcher never entirely leaves the field and another one would be that the field never entirely leaves the researcher.

HOW MUCH IS ENOUGH?

Whilst acknowledging Shaffir and Stebbins' (1991) distinction between primary and secondary involvement in the field, a decision still has to be taken about the end of primary and the consequent beginning of secondary involvement. Although it might be argued that analysis and writing should be a feature of the entire research process (Pole and Lampard 2002) it is, nevertheless, usual for summative analysis and writing to take place only after the cessation of fieldwork. The question to be posed is, therefore, are there any distinct criteria that can be used to confidently determine when fieldwork should be drawn to an end?

The literature on this topic does offer, if not a consensus, then at least some common ground here. It does not provide any objective measures to be applied mechanistically but, as one might anticipate, it does offer a range of broadly similar qualitative guides to help the researcher judge whether or not it is appropriate to leave the field. For example, Delamont (2002: 161) states that fieldwork should be 'long enough to appreciate the depth of the material' and 'the historical rhythm of the location or institution' and furthermore avoid detaching them from 'their temporal unfolding'. Atkinson (2006: 33) for example in his study of a national opera house took its immediate focus to be the construction of those performances and 'the work of the opera', but also stressed the time it takes to come to an informed understanding of that fieldwork setting:

> I do not think that it is possible to make sense of such a cultural setting without making the significant effort to become tolerably well informed about it [...] There is no advantage in rank ethnographic ignorance (Atkinson 2006: 191).

For Atkinson (2006) the internal rhythm of the opera season would have offered its own sense of conclusion, as does fieldwork conducted in institutions such as schools or universities. Glaser and Strauss (1967) in their classic text proposing a grounded theory approach to fieldwork, discuss the 'saturation' of categories and, in effect, the point at which nothing new is being learnt. In a similar vein, Hillyard in conducting fieldwork in a north Norfolk village had to evaluate whether additional information and insights gained through further fieldwork would justify the time taken to complete (Edwards and Hillyard 2012).

So far, this discussion of the end probably relates to some kind of pure or Weberian ideal type of fieldwork, where there are few restrictions placed on its conduct and decisions as to how long it should last and when it should end are those of the researcher alone. However, the reality of modern social research is such that a range of external constraints usually acts to restrict the duration of fieldwork and to a large extent limit the amount of time available for it. For example, for many researchers, the time to leave the field is determined by the level of funding for their work, which will support a specific and tightly-costed period of time in the field. Where this is the case, fieldwork has to be planned and conducted in accordance with budgetary as well as research considerations. The physical location of the fieldwork site will also be important, as a research site must be readily accessed from where the researcher is based or a period of residential fieldwork may need to be planned. Delamont discusses her own fieldwork sites and her capacity to travel to-and-from with relative ease (Atkinson et al. 2008). In joint projects, where two members of a research team are conducting their own case studies, research timetables require careful planning (Bagley and Hillyard 2011). So for Bagley, conducting research in a village in North East England close to his institutional base created different circumstances to Hillyard's case study site in the East of England. Even the weather may play a part, as you cannot, for instance, observe the School Sports Day if it has been cancelled due to inclement weather. Where fieldwork is carried out for research as part of a degree programme, there will be clear time limits for completion imposed by the university or other awarding body. These again will limit the time that can be spent in the field. Alternatively, in the case of policy-focused research, fieldwork may be limited by a timescale imposed by a sponsor, requiring a report from the researcher to assist with the decision as part of a tightly-specified policy framework. In addition, restrictions internal to the research site itself may also limit the time that can be spent in the field. For example, where fieldwork is located within an institution, as is often the case in many areas of social science, it is unlikely that an open-ended invitation for participation in that institution will be extended to the researcher. What is more likely is that a particular period of time will be offered during which it will be possible to accommodate a researcher. Whilst in some instances the timing of fieldwork may not be significant, with any particular timeframe likely to be as useful as any other, in others it will be absolutely crucial. For example, in the field of educational research, secondary school head teachers are often reluctant to grant access to their schools during the summer term fearing this might disrupt preparation for and the sitting of public examinations. Similarly so, institutions may find themselves undergoing internal or external audits, such as an Ofsted inspection, the impact of which upon a school's routine was traced by Jeffrey and Woods (1998). Here, Jeffrey was already an embedded fieldworker in the run up to the inspections and hence did not encounter barriers to access that a new researcher may have encountered at that time. In the case of a study designed to observe the full school year or more specifically the place of public examinations in the experience of schooling, timing would pose a significant problem. Clearly, it would be easy to identify likely 'hot spots' in a wide range of institutions where accommodation of fieldwork would not be possible. Ironically, it may be these very times that are of particular attraction for the social researcher. Whilst it may sometimes be possible for the researcher who has developed a very good rapport with relevant gatekeepers to persuade them to agree to access at such times, it may often be that the fieldworker is denied access to critical incidents in the rhythms of a particular institution and in the lives of its participants for myriad reasons, including space and time.

From the foregoing discussion we may conclude that opportunities to conduct open-ended fieldwork, free from internal and external restrictions, are rare. As a consequence, the time to be spent in the field will usually be specified in advance, as part of the research design. Rather than being driven by concerns for the quality and the quantity of the collected data and therefore a decision integral to the ongoing progress of the fieldwork, the decision of when to leave the field is likely to be contingent on external technical factors. This is not to argue that the decision is always predetermined and the researcher has no capacity for flexibility here, it is to emphasize the financial and political context within which much fieldwork is conducted. The fieldworker may therefore have a strong sense of what needs to be included within that timeframe (Jeffrey and Troman 2004). Whilst it may be possible for the researcher to leave the field early, that is before the time specified in the research design, it is rare for fieldwork to extend beyond the original time specified. In this respect, decisions about the ending of fieldwork may be more usefully considered not in terms of when, but in terms of how the nature of departure should be managed.

TAKING YOUR LEAVE

As with all aspects of the research process, the end of fieldwork requires careful thought and planning. As a courtesy, research participants need to be at least informed and if possible consulted about when fieldwork will end, as this will impact on them as well as on the researcher. Although a specific period of fieldwork is likely to have been agreed with at least some of the participants in advance of the study, not all of those who become involved in the fieldwork will have been informed of the arrangements. Others may have forgotten or, in cases of covert participation, the researchers' decision to leave the field may be totally unexpected and in some cases difficult to explain. Our discussion in an earlier chapter was also clear that not all people in the field can be informed or necessarily consent formally to the research. Managing the end of fieldwork may, therefore, prove similar to managing its beginning in respect of the expectations of members of the field. As we have seen above, the period for fieldwork may be circumscribed by technical factors. In some ways this may make planning for the end easier, as the researcher knows when data collection must be completed, or at least by what time he/she has to have gathered enough data to work with and with which he/she can be confident to represent the activities of the field. Knowing in advance will enable the researcher to make appropriate plans for targeting particular locations, people, activities, documents, etc., which are regarded as essential, before the end. For example, in the case of school-based research, this may mean ensuring that observations of lessons in particular subjects or those taught by a particular teacher have been completed. For fieldwork sites spread geographically across a village, it may include spending time in the different organizations or clubs within that space, meeting with residents across the village and also tracing how different areas are used and for what purpose by the people there. It may mean that the end is planned around a specific or infrequent event, such as a sports day, parish council meetings, parents' evening or the annual village charity cricket match, which is regarded as significant to the study. Whilst it may be possible for the researcher to return for such events, so long as relations with research participants have been amicable, the context of such a return may make a qualitative difference to the experience. The lead-up to the event as well as its aftermath will not be accessible and the return of the researcher may, in itself, add to the 'special' nature of the event. Clearly, these possibilities would need to be judged within the specific context before a decision to return was taken.

Deciding on or knowing the specific date of the end of fieldwork, or of the final visit to the field will help to facilitate the many simple and more routine tasks that often punctuate fieldwork. These may include ensuring that relevant documents have been collected which may be especially important where particular sequences of information are required, or where a complete set of information is important. It may be that information or books borrowed from respondents need to be returned, with thanks. It may also be an opportunity to ensure that you have reliable contact details of those you may wish to keep in touch with after the end of fieldwork. Or, quite simply, the final stages of fieldwork may produce the motivation to collect the data that, for some reason, have eluded you so far. One last attempt to talk to the one person who has so far avoided you and appeared rude on previous attempts, to catch a word with a very busy working mum or to observe the school football team at training as it had been pouring with rain on previous occasions and you hadn't fancied getting wet! The final days are, therefore, an opportunity to address those things that you had put off for one reason or another at earlier stages in the field. They reflect very clearly the fact the fieldwork is about human relationships and that you, the researcher, are not a machine able to be turned on or off at will. They come into sharper focus as you approach the end of fieldwork and prepare to distance yourself from the opportunities to continue collecting more and more data. As Delamont (2002) says, the temptation may be to go on and on collecting data in surroundings that by then will be familiar and perhaps (too) comfortable, as the alternative of prolonged analysis and writing seems far less attractive. Alternatively, as Parker (1996) found, relationships with key gatekeepers can prove antagonistic and their conclusion relieve the fieldworker from the tension involved in managing such relations.

In addition to tying up the loose ends of data collection, the end of fieldwork also means the end of relationships that will have been formed over its duration. These are likely to have varied according to the extent and nature of the contact, the formal and/or institutional status of individuals, the extent to which people have been helpful or obstructive as well as the usual conventions of social intercourse which shape whether or not individuals are able to establish a rapport. Within these particular sets of circumstances it is feasible that friendships between researcher and researched will have developed. Hillyard, coming to the end of her fieldwork in Norfolk, was invited to various informal social gatherings by staff and exchanged email addresses with some of the teachers she had worked with. Where this is the case then expectations of contact beyond the fieldwork may be anticipated and encouraged. If so, participants may also expect to continue their involvement in the research through the more informal contact with the researcher that may ensue. Whilst there may be no problem with this and such relationships may be regarded as a positive outcome of the fieldwork, it may be useful for the researcher to make clear the extent to which it will be possible to discuss the research within the context of the friendship. Clearly, the researcher has a duty of confidentiality to all of those who have participated in the study, not just those with whom longer lasting relationships have been maintained. It is not difficult to see where such relationships may present challenges to the researcher, which may have a significant bearing on the nature of the friendship. In such circumstances, it might be argued that although the fieldwork and indeed the study as a whole has come to an end, the researcher does not stop being a researcher in the sense that he/she may have had access to information that is not necessarily in the public domain and that is highly sensitive and personal. Moreover, in the course of data analysis, the researcher will also have made judgements about those with whom she/he may have come to regard as friends and may have referred to them in published work. As we have seen, even where pseudonyms are used it is often possible for research participants to identify themselves and others from the field in published work and where this happens, the researcher will need to acknowledge the possible impact of this on any future friendship. In addition, even where there is no identifiable friendship, it may also be the case that participants seek to maintain intermittent contact with the researcher. Understandably, they may wish to gain access to publications or other output relating to the study, in which they may have been key participants. Alternatively, the researcher may decide to notify participants of output and send them copies of papers, thus maintaining the relationship, albeit at a restricted and professional level. This can often be the case if the fieldwork has involved academic participants.

However, the decision of whether or not to maintain contact after the formal cessation of fieldwork may not be entirely that of the researcher. Research participants may be only too pleased that the fieldwork is coming to an end, thus allowing them to return to the way things were before the researcher arrived in the field. Alternatively, some kind of contact, perhaps in the form of reports or presentations on the findings of the study, may have been negotiated as a pre-condition of granting access to the field in the first instance. Where this is the case the researcher clearly has an obligation to prolong contact regardless of personal preference and may also feel under some pressure to present findings in such a way as to avoid creating tensions between those upon whom the findings are based and who remain in the field. The art of the post-fieldwork presentations that, whilst being true to the data also has minimal impact on the site, may be something which researchers would do well to cultivate. In addition, it is often difficult to judge what will interest the people attending, particularly if it is a public event. One further possibility may also be where participants offer to continue to feed data to the researcher after the point of departure. This may be tempting and useful as a means of adding to the stock of data. However, there comes a time in all research where it is necessary to draw a halt to data collection and where the study has to stand or fall by what there is. It is also worth keeping in mind that more does not necessarily mean better and the outcome of the research must rest on what has been collected.

AFTER THE END

RESEARCHERS

Ending the time in the field can represent a watershed in the research process. For some, fieldwork is the most enjoyable aspect of the entire project and its end may signal a return to, or the start of the more routine activities of analysis and writing. It may also signal that time towards completion of the doctorate is approaching, that funding is running out or that a sponsor will be expecting an end-of-award report. For others, the end of fieldwork may mean the beginning of serious summative analysis and writing (Pole and Lampard 2002) or where a comparative project can really come to fruition when fieldworkers return from their different sites and contrast their findings. This is the period of the research project when the hours spent in the field start to pay dividends in terms of tangible output. It may, therefore, herald the most productive phase of the research process in which there is a new or different sense of urgency, requiring a new timetable, targets or work schedules. Whichever way the end of fieldwork is interpreted, it seems likely that a period of adjustment will be required as new work rhythms are adopted at the same time as others are left behind.

For some researchers, leaving the field behind can be an emotional time. Losing contact with people, locations and situations that have been important and absorbing for what may have been a long period of time may be difficult and a time of some sadness which may even engender a sense of loss. It may also represent a 'low' spot in the research process where the researcher feels it necessary to re-charge the intellectual and physical batteries. For example, Wacquant's (2003) fitness regime in his study of boxing was highly intensive and he describes the change in his physique during that time. Towards the end of his fieldwork, his training will have diminished from the level needed for his preparations for his first amateur fight. Quite literally, his body and soul would have needed a period of recuperation after the fieldwork. On a more trivial note, the fieldworker may have been away from family and friends for a prolonged period of time. However, for many fieldworkers a period of adjustment may not be possible, as fieldwork has been conducted alongside other duties such as teaching and administration. Moreover, a period of adjustment may not be regarded as necessary. In the case of Scott (2009: 125), a self-proclaimed 'chlorine junkie', swimming regularly was already part of her schedule and hence the end of formal data collection no disruption to her routine. For many academics, for example, fieldwork has become part of the rhythm of working life and in this sense, it is not exceptional either in its conduct or its ending. The intention of this discussion is not to engender feelings of guilt amongst researchers, probably a majority of whom do not feel a sense of loss or exhaustion or relief, or even anything at all at the end of fieldwork. It is merely to acknowledge those possibilities and to give due attention to them as an aspect of the research process.

RESEARCH PARTICIPANTS

Whilst for the researcher the end of primary fieldwork may signal the start of new and different activities directed towards the completion of the research, for the research participants the situation might be very different. For some, the departure of the researcher may be welcome, signalling a return to normality, whilst for others it may result in a sense of loss and unlike the situation faced by the researcher, there may be little to compensate for it. For example, participants may have enjoyed the attention and perhaps a degree of status which participation in the research had afforded them. Some participants may have enjoyed the fact that they or their particular role within an organization was deemed to be of interest to an outsider and they welcomed the chance to participate in the study. In some instances, removal of this interest and associated status may have returned those concerned to their previous unexceptional role and hence a sense of loss may be experienced.

In exceptional circumstances, participation in fieldwork may have a long-lasting impact on the participant. For example, we discussed earlier in this text the classic example of Doc who was central to the fieldwork conducted by Whyte for the celebrated study 'Street Corner Society'. Without Doc, Whyte would have been unable to gain access to the street corner gangs of 'Cornerville' and therefore, to the activities that, for many, constituted everyday life in the town. As a result of the attention the book received over many years Doc, whose real identity was eventually revealed, enjoyed a minor celebrity, appearing in newspapers and on US talk shows. However, other gang members took exception to Doc's new-found status and ostracized him, suggesting that he had betrayed them and their way of life. Doc eventually suffered some kind of breakdown which Boelen (1992) argues was the result of the difficulties he encountered with former friends. For Doc, the consequences of such close involvement with Whyte's fieldwork were felt long after it ended and Whyte had left the field. For Whyte, 'Street Corner Society' provided the foundation for a highly successful academic career and therefore, represented the beginning of things. For Doc it was the end of an episode of his life and although his participation also led to other things, not all of these were by any means positive. A final, more recent example can be drawn from Deem and her team's research on new managerialism in UK universities (Deem et al. 2007). The team was interdisciplinary and included four professors and two researchers. In negotiating access that required research across all levels of the organization the team, on occasion, drew upon their own personal and research networks to make initial approaches. This alone was not problematic for, as we have discussed earlier, rapport is an inter-personal process cultivated across the data collection process. Nevertheless, clear instances emerged where the research uncovered instances of conflict or criticisms directly relating to or addressing those who had acted as initial gatekeepers. This required tact and diplomacy, both in the dissemination of the project to case study sites and also in subsequent publications where the individual characteristics of institutions can render them – and their employees – identifiable.

Whilst such situations are rare they do, nevertheless, serve to demonstrate not only the potential for lasting impact of fieldwork but also the uncertainty that surrounds it. The case of Doc raises a broader ethical issue relating to the extent to which responsibility for Doc's unfortunate situation could be attributed to the demands made upon him by Whyte, in the conduct of the fieldwork. Whilst it would be possible to argue that Doc took it upon himself to engage with the media after the publication and success of the book, a question remains about the responsibility of Whyte to alert Doc to the possible consequences of doing so. This would assume, however, that Whyte himself was aware of the possibility of such consequences, which may not have been the case. In the case of the new managerialism project, Hillyard was the interviewer in one interview with a respondent who had also been an initial gatekeeper. In this case, the respondent was reflexively aware that they were an 'uncomfortable presence' inside their own organization and curious as to the future of the project and its findings. In a context of profound and enduring change across the Higher Education (HE) sector, they would not have been able to foresee the longer-term consequences for their institution nor their own career. Such examples serve to emphasize the uncertainty surrounding life after fieldwork and its wider impact. It could be argued that the sixty years since Whyte's study have resulted in a far greater awareness, amongst researchers, of the role of the media in their work and of its potential for interest beyond the academic world in which it is located. This may be the case and there are certainly attempts, for example, by the research councils and other funding bodies, to encourage researchers to give due attention to the likely impact of their work (although this may be measured differently). However, increasing the awareness of and attempting to manage the wider ramifications of research outcomes does not necessarily mean that it is possible to control for all of its likely consequences. Moreover, there may be many different kinds of consequences, some of which will be easier to manage than others. For example, whilst researchers may be able to alert and thus prepare participants to the likely consequences of speaking to the media about the research, they would not be able to offer protection against more personalized consequences of participating in the research. The example of Heley's research in his home village in Bedfordshire, England had been discussed already as Heley (2011) himself did not see his familiarity with the town as necessarily problematic, even though members of his family still lived there and during the course of the fieldwork he had been invited into the homes and to social activities (for example, golfing) of this group. Whilst originally presented anonymously in journal articles, the village's real identity was exposed by the media. This led to a sense of betrayal amongst his respondents, the new incoming and wealthy village residents. In contrast, during another project exploring the social and cultural impact of the 2001 UK foot-and-mouth disease epidemic, Hillyard, as a member of the research team, was involved in fieldwork trips and conducted several interviews with key policy and governmental figures. In such cases, a great deal of what was reported was discussed 'off the record' and/or could not be included in subsequent publications for it would have revealed the identity of the source. However, as should be clear from the discussion throughout this volume so far, it is never possible to give categorical assurances of anonymity, confidentiality or the impact that a study might have. Whilst all reasonable precautions can be taken there will always remain the possibility of things going awry. In addition, taking the view that what participants never know will not hurt them, does not address the more fundamental question of whether those involved in studies based on fieldwork should have the right to know precisely that.

THE DATA

Although it is rarely discussed explicitly in methods texts or accounts of research more generally, perhaps the most important responsibility the researcher has after fieldwork has been completed is to the data. As we have seen, there may be a substantial amount of primary data, in various formats, that have been collected and generated during the fieldwork. In addition, there will also be documentation produced to support the fieldwork in the form of access and permission correspondence, research tools and in many instances the primary data will have been supported by secondary data in the form of documents collected as the fieldwork has progressed. The researcher's responsibility to all of this falls into three related categories of storage, security and access. In short, the researcher will need to ensure that data are stored securely and that only those with an agreed and legitimate need will have access to the data. Expressed in this way these responsibilities appear quite straightforward. However, in practice they present a number of challenges for the researcher.

Whilst the capacity to digitize all kinds of data has largely dispensed with the need for physical storage of hard copies of data, it has not removed issues of security and who should have access to the data. For example, whilst it may be reasonable to assume that the principal investigator(s) would have long-term access to the data, would the same access be extended to all members of the research team and if so for how long? Would conditions also need to be applied to the access? For example, that any member of the research team be obliged to at least inform his/her colleagues of output produced on the basis of access to the data, or perhaps to collaborate with them in such output? What capacity should there be for discussion prior to publication, if the analysis presented by one member of the research team is not shared by the others? Moreover, storage of electronic data presents questions not just about access but also about security. For example, in how many locations should files be stored? If hardcopy of some documents exists, who should be allowed to take copies and how should their safe handling be ensured? If electronic copies, of papers, pictures or recordings exist, what arrangements need to be made for shared access to files which ensure that only those authorized to do so gain access? Should these be on a university central computer network, in The Cloud or even via an international software package, such as Nvivo, that may require regular software updates? What responsibilities for security will be in place if individuals then download material to individual hard-drives, USB devices or smart phones? Even the disposal of physical hardware on which files may have been stored needs to be addressed in order to be as sure as possible that those without good and approved reason to do so, do not access material. Shredding paper, for example, is more straightforward than irretrievably erasing a hard-drive.

Issues of storage, security and access need to be addressed not just in relation to those conducting the research and those from whom data have been conducted but also to a number of third parties. Most readily identified in this category are the sponsors or funders of the research. With some, for example, the research councils in the UK, there is often a contractual requirement that the collected data be offered to a relevant and specified data archive for use by other researchers for secondary analysis in the future. When the archive wishes to accept the data there are certain conditions. For example, they may embargo any use of the data for a specific length of time and in some instances it is possible to specify the kinds of organizations to whom access should and should not be given. For example, whilst other bona fide academic researchers may be granted access, organizations seeking to use the data only for financial gain may perhaps be denied access. There are also a number of difficult issues here relating to access by various official and quasi-official organizations and bodies such as, for example, the police and social services. Such organizations may seek access to data for perfectly legitimate and laudable means. For the researcher, however, even though the data will have been completely anonymized before placing it with the archive, there remain issues about providing information about particular lifestyles or events that may be used against certain groups of people in ways not intended at the start of the study.

Access to data is, however, carefully regulated in statute by the Data Protection (1998) and the Freedom of Information (2000) Acts. Collectively, this legislation specifies the conditions under which personal data may be stored and the purposes for which it may be used. Additionally, it makes clear an individual's right to access any information held about them. Whilst it is not appropriate to enter into the detail of this legislation here, it is, nevertheless, important to emphasize that all researchers need to be familiar with the regulations on data protection and access to information, in order to ensure that their work is conducted within the law.

Storage, security and access to data remains an issue long after the end of fieldwork and indeed, long after the particular piece of research to which it pertains may be deemed to have been completed. For example, we are sure that the great majority of social researchers hold on to data long after they have finished working on a particular project. Moreover, we are equally sure that there are data in both formal and informal archives which have been all but forgotten by researchers who may have moved on from the particular institution which still holds the data or in some cases the researcher(s) responsible for depositing the data may be dead. Such situations present interesting test cases for the legislators and for the institutions that continue to hold the data. Whilst there may be good reason to dispose of such data there are examples of very old data being rediscovered and put to good and legitimate social scientific use. The work of Goodwin and O'Connor (2005) and O'Connor and Goodwin (2004) is a case in point. After discovering a collection of some 400 unanalysed questionnaires completed during the early 1960s, Goodwin and O'Connor set about contacting those who had completed the questionnaires as part of the Young

Workers project (Ashton and Field 1976) conducted by, amongst others, Norbert Elias (1961) some forty years earlier. The completed questionnaires had, at some point, been stored in a loft in a property belonging to the University of Leicester and forgotten about. Ironically, one of the final questions on the original survey asked respondents whether they would agree to a follow-up interview and many had done so. However, it is doubtful whether they expected to wait more than forty years for that interview! Goodwin and O'Connor traced people via addresses on the original questionnaire but also via snowballing techniques and the website Friends Reunited. Finding the questionnaires provided a fantastic opportunity for longitudinal study, underpinned by a romantic methodological account of access and analysis. However, such examples are rare and are not without their ethical challenges. Re-visiting data and people forty years on posed a range of ethical issues which the twenty-first century researchers had to confront. Ultimately, after careful consideration, they felt the risks of harm could be minimized and there was much to be gained from contacting the original participants again. We should also note the complexity of revisiting data or conducting re-studies (Charles and Crow 2012, James 2012). Savage (2010), for example, sought to contextualize the fieldwork underpinning several landmark sociological studies. Moreover, he sought to see the implications of fieldwork for the public academic or intellectual emerging during that research era – to unravel the politics of the method. However, he failed in the eyes of some key figures embedded in those contexts to capture the nuances of those intellectual traditions (Pahl 2011). There is a real danger that retrospective work can lack a contextual appreciation of how and when the data were collected (Hammersley 2012b, Pahl 2011, Phillipson and Thompson 2008). This, and the issue of familiarity with your dataset, is something we discuss in relation to analysis later. With the requirements of present-day data protection legislation governing the storage of information, it is also doubtful whether 'finds' such as Goodwin and O'Connor's will be possible forty years from now. It is also intriguing as to whether projects employing software packages will lay as clear an analytic pathway as the index card system used by Chicago sociologist W.I. Thomas in the early part of the twentieth century (Janowitz 1966). Perhaps only if the software manufacturers ensure full compatibility across versions.

CONCLUSION

The intention in this chapter has been to raise awareness of the need to think carefully and systematically about leaving the field and to avoid the temptation to assume that there is no need to attempt to manage the end. Above all, it is essential to recognize that the end is not simply the end for the fieldworker, but also for those at the centre of the fieldwork and from whom the data have been collected and generated. Moreover, the definition of the end of fieldwork has also been considered in the sense that the end seems not only difficult to determine, but also unlikely to be pre-determined as a particular date and time. There may be many ends to fieldwork that, in turn, lead to new beginnings in the form of other aspects of the overall research process. Without wishing to be over-romantic or clichéd, it does, however, seem reasonable to assert that research rarely comes to an absolute and final end. We may reach the end of data collection but continue to work with the data for many years and by doing so, continue to interact with the field. Furthermore, as we have seen through the work of O'Connor and Goodwin, data may lay dormant for several decades before being taken up again and further engagement with the field ensues. For every project that faces immediate and unforeseen difficulties even before the research takes place,[1] fieldwork still presents new opportunities. These are inevitably varied, drawn variously from personal affinities (Atkinson 2005, Sanders 2008, Scott 2009), the challenge to immerse in unfamiliar fields and explore new techniques (O'Neill 2012, Wacquant 2003) or to capture insider nuances (Stephens and Delamont 2006). As Geertz (1988) argued, fieldworkers will always have the suspicion that they haven't got quite right 'that' element of the field. In that sense, there is always more 'for lust of knowing' fieldwork to be done (Delamont 2002: 1).

NOTE

1 For example Cox et al.'s (1996) ESRC-funded project, where most of the research team had moved institution before the data collection process began or where, in the case of Deem's new managerialism ESRC project, members of the team had taken on unanticipated senior management roles themselves before the fieldwork commenced. As Deem (2002) later noted, those who conducted the interviews influenced the focus and content of the material collected.

FURTHER READING

Delamont S (2002, 2nd edition). *Fieldwork in Educational Settings: Methods, Pitfalls and Perspectives*. London: Routledge. (Opening and concluding chapters.)

Jeffrey B and Troman G (2004) Time for ethnography. *British Educational Research Journal*, 30(4): 535–48.

7

ANALYSIS

Chapter overview

- Analysis is not a distinct stage of the research, but takes place across the entire research process – not just at the end.
- A comprehensive familiarity with your dataset is vital.
- Analysis involves transforming and interpreting qualitative data in order to capture the complexities of the social world we seek to understand – making sense of the processes we have experienced and/or witnessed.
- The analytic process, guided by the research focus/problem, involves moving from tentative to more confident understandings of social worlds.

To this point, we have discussed a range of research methods and techniques and also key principles involved in their application. Along the way, we have also alluded to a much wider orientation which we feel fieldwork involves. Namely, it is an alignment with the interactionist tradition, interpretivism and also social constructivism. We have also stressed the importance of reflexivity throughout the research process, for example, in Chapter 5 we highlighted that fieldwork is produced by the judgements of researchers, not something occurring neutrally. In this chapter, all of these come together in the analytic process.

Our approach has probably already revealed that we do not consider analysis to be a separate research phase, rather it is something that involves careful reflection right at the outset of any research (as we discussed in Chapter 2 on 'Finding the field'). As Hammersley and Atkinson (2007: 158) argue, 'the analysis of data is not a distinct stage of the research' and by that they mean that analysis and writing take place across the entire research process – not just at the end.

Therefore analysis is absolutely intrinsic to research – it is what makes research count and makes it more than just the meaningless collection of 'facts'. Data analysis was perhaps once seen as the territory of more quantitatively-orientated social researchers and qualitative researchers neglected the idea of analysis until relatively recently. For example, Atkinson et al. (2008: 52) remind us the 'root metaphor of triangulation' was originally to prevent the risk of one method introducing bias. The use of multiple methods would reduce measurement flaws. This reveals how some concerns have been inherited from quantitative research terminology, rather than reflecting our own distinct, contemporary concern with multi-strategy research. In the mid-1990s, an important flurry of publications redressed this absence within qualitative research (cf. Bryman and Burgess 2002, Coffey and Atkinson 1996, Denzin 1997, Miles and Huberman 1994, Wolcott 1994). These took the work of Glaser and Strauss' (1967) *Discovery of Grounded Theory* (itself a significant landmark) a step further. This body of work served to place analysis more prominently in discussions about fieldwork, in the same way that Thomas and Znaniecki's (1918–20) 'methodological note' at the beginning of the *Polish Peasant in Europe and America* study was instrumental in raising the importance of talking about the research process in general (to the extent that it was read more widely than the original study!). There is now a substantial research literature available, but it is useful to remember that this was not always the case and it has only relatively recently received special attention – opening up what had arguably hitherto been the 'black box' of analysis. Simply because it now receives more discussion and is almost a standardized aspect of the research literature, does not mean it should be taken for granted or that we should become complacent.

In this chapter, we support the argument established by the analysis literature that emerged in the mid-1990s and stress that the analysis of fieldwork demands careful thought. We focus upon the analysis of fieldwork *per se*, but later reflect upon the data that come from fieldwork in the concluding chapter. An opening question to address here is – what do we mean by analysis? What are the key issues researchers face when managing their fieldwork dataset? What are the different elements fieldworkers highlight in seeking to unlock their fieldwork sites? There are a number of approaches or techniques available and we outline these as well as stating our own position.

Silverman (2013) offers a cautionary tale:

> *Sequence* is consequential for what we say and do [...] qualitative research is not [...] just a set of techniques but an analytic project, different from journalism (Silverman 2013: 54, original emphasis).

For us data analysis involves transforming and interpreting data in order to capture the complexities of the social world we seek to understand. For Hillyard and Bagley (2013: 413) it was 'looking beyond the school gates' that enabled them to unlock the circumstances informing long-term lack of a head teacher in one village's primary school:

> This school (and its absent head) therefore acted as a lens through which to see broader changes through the lived reality of one, rural village environment 'in the round' and also place a value upon the perspectives of those embedded in that locale and milieu—both its 'peasants' and its (new or otherwise) 'squirearchy' (both respondents' terms) (Hillyard and Bagley 2013: 413).

This immediately offers two distinctions. One holds that the analytic task of fieldwork is to make sense of the social world we are studying (to ask 'What is going on here?' Silverman 2013: 50). The second is that it is also about seeing into the working behinds the scenes. Our stance is that the task of analysis is both: to understand and see what is ordered out of what may at first appear messy and chaotic. We have already acknowledged that research is a messy, complex process, which (no matter how carefully planned in advance) rarely runs smoothly or in a straightforward way. We also know that we are fighting familiarity (Delamont et al. 2010) in seeking to de-familiarize the very social world of which we are a part. The main aim remains to make sense of your data. But we need to unlock, or find a key to, the way in.

Now is also the time to be clear that there are assumptions underpinning our own stance. Foremost is the supposition that fieldwork is capable of delivering insight into the social world (Hammersley 2012b, 2013). This holds fast to 'the possibility of discovering what people's attitudes *actually* are and what is *really* going on' (Hammersley 2012b: 159, original emphasis). Therefore, it is – at its most basic level – an applied social science (Byrne 2011) because it evokes this language of subtle realism (Brewer 2000). It is therefore timely now to clearly state our own principles and then to outline alternative stances (such as grounded theorizing) and what they seek to achieve.

PRINCIPLES

THE IMPORTANCE OF THE RESEARCHER

We highlighted earlier that the researcher is the research instrument *par excellence* in our chapter on fieldwork tools. So across the entire research process, social research techniques remain nothing on their own, but rather are what the researcher makes of them. As Hammersley and Atkinson (2007: 151) observed, 'there is a constant interplay between the personal and emotional on the one hand, and the intellectual on the other.' For example, Crossley's (2008) study of his own gym and the exercising of social capital by some of its membership involved a personal closeness (literally being in the gym, pool and sauna with participants), but also the recognition that 'the details of wider roles were screened out and agents enjoyed a degree of autonomy in "self-presentation"', to borrow Goffman's (1959) term, because they were the only source of information about their "outside life" (Crossley 2008: 486). Here, Crossley (2008) used Goffman's theoretical ideas as a means to maintain an analytic distance – to keep a critical purchase – despite his personal and physical closeness to his research group. Here there is a close dialectic between theory and method in analysis:

> Ideas are emergent from one-experience in the field, and from one's preliminary analytic reflections on the data. As this should make clear, emergence is a function of the analytic work one puts in: it does not 'just happen' (Hammersley and Atkinson 2007: 159).

So here, the sociologist's role is explanation and interpretation via analysis, but does not dictate the form that analysis takes. Rather, as we reviewed in our chapter on finding the field, there is a process of identifying a conceptual framework to 'guide' the direction of the fieldwork. It is this conceptual framework that aids our interpretation of the data and moves it beyond the research subjects' own understandings of their actions. This is thinking in a hierarchical sense, of levels of concepts and orders of knowledge. On the first, 'lowest' level in this order is the data. What qualitative data analysis delivers is the next level up: second-order knowledge that conceptualizes the social world (echoing Robert K. Merton's notion of middle range theory). This is not radical or unduly daunting for, as Craib (1992) points out, we are all involved in thinking theoretically in our everyday lives when we make sense of what is going on all around us.

GENERATING LANDMARKS

A very early stage in this conceptualizing process – thinking theoretically – is when we start finding or generating concepts that help us understand what is happening in the area we are studying. Silverman (2013: 50, emphasis added) captures the move between these levels of thinking: '*What is going on here?* In the analytic process this then becomes *how can I **make sense** of what is happening here?*' So here you are unlocking or making sense of what is occurring and this is a fundamental aspect of doing analysis.

The methodological literature uses a wide variety of terms for how we identify these kinds of first and second order concepts: coding, classifying, creating typologies, memo writing, diagrams, themes, categories and nodes. These develop via the continuous interaction between data and thinking by the researcher. Plenty of analogies are available. Hammersley and Atkinson

(2007: 160) use the metaphor of a funnel in their discussion of ethnography. This captures the refinement of the initial research problem across the course of the research and also that analysis involves making what is, or can be, very unstructured datasets into 'the development of a set of analytic categories that capture relevant aspects of these data, and the assignment of particular items of data to those categories' (Hammersley and Atkinson 2007: 161). The capture of that analysis is a cyclical process that requires thinking about interrelationships across your dataset. Blumer (1954) summarizes the process as moving from the tentative 'sensitizing concepts' to more confident 'definitive concepts'.

It is sometimes difficult to see how to start this process, for example, what to code in the first place. Delamont (2002) suggests code anything that interests you. Atkinson et al. (2008: 46) also appeal to Blumer's recommendation 'that research should be "faithful" to the phenomena under investigation' so here you might pursue what is of concern to those in the research field. For example, Payne (1996) makes the very well-observed point that fieldwork almost cannot avoid picking up on the issues that are important to the people being researched. Silverman (2013: 49) seeks 'to reveal what is extraordinary about the ordinary features of everyday life'. The analytic process needs to note the intriguing and regular or irregular features of the dataset.

All of these could be almost anything, but will of course be dependent upon your research focus and the research problem you are investigating: in sum, looking for landmarks and creating your own landmarks as well as capturing the capacity of fieldwork to surprise. These are all potential landmarks to explore.

AN INTIMATE KNOWLEDGE OF YOUR DATASET

What is vital across all of these issues is a comprehensive familiarity with your dataset (Atkinson 2015, Delamont 2002, Hammersley and Atkinson 2007):

> It is not good enough to skim a transcript or set of field notes and to have a broad sense of 'what it's all about', cherry-picking bits of data for quotation. Thin descriptions and unconvincing analyses derive from cursory reading and inadequate acquaintance with the data (Hammersley and Atkinson 2007: 162).

The sheer volume of a dataset, given that a single interview can yield a document of twenty or more pages per respondent, can make this a daunting prospect. Yet amongst the research teams within which we have worked, we have seen it is possible to have an intimate command of a dataset even when others have collected some of that material. Fortunately, in categorizing and classifying data, there are also now far more computer-based methods of data storage to help than was the case even ten years ago. Some are Cloud-based (such as the sharing capacity of Dropbox) that allow a team password-protected access; some simple category analysis software packages (cf. Filemaker or even Word) and Nvivo is a more sophisticated package, but rendered problematic due to frequent upgrade requirements. Like Tummons (2014) and Wolcott (2010), we consider these great aids and agree that they do not perform the thinking for you.

In discussing computing, we must acknowledge that our lives are now permeated by ubiquitous technologies and in our view this has led to some confused thinking about the role of data. Hand's (2014) overview of the 'big data' literature is very clear here. There is a considerable difference between seeing the parallels between Simmel's cosmopolitan and the online gamer/'flâneur electronique' and setting up such 'big' datasets as a means to predict our behaviour (Atkinson and Willis 2007: 818). Atkinson and Willis' (2007) analysis shows how we experience space is also mediated by our encounters with technology – they come together to inform our lived realities (even if this reality takes place online). Hand (2014) powerfully argues, we want to study this, rather than think that 'big data' will deliver the answers for us. Living in a 'big data bonanza' means that fieldwork must acknowledge the role such technological systems (or knowing capitalism) holds for our everyday lives, but it should not detract from being clear about the analytic status of electronic datasets that 'big data' proffer us. Lyon and Back (2012), whilst talking about the working practices of a London street vendor – and the very movements of their hands – still carefully situate their fieldwork within changing global consumption. The analyses of bin usage datasets in a sentient city or what city traders are buying for lunch in expenses-restricted times will only tell us so much. We can reach into electronic and social transactional datasets, but we should not fetishize nor suggest they will yield privileged insight – or answers.

There is a history of over-promising in relation to new techniques of social research. Travers (2009) argues that technological developments often result in innovation claims, but that does not equate to developing methods to better understand the social world (see also Wiles et al. 2011). For example, the strong case made by Strangleman (2004) regarding the illuminating insight visual methods can yield for the sociology of work has yet to waken the sub-discipline to non-traditional techniques of data collection (Roderick 2014). We would suggest, as Atkinson (2013) noted of his own practice of making his notes only after leaving the field, that capturing information 'in the moment' will always be selective whatever the medium (and he uses digital video-recording) and hence is not essential for good practice. What is key is the analytic thinking that goes on around that information. So when Delamont (2006) began her fieldwork exploring capoeira, it was both careful observation of that activity and analytic thinking that enabled her to write about the authority of the different teachers – working out which t-shirts demonstrate displays of loyalty, that is, the meaning of the data.

THE IMPORTANCE OF A REFLEXIVE OUTLOOK

This reaches across all principles. It is vital to maintain throughout the process of analysis (and the entire research project) a reflective stance (cf. Atkinson 1990, Hammersley and Atkinson 2007). This involves the constant questioning and reflection upon what you are doing in the field, through the analysis and too in the writing-up. This involves asking questions such as:

1 What was your basis for selection? (What you are omitting?)
2 Access (Who granted access and does this skew your own analysis in any way?)
3 What counts as data? (Both informal and formal situations?) Following that, what status do you give to each and what are the implications of that thereon?
4 Have you collected enough data? (A qualitative dataset need not be vast. Glaser and Strauss (1967) argue that this process of data analysis finishes when the data are conceptually exhausted. Delamont (2002) is perhaps more accurate when she suggests it finishes when the researcher is exhausted!)

Being reflexive is vital because all decisions impact upon the fieldwork product as a whole. For example, the roles you occupied during your fieldwork will lead to different vantage points – and these will then impact upon your analysis and the representation of the field that you ultimately offer.

So, in summary, opening principles of analysis involve:

- Becoming completely familiar with your data (whilst acknowledging the wide range of data this may encompass).
- Re-engaging (by watching/listening/experiencing again) with the data you have collected (using your initial research problem or 'foreshadowed problems' to guide you).
- Looking beyond the obvious.
- Looking closely in order to be surprised.
- Exploring anything of interest or regularity.
- Categorizing and classifying the data (what patterns emerge? What surprises or puzzles you?).
- Are there any inconsistencies or contradictions?
- What similarities and differences are there?
- Noting the context in which the data were collected (as meaning is inter-bound with context).
- Maintaining a reflexive outlook.

We now move to situate these opening principles with three approaches often utilized by qualitative researchers: grounded theorizing (GT); analytic induction (AI) and; critical ethnography.

THREE APPROACHES TO QUALITATIVE DATA ANALYSIS

I. GROUNDED THEORIZING

Grounded theorizing (GT) is the most cited and arguably most famous approach to the analysis of qualitative data. It is inductive, in that the data provide the steer through which the theory is built. In that sense, it cannot be wrong because it was iteratively generated by/through the data. The analysis is therefore extremely important – effectively what the whole project is about.

Glaser and Strauss (1967) first outlined the grounded theory approach in their seminal text *The Discovery of Grounded Theory* and this is the original reference point. However, this immediately leads to some problems for those choosing this style of analysis. Namely, it has evolved in different ways since. As Atkinson (2012) noted of the time when Strauss taught him in the States, there is a difference between the way the approach is communicated first hand and the textbook account. To further complicate matters, Glaser and Strauss themselves subsequently took up different approaches to grounded theorizing (cf. Charmaz and Mitchell 2001). The danger emerging might be that there are as many versions of grounded theorizing as there are grounded theorists!

Space does not permit us to go into a detailed account of all the nuances between Glaser, Strauss and their followers' versions of GT, but these debates lead us to feel that grounded theory is best described as an ideal type of inductive analysis. It places an importance upon the definition of the situation of the research participants themselves and attempts to build an analysis from there. Yet, as the preceding chapters on reflexivity and the process of defining the field have shown, fieldwork is not a simple process of allowing the data to 'speak' for themselves. So one way to see how the approach has worked is to look beyond the classic text by Glaser and Strauss to see a more recent form used by one scholar. This version of GT operationalized by a former student of Strauss' is well represented in the methods literature by Charmaz (Bryant and Charmaz 2007, Charmaz 2006, 2014, Charmaz and Mitchell 2001).

The core principles of contemporary grounded theorizing are straightforward and we are resistant to attempts to over-complicate or mythologize them. Key – indeed absolutely vital – is flexibility for reasons that we will explain. The approach emerged from the symbolic interactionist tradition (see Rock 1979) and this informs two features of GT. Firstly, its interest in theorizing and, second, the type of theorizing that is interested in how action and meaning are constructed. Charmaz, too, acknowledges that multiple interpretations are possible. So, taking a step back, we can see that grounded theorizing has an ambition to: make sense of the data; to interpret them and; to use them as a basis for explanation of the processes they have captured. It is therefore ambitious – it wants to do more than simply understand or describe (although these are important steps on the way), it wants to produce grounded theory.

This metaphor or moniker of 'grounded' emphasizes flexibility and too reveals the importance of being open-minded. That translates as a curiosity about issues that arise and develop during fieldwork whilst 'suspending your disbelief' (to employ the phrase used in literary studies). Here you want to see the *weltanschauung* or worldview of the people studied and this might well involve challenging your own. Charmaz is certainly resistant to any prescriptiveness in the process of use of research tools and celebrates that grounded theorizing is only one approach amongst many, so whilst she clearly is a champion of GT, she is no methodology zealot.

What is particularly distinctive about this approach compared to others, or Charmaz, is that grounded theorizing is aligned to ethnography more so than fieldwork. She perceives here that fieldwork is often targeted at a particular issue or question (i.e. forms of assessment in schools or the role of the school in a village community). Ethnography tends to look at an environment or setting in its entirety (i.e. a whole school or a whole village). Such social worlds do not need to be geographically large, but they involve more than the participant observation of face-to-face behaviour and co-presence.

Whilst we might take issue with this representation of fieldwork that is issue-based or has a pre-defined research question at its core, the point Charmaz is making is that GT's focus upon a 'whole' social world is a strategic one to do with what GT seeks to achieve. It seeks to see the interconnections. Right from the outset, the challenge is to see what categories and concepts emerge when trying to make sense out of what is happening in that relatively-contained social world. GT then uses the technique of comparison and contrast to see what relations and relationships operate across these categories and concepts. It then asks whether these original categories and concepts hold, or need modification in the light of new data? The strategy necessitates having a grasp of the whole in order to see its interconnections.

Charmaz and Mitchell (2001) outline some useful procedural steps for grounded theorizing in greater detail than we can offer here, but identify the following five strategies as core to the approach:

1 simultaneous data collection and analysis;
2 pursuit of emergent themes through early data analysis;
3 discovery of basic social processes within the data;
4 inductive construction of abstract categories that explain and synthesize these processes;
5 integration of categories into a theoretical framework that specifies causes, conditions and consequences of the process(es) (Charmaz and Mitchell 2001: 160).

The grounded theory analyst is therefore constantly asking questions in two senses: in the field and of the emerging dataset. It involves the kind of 'thinking theoretically' we mentioned earlier that Craib (1992) talks about. Here, thinking theoretically whilst doing GT helps the fieldworker consolidate their ideas through a cyclical engagement and re-engagement with their dataset. What initially starts with making descriptions moves to the generation of abstract concepts that then are reinforced to become *theoretical* explanations. This happens as the initially abstract concepts are compared to the data and found to 'hold' across a variety of insights the fieldwork has generated. They become more confirmed or solidify into theoretical explanations that hold across the different social scenes studied. The data therefore do not speak for themselves, but this analytic engagement with them is absolutely intrinsic to the account that emerges. It is cyclical and only becomes solidified once the abstract concept holds across the dataset that is being worked with. The claim is not towards generalization, but rather that if you are looking across three teaching groups in a school, it would successfully capture what happens in all three.

One of these steps marks out a clear distinction between GT and the approach of analytic induction we now introduce. For Charmaz' grounded theorizing, the review (of the data) comes *after* concepts and categories have been modelled into a theoretical framework. For analytic induction, as advocated by key proponents such as Hammersley, the review comes much earlier and (like GT's interest in flexibility) for strategic reasons.

II. ANALYTIC INDUCTION

Hammersley has been a central figure in the description and advocacy of analytic induction within qualitative research (cf. Hammersley 1992, 2010b, 2012a, 2012b). We agree with his argument that a reflexive position should include metaphorically laying your cards on the table (i.e. being very clear about where you stand) when it comes to making causal claims based on qualitative research (Hammersley 2012b). His point is an important one. With the recognition that, (a) multiple representations are possible from one research site, and (b) that when we are constructing an account as much as presenting any 'reality' comes the danger that we might lose sight of what qualitative research can and should produce. In response, some researchers have rejected the grounds for making causal claims, whereas Hammersley (2012b) points out in practice they often do. For Hammersley (2012b), a lot of qualitative researchers are in denial.

It is in this argument that Hammersley's calls for clarity in the analytic process (cf. Hammersley 1992, Hammersley and Cooper 2012). For example, he reminds us that AI actually pre-dates GT and offers a very accessible introduction to what AI is by contrasting it with GT (Hammersley 2012b). First, both approaches favour the use of case study datasets (echoing Charmaz' point about ethnography working best with GT). Secondly, they share an inductive flavour, that is, use the data to help explore and unravel what is significant and important about the given social phenomena. Finally, neither sample with an aim to be representative or towards generating probabilistic generalizations, but rather for AI the aim is about working out deterministic laws and for GT sampling strategy is all about finding cases that help further crystalize the emerging theory. This last point or feature of AI – its concern with deterministic laws – seems quite strong at face value, but what it means is that the challenge is to look at samples that can help really improve or narrow down the issue or phenomenon explored: that make it manageable in research terms. You sample to help you to look at examples that will help refine your working theory. So, it is only when the point of 'theoretical saturation' is reached (and no further sampling or cases would provide valuable information because your data have already captured that issue or aspect of the field), that your work is done.

So if AI and GT share many characteristics, what merits the distinction between the two? It lies right at the starting-point, or initial source of inspiration for the research, what we termed finding the field (Chapter 2). For AI, there is *already* a burning issue or interest, whereas for GT the concern is more about what is taking place in a more generic setting or scene. This difference at the start is reflected in their subsequent conclusions. AI is narrower and very specific in the conclusion or knowledge that it offers (i.e. it would be about a form of behaviour in particular circumstances or an exact situation), whereas GT would seek to explain a set of behaviours in the context of a setting or system. This is a key distinction for Hammersley (2012b) for it affects the precision of language deployed. AI favours binaries (i.e. *xyz* does or does not occur), whereas GT tends towards degrees (i.e. a change of behaviour occurs, but varying). Here we can see that the ambitions of both approaches (what they seek to achieve) impacts upon what each approach initially wants to explore. So for AI, questions could be: does it hold in this new setting (yes or no) and, if not, what causal factors account for why? For GT, there is more scope to refine the theory, to explore perhaps why things do not seem to fit or further explaining why they do.

This nicely summarizes a key distinction: GT is developmental; AI is about testing (that can then help theory development, too). GT holds fast to the logic that, if the approach is used correctly and the theory inductively developed throughout, it is valid in its own right and therefore does not need further testing. Put simply, because it has inductively arisen from the data it cannot be wrong.[1] For AI, because it 'thinks' in binaries, it needs to fit or be well-aligned, or otherwise be re-worked to explain the discrepancy.

We can see now that there are two, quite different approaches. These very different styles stretch across the whole research process and echo what we stressed earlier about analysis – it begins even before the fieldworker enters the field. To ignore thinking about what analytic approach you are going to use simply will not wait until the fieldwork is underway – you must have thought long and hard about it beforehand. Of course, and as Hammersley (2012b) reminds us, there is still the act of interpretation by the researcher taking place. If you are in the business of causation, which GT or AI are, then it is essential to remain reflexive towards how you are shaping your data as much as your data are shaping your account.

The orientation of AI towards causation, in our view, is one of the particular strengths of AI. It maximizes the synergy between fieldwork and the development, testing and cumulation of theory. A reflexive analysis would not become refined or isolated to the degree that it does not speak to broader, more abstract social forms or sociological theory. Hammersley (2012b) is very critical of such insular work and perceives it as a form of naïve realism, naïve because GT does not need to look hard at confounding or outlying data. Whilst a critical point, this does ensure that fieldwork does not become divorced from the issues that preoccupy its parent discipline of sociology. We feel fieldwork has the capacity to help inform and even shape the latest debates in sociology and it would be a waste to miss this by solely using GT. There are parallels with Gane's (2012) use of Weber's work to analyse contemporary capitalism. Weber's output is that of an early twentieth-century scholar writing during the industrial revolution, not one who is inside contemporary 'knowing' capitalism (Thrift 2005). Yet Gane uses (even transgresses) Weber's ideas to lever insight into contemporary social and cultural dynamics. Fieldwork can be used in a similar vein, but not if it only looks to itself.

In summary, AI involves the following stages:

1 An initial description of the type of outcome to be explained is formulated.
2 One or a few cases where this outcome occurs are investigated.
3 Data from these are analysed in order to identify common elements, and to generate an explanatory hypothesis [...].
4 Data from further cases are collected and/or analysed in order to test this hypothesis [...].
5 If the hypothesis is not confirmed, there are two options [...] the hypothesis can be revised [...] [or] revised in such a way as to exclude discrepant cases [...].
6 This process of modification [...] continues until the explanatory hypothesis fits all the data from new cases as well as that from previous cases (adapted from Hammersley 2012b, in Cooper et al. 2012).

The capacity of fieldwork to be relevant links to the goal embedded in the next analytical approach we discuss – 'critical ethnography.' Critical ethnography is all about speaking to the contemporary issues, be they theory, power, inequalities or even consciousness-raising. The result is a very different set of orientations and predispositions and of course analytic principles. We now outline the approach and then evaluate how it sits alongside the broader fieldwork canon – for better or for worse.

III. CRITICAL ETHNOGRAPHY

An early point to clarify is that in discussing critical ethnography (CE), no suggestion is made that GT or AI are *uncritical*, but rather they have different ambitions. CE takes Marx's maxim – that sociology's task is not just to understand society, the point is also to change it – and this applies to fieldwork too. So rather than the interactionist research tradition that informs our own approach to fieldwork, CE injects postmodern literatures and ideas (the work of Foucault, Derrida and Butler) alongside its Marxist concern with praxis (to not only understand the world, but to change it too). If we return to our earlier description of *verstehen* and the importance we placed upon it, the value of *verstehen* is not sufficient for CE. The theoretical territories of CE align it with global post-colonial research and towards a public sociology. These theoretical ideas avoid the perceived 'shallow romanticism' of early anthropological work (Madison 2011: 144). CE's engagement with postmodern literatures therefore leads it to be critical of past, early forms of anthropological fieldwork. What CE takes from its reading of new theoretical ideas is a strong synergistic relationship between theory and method and a more proactive, interventionist stance.

CE blends theory and method and concludes with the argument that social justice, critical analysis and the ethics of fieldwork are intrinsically intertwined. So whereas GT draws inspiration from interactionism's social construction of reality by actors to narrow its focus, CE wants to use that knowledge to make a difference. To use the metaphor Goffman (1974: 14) uses to describe the task of his sociology – 'to sneak in and watch the way people snore' rather than to wake them from their ideological slumber – CE is setting the alarm clock! So rather than an inductive model, CE argues that the very opening research question of what is happening in a setting is a 'critical and moral question' of representation (Madison 2011: xi). Madison's own professional field is that of performance studies and anthropology and draws upon the work of Stuart Hall. Hence representations matter and there is a 'responsibility to address' societal inequalities alongside fieldwork's concern to understand, study and comment (Madison 2011: 5). The task is to move from merely laying bare the processes of what is, to see what could be.

This stance determines every aspect of fieldwork conduct. CE is highly attuned to the 'positionality' of the researcher and highlights the need for them to 'resist domestication' (Madison 2011: 8). This is more complex than it first appears. CE is against objectivity *and* subjectivity because of its political charge or desire to make a difference. Whilst we discussed in Chapter 1 that there is often something that attracts the fieldworker to the research site, for CE through dialogue and representation the task is to make a difference to that fieldwork site. This is CE modifying its Marxist antecedents for the contemporary fieldworker and the metaphor of dialogue becomes key here for achieving its aims (dialogue representing the relationship between researcher and researched).

This is presented as the key means by which the othering of the researched of early forms of anthropology can be corrected (and hence is very different to the lineage and analytic principles of GT and AI outlined above). We can also see parallels here with action research, with its twin objectives to work with the researched and also have an (positive) impact upon their lives as a direct consequence of the research.

The different theoretical lineage of CE distinguishes it from both GT and AI and also shapes its analysis. With CE, its opening theoretical ideas position the researcher *beforehand* – CE is in effect the fieldwork application of critical theory. Critical theory then defines what constitutes the 'just purposes' to which CE should be applied to make a difference (Madison 2011: 15).

What constitutes such responsible research purposes and what would be a just outcome is, we would argue, relative. The combination of theoretical orientations (some nine heritages are discussed by Madison) make for a heady mix and we would question to what degree these would or could possess the same sense of just purpose. There are many procedural strategic similarities between CE and analytic induction, both for instance emphasizing a circular ontology. Madison's (2011) stylistic choice to introduce three hypothetical researchers – to discuss how they each grapple with issues of theorizing and analysis – is less illuminating than the examples grounded in practice used by both Charmaz (reviewing her own work) and Hammersley (applying Znaniecki, Cressey and Lindesmith). The chapters by Madison (2011) outlining the practice of fieldwork are also thinner than her highlighting of CE's opening or core theoretical position. Neither does fieldwork enjoy the same status GT accords it. We are with Hammersley when he argues that whichever strategic technique is used – it should be used well. In summary:

- 'research should operate within a framework of political assumptions, and should be geared to serving political goals' (Hammersley 2013: 34).
- 'it means that a comprehensive theory of society is required [...] [and] it implies that the researcher is not located outside of the socio-historical process but is necessarily part of, and shaped by it. As a result, he or she cannot but operate within some perspective that has been generated by the process of social development, and this carries with it the dangers of bias, and therefore error, *but also the only potential for true understanding that is available*' (Hammersley 2013: 32, original emphasis).
- [it is therefore about] 'achieving particular kinds of political goal: reducing or eliminating exploitation and oppression, and bringing about emancipation' (Hammersley 2013: 30).

In times of increasing complexity and speciality amongst forms of analysis, the addition of CE as a choice of qualitative research analysis for contemporary fieldworkers we would argue, is a useful one. Yet, like others, it has advantages and disadvantages.

IV. CONVERSATION ANALYSIS

Finally, we wish to overview the contribution of the tradition of analysis known as conversation analysis (CA). It enjoys less of a profile than the others, but could be argued to be enjoying something of a renaissance given the attention 'big data' analysis has attracted (for example, twitter feeds). CA has been thinking on these matters for many decades and hence it would be an omission not to consider what this stance upon analysis has evolved into and why.

CA stems from an ethnomethodological theoretical standpoint (Garfinkel 1967); it researches people's methods of making sense of the world around them. CA therefore has a different flavour or orientation to theory – it is far more micro. It looks *inside* conversational exchanges to seek how people are making sense of their social world – during the very doing of conversation. That moment of conversation exchange or interaction is the primary focus. They make no assumption that it will be successful, but rather see any outcome as a product of the moment or exchange itself. Sequences and pauses – even conversational stumbles – are therefore key here.

Earlier in the chapter, we argued that Charmaz was no methodological zealot. When we contrast her version of GT with CA, we see there is a purist character to CA stemming from its association with ethnomethodology. By looking to the moment of interaction (or conversation) as where meaning is achieved (its advocates do not recognize structure in the same way CE would) this then influences the methods they choose. Their unit of focus is inevitably the conversational exchange. Therefore, the depth of an analysis of that very unit is much richer – *every* utterance is noted, including non-verbal clues (nods, winks, for instance) as well as over-lapping talk. The CA transcript (and key) is therefore far richer than you would find quoted in most methods textbooks.

CA has come under attack for being too micro-focused and that this had detracted from its ability to acknowledge other important aspects of how interaction is ordered. However, Silverman (2013) carefully notes that, for him, such an interest in this kind of sequential analysis does not put CA at odds with other approaches to qualitative research. He importantly stresses that interviews need to be contextualized, not just taken as fixed lumps of data for analysis. Mair et al. (2012) is a strong case-in-point. They used a CA-informed approach to analyse an instance of 'friendly fire' in 2007 during the Gulf War. They do so by looking at the ground-to-air communication and the air-to-air communication and exchanges:

> we see the chaining and amplification of problems stemming from the locational confusion we focus on in Excerpt II.9 Once POPOV36 [pilot] received confirmation from POPOV35 [pilot] (via MANILA HOTEL) [ground control] that there were no allied troops in 'the area' (with both the ground controller and the pilots laboring under different understandings as to where 'here' was), he

> erroneously concluded, by a process of elimination, that the 'orange panels' he had observed on the British vehicles could not be markings signalling an allied force (as they standardly are). Instead, they had to be something else, orange 'rocket launchers' attached to Iraqi vehicles. In this way, the 'four ship' came to embody not merely a potential enemy force but a potentially threatening enemy force (Mair et al. 2012: 91).

Mair et al. (2012) were here looking into a conversational exchange that was also situated in a wider context of shared (or mis-shared) knowledge (where 'here' was). They looked at the conversational exchange to note when this breach or disjunction in the accuracy of knowledge occurred – in flight, via a conversational exchange. Therefore, their application of CA was successful in capturing and detailing that particular, critical moment. In this case, CA as an analytic technique was perfectly matched to the subject matter and task at hand.

SUMMARY

This discussion of alternative approaches has revealed that our own stance distances us from a postmodern discourse that, some have argued, severs the arteries of field research (Pole and Morrison 2003). We would therefore summarize our own stance towards analysis with a few broader comments and observations.

Firstly, we resist the tendency towards something alchemic in the analytic process. Rather, foreshadowed problems inform the analytic process (Delamont et al. 2010). In the current climate in which fieldwork now often incorporates a wide array of tools and new digital technologies, there is a risk that something magical or mysterious has become associated with analysis. Delamont et al. (2010) argue that actually working hypotheses (said foreshadowed problems) are key to fighting familiarity. Careful questions and demystification needs to be asked of all the resources that fieldwork appeals to – whether traditional tools or the ever ubiquitous technologies, such as photographs and other visual media. Beer (2012) for instance notes how algorithms predefine Big Data outputs. We therefore cannot take these techniques, nor the knowledge that they yield for granted or think they have any more privileged access to social reality than the more traditional techniques associated with fieldwork.[2] As Hand's (2012: 24) discussion of the permeation of photography across our everyday world recognizes, 'Photography now has many lives, each of which may be related, but all are part of different trends and may have rather different trajectories in the future.' For fieldwork, you will need to think about the very 'life' or trajectory of the medium you are looking to include and why. Rich as new resources may be, they provide no analytic shortcut. Unlike CA, it is rare that analysis consists entirely of a text-based dataset. Therefore analysis will always be done on a portfolio of material, some you have generated, and others you have adapted to your own needs or even stumbled upon. Increasingly, this will include open data – that is, data which are already there – the kind of data shadow we all possess in the digital age. For the purposes of analysis, a more fruitful way to respond is to invite fieldworkers to explore how such new technological developments can better aid our understanding of the social world (Travers 2009). The fieldworker here proactively uses New Social Media (NSM) *for their own ends*, rather than simply scraping or mining from what is already there (after netnography). Our preference would be to see the social science community work in synergy with new and established methods to see the presentation of self both online and in co-presence, but there is a danger we may miss the boat. To paraphrase Kelly and Burrows (2011: 140), 'it's play or get played'.

Our second point overviews the evolving 'life' or status of fieldwork within the social sciences. Qualitative analysis has now become a broad church, containing a variety of approaches each with advantages and disadvantages (Atkinson et al. 2008). For instance, Atkinson (2009, 2013) was instrumental in revealing the rhetorical devices underpinning ethnographic representations, yet has remained cautious about some forms of narrative analysis (such as autoethnography). Nevertheless, such new forms (cf. Smith 2013, Sparkes 2007, 2009) or those that privilege the interview (Forsey 2010) are well established. The broader cultural context in which fieldworkers are trained and work has had its own impact. Atkinson and Silverman (1997) and Silverman (2013) argue we live in an 'Interview Society' akin to a sound-byte society in which the interview is reified as the best or only way to access the complexity of an individual's world. Fieldworkers risk becoming complicit with this, for example, Atkinson (2013) is particularly cautious about how we have come to neglect the situation within which the individual is located (instead focusing more upon their biography – or further even auto-ethnography).

A discussion of these debates in full is beyond our task here, beyond noting the tendency to over-claim methodological innovation (Travers 2009, Wiles et al. 2011). We prefer Goffman's (1983) modest wish for a few conceptual distinctions (and a cold beer) that will help 'unlock', explain and illuminate our fieldwork sites alongside Delamont's (2002) metaphor of fieldwork as a journey. These both capture the excitement – and challenge – of fieldwork as a social science research approach is evolving as well as offering the fieldworker a sharp learning curve. Delamont et al. (2010) use classic examples from the literature to dispel the mysticism or 'magic' (Geer's original metaphor) of getting an analytic grip on a fieldwork setting. In a similar manner, we now conclude with a few celebrated (and varied) examples of the analytic insight yielded by distinctive fieldwork. In the spirit of Atkinson (2015) and Atkinson and Housley (2003), classics may appear dated, but we feel should not be forgotten for danger of reinventing the wheel.

EXAMPLES OF CONCEPT USE IN RESEARCH MONOGRAPHS

There are many examples in the literature where analytic concepts have been drawn from the terminology of the research participants. Wieder (1974) is a seminal case and more, using the inmates' own notion of 'telling the code' in his study of an American prison. However, importantly, he moves beyond the way the inmates employed it to use it as a tool of both description and explanation. Where an inmate refused to provide a prison guard with information about a fellow inmate, they explain their actions with reference to the prison code. Here it becomes more than an informal code to become something that is directly appealed to as a means to (legitimately) explain behaviour (even if it places them at odds with the prison rules). To fast-forward to a more contemporary piece of fieldwork, O'Neill (2012) used 'walking ethnographies' with workers and residents of Vancouver's downtown east side. Here, alongside physical maps drawn by participants and their verbal accounts during the walks, O'Neill pieced together local knowledge of the place, both the no-go areas and safe spaces. This was richer than a physical map or even transitional zones of a city in terms of capturing the 'experiences and presentations of communities of interest, well-being and connection' (O'Neill 2012: 165). O'Neill's account was dependent upon the analytic interconnections possible across her dataset, from interviews, walking tours and observation techniques in order to make sense of 'the workings of "community"' (O'Neill 2012: 166). This multi-strategy approach relied upon the most marginalized informants' deep familiarity of their locale.

Pryce (1979) is a second example of a seminal fieldwork monograph that used participants' terminology and adapted them into a more formal sociological language. Pryce (1979) created six categories, or typologies, which described the differences between people in the Afro-Caribbean community in the St. Paul's area of Bristol and captured their orientations towards criminal activity vis-à-vis respectability – from the piously religious to the teeneyboppers. To again fast-forward to a more contemporary scene, Lyon and Back (2012) were similarly interested in the multicultural city environment. Employing an array of ethnographic techniques, including visual and aural recordings, they sought to capture urban multiculturalism in a street in South East London. Here they focused upon the craft of the occupational group – fishmongers – but the contemporary context demanded they opened up their analysis to understand the particular circumstances of two retailers in both the setting (a high street) and the social history of that section of London (the embedded third generation local vis-à-vis a migrant from Kashmir – where there is no sea!). Lyon and Back (2012) looked beyond craft (fishmongering) towards its becoming a skill of embodied local knowledge that was embedded in the new landscape of a global, multicultural city. 'Knowing your fish' becomes diversified to shaping the product to fit the consumers' world (using ideas drawn from actor network theory) (Lyon and Back 2012). The situation of the working lives of the two case study individuals could, their analysis found, only be understood as part of a global landscape situated alongside the sensuous activity of their labour. This is a theoretically-informed example of global ethnography.

Metaphors are an alternative technique for extrapolating data. A famous example is Goffman's (1959) use of a dramaturgical model. In this Goffman conceptualized social interaction as analogous to a drama on a stage, with social actors taking the role of performers. Goffman then applied this drama metaphor to understand their actions and behaviour, informed by fieldwork conducted in the Shetland Islands. Here he was able to represent how people, in a very small and remote community, adopted 'masks' of sociability upon entering public spaces (such as the pub). The metaphor works on a number of levels. One, to invite the audience to see how we represent ourselves in a more critical light (we are all performers) and, secondly, to see the influence of the audience upon us (whether we get good reviews or not). To again introduce a more contemporary study, Keenan (2012) found various readings and misreadings of his own sexuality during his largely interview-based research upon self-defined homosexual clergy. Rather his 'interesting perspective for a straight researcher to have their gayness presumed when professionally reflecting on the effects of the presumption of heterosexuality on gay lives' forced him to think reflexively about his own disclosure and presentation of self during the research process (Keenan 2012: 92). Here, Keenan's backstage persona could not avoid being intertwined with his facework and front-stage demeanour, during the informal conversations and communication with his respondents before, during and after his research that fieldwork visits included. His front-stage habitus as a young, white man from Northern Ireland overlapped with his more personal, backstage persona as a 'clergy kid' and heterosexual man. Sexual identity, he concludes, is 'a rather complex whole' (Keenan 2012: 93). Roles and masks therefore infiltrate both the way we think, make sense of our fieldwork and also how we conduct it.

Finally, researchers can also use what does not happen or absences in the field as an analytic strategy to understand a research site. Atkinson and Delamont (1977), in a classic classroom observational study of science lessons, argued that in order to produce 'successful' learning outcomes, certain experiments were effectively staged. The model of allowing pupils to follow instructions to conduct a science experiment could not guarantee the results that would sufficiently demonstrate the 'right' outcome. Hence 'mock-ups' were better learning experiments than the 'cock-ups' of when pupils were left to conduct experiments autonomously. The right outcome needed to be staged, rather than risk not getting the right results. In a more contemporary school study, Hillyard and Bagley (2013) found during their fieldwork in a Norfolk primary school that it lacked a permanent head teacher and began to question and analyse why. It could not be explained by issues inside the school gates, but linked into the recent political-economic change and expansion of the village itself. The absent head teacher was therefore symptomatic of a much broader social phenomenon.

The above examples use concepts derived from fieldwork and observation, but move beyond the data via their analyses. It is this that makes their work sociologically distinctive. We would argue that without such an analysis, it would not be sociology. There is a risk of making mistakes along the way, Alex Allan (2012), for example, talks frankly about her inclusive ambitions for her fieldwork. Yet during the research, not only did her judgements about what would be possible change, but also her standing in the eyes of her own respondents:

> Seeing as though Hetty had never used the camera or the tripod before, I attempted to leave her with some basic instructions about their use. As I did this the camera and tripod accidentally fell to the floor. This was met with a disdained look and a dry remark from Hetty: 'Come on Alex ... you don't really know how to use this equipment do you! It's probably best if you leave it to us experts!' (Allan 2012: 4.5).

Here, Allan's (2012) reflexive orientation made her only too conscious of this changing balance of power across the research.

CONCLUSION

We can see that qualitative data analysis is not an easy or straightforward task. Data analysis is messy, complicated and often uncertain. Unlike Glaser and Strauss' (1967) metaphor of discovery implies, theory and concepts will not 'magically arise' out of the data for you. It involves (to borrow C. Wright Mill's term) exercising your 'sociological imagination'. The process acknowledges the human element of research, namely, that we are intrinsically a part of the social world we study and hence cannot be separated from it. As Hammersley and Atkinson (2007) remind us, this is not a part of a methodological commitment: it is an existential fact and is fundamental to the notion of reflexivity. However, this is not to suggest theory is the only aim or outcome of research. Your aim may be to make a difference, to speak to a specific goal or task or to explain a particular social phenomenon – all of which are valuable qualitative research enterprises.

NOTES

1 Even contemporary thinkers, influenced by postmodern thinking, would not entirely disagree – they would just argue that it holds *only for that moment in time* (Thrift 2008).
2 Simply 'so that we understand the software and its automated sorting processes, and so that we might use such a dialogue in order to morph versions of this software to suit our own critical and comparative interests' (Beer 2012: 5.3).

FURTHER READING

Weider DL (1974) Telling the code. In: Turner R (ed.) *Ethnomethodology: Selected Readings*. Harmondsworth: Penguin Education, pp. 144–72.

Smith RJ (2011) Goffman's interaction order at the margins: Stigma, role, and normalization in the outreach encounter. *Symbolic Interaction*, 34(3): 357–76.

8

CONCLUSIONS

Chapter overview

- Fieldwork involves paying very close, serious attention to the lived experience of people's lives in all their different manifestations.
- It involves craft, verve, curiosity and an entrepreneurial spirit.
- Reflexivity is a hallmark of good fieldwork – laying your work open to inspection, evaluation and critique.
- Fieldwork both has its eye on the minutiae of our everyday lives and the broader social-historical circumstances that inform that situation.
- Fieldwork is more than a stand-alone, individual product or output, but involves a dialogue between theory and evidence.

Throughout this book, we have tried to capture what we consider to be the essences of doing fieldwork – its excitement and its challenges:

> Fieldwork is not only a way of doing research; it represents a wider commitment to engaging with people in their everyday lives, and in their work settings, in order to pay very close and serious attention to their doings (Atkinson 2005: xi).

We now return to highlight a few themes we have discussed across the book, and comment on some of the challenges of the present research climate before finally drawing together some core characteristics we perceive to be at the heart of doing fieldwork.

From the outset, we outlined an approach that applies research tools (methods) strategically. The aim is to generate an insight into 'social life' in rich detail. We stressed that it is not a neutral research medium. Chapters 5 and 7 particularly demonstrate that fieldwork is more than the simple collection of data. Through the process of doing fieldwork and constantly thinking analytically, we come to offer explanations/make decisions about data and what they say. Therefore, research is also about ethics and politics. The social world is descriptively inexhaustible and fieldwork selectively represents one account or interpretation of the social world. Yet in the very act of doing fieldwork we make an assumption aligned to a Simmelian sociology in which 'aspects of culture and the mundane organization of social life have their *intrinsic formal properties*, and that the analysis of social life should respect and explore these forms' (Atkinson et al. 2008: 35, original emphasis).

The task, as we have communicated in our discussions, then becomes the ambition to do good, rigorous and thoughtful fieldwork capable of exploring these social forms or everyday patterns and rituals of social life. Pole and Morrison (2003), for instance, talk about the 'nerve' to do a thorough analysis, Atkinson (2013) mentions the fear or desperation ('the silent cry "How on earth do I *make* something out of this?"') and to this we would add a metaphor of fieldwork apprenticeship – what Atkinson calls the craft of fieldwork (Atkinson 2013: 57, original emphasis). This asserts that, through application, you will become more familiar with the fieldwork toolbox of techniques and also be aware of what kind of knowledge your use of them can yield. As Alasuutari (2004) notes, each user leaves their marks on the tools that they use.

In our opening remarks, we talked about how embedded fieldwork is in our everyday lives – we are all consumers of fieldwork. This is not to be confused with claiming that fieldwork has any automatic claim or privilege towards generalizability. Rather that reaching the end of a project invites you to reflect upon the fieldwork in its entirety – the total experience of your fieldwork. This is thinking about fieldwork as something you have produced, but also as something others will consume. A fieldwork project is not fully finished until it is disseminated and how you communicate your ideas (through writing or other formats) is just as important as the techniques you used to collate the data upon which it is based. This process of reflecting upon this experience as a whole (including how it will be consumed) is what Atkinson (1990) defines (and most comprehensively in our view) as reflexivity. Here, you need to lay your work open to inspection, evaluation and critique. Expressed more simply, you need to defend the decisions that you made before, during and after your fieldwork and how they speak to the initial goal or objective you had at the outset of the research.

A reoccurring theme across the preceding chapters is flexibility in the fieldwork process. We view this is a core strength and Silverman (2013) likewise discusses how the task is to 'document properly the choreography and scenic resources of any milieu, it is usually necessary to look out for new cases and new sources of data while we are in the field' (Silverman 2013: 50). (By scenic resources, Silverman means the frame or setting of that place – like the props, costumes and staging of a theatre performance.) Flexibility is a generic principle that bridges all of the differing uses or applications of fieldwork. This is not to say that the field dictates your actions, but it often leads you to explore new avenues of investigation or requires you to alter your plans in order to best capture the complexities of the given research setting.

This is where we see that fieldwork itself contains an orientation – it has a passion to explore how action gets done. This is not to suggest it has a life of its own, beyond the good fortune of serendipity, but rather it has a deep-seated curiosity about interactional encounters. So for example, whilst some scholars have a commitment towards a plural theoretical stance (such as Giulianotti's (2005) use of Simmel to explore the sociability of the Tartan Army) and others have a coherent intellectual programme of engagement (such as Pahl's (2008) with space and class), for us, fieldwork contains an interpretivistic orientation. That is, 'how people interpret and make sense of their world and act on their interpretations' (Hammersley 2013: 27). But we also temper this interpretivism by agreeing with Hammersley's (2013) own stance that the aim of 'social science must be to produce knowledge about social institutions, policies, and/or processes, their character, sources or consequences' (Hammersley 2013: 98). Therefore, whilst fieldwork has its eye on the minutiae of our everyday lives, it must also remain attuned to the broader social-historical circumstances that inform that situation. That is, the intrinsic formal properties of Simmelian sociology also to be found in the dramaturgy of everyday life (Goffman 1959). This is neither profound nor radical, rather it celebrates the value of the insight that fieldwork can offer:

> We do not need to *define* the key elements of social life, nor to reinvent a theory of everyday life in order to demonstrate how close attention to its multiple forms can inform an ethnography that is densely responsive to the complexity of social life (Atkinson et al. 2008: 3, original emphasis).

Atkinson's point here is that fieldwork can offer a richness of insight into everyday life whilst also keeping an eye upon broad themes or changes taking place in society. It may be small-scale, but it is capable of speaking to the big themes of our times in all of their complexity. As such, we feel fieldwork is well placed to accommodate innovations within digital sociology and Big Data resources (such as new social media). Whilst Atkinson et al. (2008) declare themselves unashamedly modernist, we see less of a disjunction between the traditions from which fieldwork has emerged and the contemporary research climate. These do not demand a reorientation. However, Hammersley (2013) does make an interesting observation. He is unhappy with 'qualitative research' as a category, perceiving it more a matter of degree in practical terms, rather than any fundamental clash with quantitative research. In fact, his careful tracing of core elements of both shows an oppositional dualism is both inaccurate and unhelpful. So, something more subtle and realistic that captures differences in practical conduct (the doing of fieldwork) would be more helpful and we would say the same applies to new forms of data now making themselves available to us. As Christensen et al.'s (2011) study showed, children write text messages and hence using that medium can be useful in getting to understand children's worlds. It is not so radically different from looking at the notes they write to one another, as Hey's (1997) ethnography did.

What is clear is that we live in interesting times and fieldwork is an approach well placed to engage with process and change. Yet Atkinson et al. (2008) and Hammersley (2013) are right to express some concern in their respective ways. Whilst fieldwork and 'qualitative research' has for many years been on the ascendency, funding councils in the UK context are currently more attuned to a more quantitative-orientation and this in turn shapes what empirical research gets done. It is our belief that the quality of our understanding about the changing social world around us will not be enhanced if less fieldwork is done and therefore we know empirically less as a result.

Unsurprisingly, our stance is to resist any essentialist position that categorizes fieldwork as a single way of doing social research. Research boundaries or labels can be distractions rather than means of enhancing good fieldwork. For us, fieldwork is a practical activity that will, to a certain extent, demand adaptions. For example, if you are researching children's social lives and a lot of their time is spent online, then perhaps the fieldworker needs to follow suit. As Wiles et al. (2011) note, this would be adaptation rather than methodological innovation. We would encourage a more entrepreneurial spirit that is mindful of the political climate in which fieldwork is situated. Fieldwork now, perhaps more than in the last twenty years, needs to make itself relevant and not retreat into its own silo.

We now end on a series of comments or food-for-thought issues of which the outward-facing fieldworker should remain mindful. These debates are now core to the fieldwork enterprise. We look forward to seeing how they unfold via new fieldwork project designs and conceptualizations; the dissemination of research findings; and through continued sustained methodological reflection.

I.

Fieldwork is a creative process. Sometimes this may entail thinking tangentially and eclectically. For example, much is to be said for eclecticism as a means to unlock your data. Strong (1988) used the *deviant case* as a means to get a critical purchase on a substantial dataset of over one thousand observations of paediatric consultations; Atkinson (2013) *inverted* Sudnow's focus upon the hand in piano playing to look at the feet (in the movement of glass-blowers in their workshops); Atkinson and Willis (2007) used the notion of the flaneur, but applied inside a computer game as well as an urban context to explore contemporary identities and experiences. Thinking tangentially and using resources eclectically can yield insight. New combinations can emerge from reading beyond your immediate sub-discipline or from a broader field. What is key is not to expect thinking eclectically to magically resolve your query or impasse, but it may give you additional critical purchase upon the problem at hand. It may serve to get you over the fear or worry about what your data are actually telling you. We are not suggesting that the tail should wag the dog, nor attesting to the promise of the latest technological fashions, but rather that the fieldworker can imaginatively use a wide array of analytic strategies. This is Burgess' multi-strategy research in a more interdisciplinary and twenty-first century technology-savvy context. All methods still have advantages and disadvantages and this holds for all alternative or emerging techniques.

II.

Fieldwork emerged from a particular theoretical 'moment' or canon and it is important to remain aware of that antecedence. As Silverman (2013) notes, the 'overwhelming number of my students seem unaware of the theoretical basis of their approach' (Silverman 2013: 50). The knowledge that fieldwork yields has not just fallen from the sky, blue or otherwise. It is a way of thinking about the world that places a value upon particular forms of information and ways of knowing. Ethnography and fieldwork, we would argue, have become a victim of their own success. They are no longer subject to the same criticism as experienced by those first using sustained fieldwork and are even the dominant paradigm in some sub-disciplines which may have fostered complacency. Hammersley's (2013) concise tracing of the various lines of intellectual development around qualitative research highlights what some research has come to be missing. There is also a second element to this, relating to practice and the need to demonstrate competence in the field. It is worth remembering 'a coquette is in a much better position to learn about men than a nun' (Dingwall 1980: 880, quoting Wax 1971). Whilst there is an advantage on occasions to play the naïve card in order to invite a full explanation of an event, for the most part 'to be too ignorant of the setting and current affairs, to be a total ingénue, may convince elites that you are too unconcerned or uninterested to have done your homework for them to waste their time with you' (Hunter 1993: 51–52). With more candour, Atkinson (2005) argues:

> I do not think it is possible to make sense of such a cultural setting without making the significant effort to become tolerably well informed about it. Part of the work, therefore, that goes into an ethnography like this one [of the Welsh national opera] involves not just participant observation in situ, but also a commitment to pay attention to such specialist knowledge. There is no advantage in rank ethnographic ignorance (Atkinson 2005: 191).

If we accept this argument for competence in the field, then it follows that we should also know what drew us to be interested in generating that kind of knowledge about the social world in the first place.

III.

We argued earlier that flexibility (during fieldwork) is one of the strengths of the approach, both in the sense of freedom to follow new avenues of investigation and also make the most of opportunities that arise (such as being invited to a staff leaving-do; the school end-of-year barbeque; or out for a post-work drink with the teaching staff). These are options: you don't have to – nor is it always useful or sensible to accept such offers – but the capacity of fieldwork to enable the fieldworker to adapt is a core strength and challenge. More strategically, we would add that fieldwork needs to include not only those who might want to collaborate, but also those who do not. This is not to advocate coercion, but more to put your fieldwork into a position where there is a capacity for you to come across divergent points-of-view. For example, as Neal and Walters (2008) acknowledge, inviting discussions about rurality amongst groups such as the Women's Institute and the Young Farmers' Club is a Goffmanesque front-stage performance of the versions of reality (in this instance, rural lifestyles) that actors are prepared to share with the research team. The backstage also, as best we can access it, also demands attention; that is, what people do in everyday life, as well as what they say they do.

IV.

There is a new imperative we want to comment upon that seeks to update and further develop research that has already been done. Sometimes this is by those originally involved (James 2012), or alternatively can be a re-study of a 'classic' study of a geographic area or locale (cf. Lyon and Crow's (2012) restudy of Pahl's work on Sheppey and Manchester sociologists' re-engagement with the *Affluent Worker* study of the 1960s; cf. Savage et al. 2013). Charles and Crow (2012) observed that re-studies are uncommon but it seems to us that they offer an opportunity, not least for analytic contrast. The danger remains that retrospective studies miss the nuances of the research during data collection, as Pahl (who was placed within that research moment) considered to be the case with Savage's (2010) account of social science research in the past. Whilst we would not go as far as to agree with the argument put forward by Thrift (2008) that (fieldwork) accounts hold but just for that one moment, we see that fieldwork has its roots in a research tradition. That is, it emerged from the influences of two strands: American interactionist sociology (such as the Thomas and Znaniecki 1919–20) within the very early Chicago School and also British anthropology (and Malinowski 1922). Both the tradition and the research setting are changing and hence any re-engagement must be familiar with how both have been reconfigured.

Charles and Crow (2012) offer a measured and important reflection upon the possibilities of re-study research and James (2012) is also supportive. Claims towards innovation as we have acknowledged earlier can often be over-cooked

(Travers 2009, Wiles et al. 2011) but we also agree with James (2012) that the potential for re-use is currently neglected. What must be key is the awareness of that moment or the politics of the method when that account was created. The impetus for a study is inevitably grounded in a particular moment and context and something of its original intent/direction will change with time (even if the same research team is used). Wiles et al. (2011) argue that in practice, most re-studies adapt rather than simply adopt the same approach as an original study. The new imperative towards improved archiving offers strong encouragement and an important resource for all social scientists.

V.

There are now more opportunities to publish and disseminate research in a variety of formats and styles than has ever been possible before. It would be hard to imagine a fieldwork project dataset that did not include a wide array of textual, visual and digital materials. Yet fieldwork is richer than a variety of formats. Abrams (1980) in a classic paper called for work in which 'narrative and theory, evidence and concept really do maintain a close, fluent dialogue with no bullying' and cited Goffman as 'manifestly our best stylist' (Abrams 1980: 15). There are two elements to this argument. First, we know now (as did Abrams) that form and style are wedded. So format and style come together in bringing alive the field to the reader, viewer or consumer and this includes new formats. Stylistically, Atkinson et al. (2008) advocate retaining 'something of the texture and the flavour of the original ingredients' (Atkinson et al. 2008: 54). He inverted dramaturgy – everyday life was not like a drama, rather drama was like everyday (working) life. Some scholars have utilized poetry, some plays or narrative scripts. However, like Hammersley (2010a), we suggest such performances remain the preserve of the professionals, rather than the social scientist amateur. More specifically on the communication of an argument, metaphors have often been used as an analytic device to generate a jolt of surprise or evoke a comparative analogy, but ultimately the scaffolding must come down (Goffman 1959). (The metaphor stopped for Atkinson (2005) and he did not see fit to disseminate via the medium of dance, theatre or song.)

Secondly, whilst format and style are key parts of fieldwork, collectively fieldwork is more than a stand-alone, individual product or output as Abrams (1980) realized in his advocacy of a fluent dialogue between theory and evidence. This places fieldwork within a much wider picture of its contribution to a body of knowledge (or theory). Of course, the centrality of theory or conceptual ideas will vary with the remit of fieldwork studies, but where it sits and contributes vis-à-vis the theoretical canon to which it feels it belongs is equally important. Our point here is that there is nothing wrong with highly varied formats and styles, but sometimes their role and status in the presentation of research conclusions has become blurred. Like Hammersley (2013) suggests, we should be very clear about what activity we are involved in – or run the risk of doing nothing well. Format and style are vital in the communication of fieldwork ideas, but run the risk of reification – the medium becoming more important than the message.

Novelist David Lodge (1984) makes an interesting and relevant point about the ambitions of texts, when one of his characters (an academic) suggests that reading a text is analogous to a striptease. This metaphor holds that accounts are persuasive, leading you on, taking you down a certain route with the promise of ultimate revelation (in the conclusion). Lodge's (1984) character is a postmodernist and suggesting that perhaps we should not look so hard for 'the truth' or categorical statement of meaning (for as we know, multiple interpretations of the field are possible) but 'instead [...] we should take pleasure in its teasing' (Lodge 1984: 27). The argument should only be taken so far, as there remains a danger in the recognition of diversity and ambiguity that we give up our ambition for fieldwork's capacity for knowledge and impact. Acknowledging that how an argument is presented is as important as the message it seeks to communicate does not mean rigour should be abandoned. Yet in the light of the observations we have made about the contemporary zeitgeist permeating qualitative research, we consider that a loss of rigour has occurred but we are not yet in an empirical crisis. Furthermore, social science in the past produced fine work whilst under attack. For example, the 'new' sociologies of childhood, education and deviance and recent turns (object, affect, mobilities) produced many papers and monographs before they became established as legitimate canons complete with their own distinct literatures and celebrated papers.

There are analogies with contemporary critiques and we advocate the need to participate in those debates, rather than to ignore them or allow them to overrun us – namely, the dilemma of accessing everyday dramaturgical life – be it online, co-location or co-presence. The metaphor of the striptease is too complacent and now is not the time for complacency. To answer Silverman's (2013: 55) question – there is nothing wrong with the ability of fieldwork or ethnography to access and engage with the manifestations of social worlds and experiences. We look forward to seeing where the challenge to explore all facets of social life takes fieldworkers next.

FURTHER READING

Atkinson P (2015) *For Ethnography*. London: Sage.

Hammersley M (2013) *What is Qualitative Research?* London: Bloomsbury.

REFERENCES

Abrams P (1980) History, sociology, historical sociology. *Past and Present*, 87: 3–16.

Agar M (1996, 2nd edition) *The Professional Stranger: An Informal Introduction to Ethnography*. San Diego: Academic Press.

Alasuutari P (2004) The globalization of qualitative research. In: Seale C, Gobo G, Gubrium JF and Silverman D (eds) *Qualitative Research Practice*. Thousand Oaks, CA: Sage, pp. 595–608.

Allan A (2009) The importance of being a 'lady': Hyper-femininity and heterosexuality in the private, single-sex primary school. *Gender and Education*, 21(2): 145–58.

Allan A (2012) Power, participation and privilege: Methodological lessons from using visual methods in research with young people. *Sociological Research Online* 17(3) http://www.socresonline.org.uk/17/3/8.html

Anderson N (1923) *The Hobo: The Sociology of the Homeless Man*. Chicago: Chicago University Press.

Archer MS (1995) *Realist Social Theory: The Morphogenetic Approach*. Cambridge: Cambridge University Press.

Archer MS (2007) *Making Our Way Through the World*. Cambridge: Cambridge University Press.

Ashton DN and Field DJ (1976) *Young Workers*. London: Hutchinson.

Atkinson P (1981) *The Clinical Experience: The Construction and Reconstruction of Medical Reality*. Farnborough: Gower.

Atkinson P (1990) *The Ethnographic Imagination*. London: Routledge.

Atkinson P (1995) *Medical Talk and Medical Work*. London: Sage.

Atkinson P (2005) Qualitative research – unity and diversity. *Forum Qualitative Sozialforschung/Forum: Qualitative Social Research*, 6(3): Art. 26.

Atkinson PA (2006) *Everyday Arias: An Operatic Ethnography*. Lanham, MD: AltaMira Press.

Atkinson PA (2009) Illness narratives revisited: The failure of narrative reductionism. *Sociological Research Online* 14(5).

Atkinson P (2012) An accidental anthropologist, a sceptical sociologist, a reluctant methodologist. In: Denzin N (ed.) *Blue-ribbon Papers: Behind the Professional Mask: The Autobiographies of Leading Symbolic Interactionists*. Bingley: Emerald.

Atkinson P (2013) Ethnography and craft knowledge. *Qualitative Sociology Review*, 9(2): 56–63.

Atkinson P (2015) *For Ethnography*. London: Sage.

Atkinson P, Coffey A, Delamont S, Lofland J and Lofland L (2001) Introduction. In: Atkinson P, Coffey A, Delamont S, Lofland J and Lofland L (eds) *Handbook of Ethnography*. London: Sage, pp. 1–8.

Atkinson P and Delamont S (1977) Mock-ups and cock-ups: The stage management of guided discovery instruction. In: Hammersley M and Woods P (eds) *School Experience: Explorations in the Sociology of Education*. London: Croom Helm.

Atkinson P, Delamont S and Housley W (2008) *Contours of Culture: Complex Ethnography and the Ethnography of Complexity*. Lanham, MD: Rowman Altamira.

Atkinson P and Housley W (2003) *Interactionism: An Essay in Sociological Amnesia*. London: Sage.

Atkinson P and Silverman D (1997) Kundera's immortality: The interview society and the invention of the self. *Qualitative Inquiry*, 3(3): 304–25.

Atkinson R and Willis P (2007) Charting the ludodrome: The mediation of urban and simulated space and rise of the flâneur electronique. *Information, Communication and Society*, 10(6): 818–45.

Bagley C (2009) The ethnographer as impresario-joker in the (re)presentation of educational research as performance art. *Ethnography and Education*, 4(3): 283–300.

Bagley C and Hillyard S (2011) Village schools in England: At the heart of their community? *Australian Journal of Education*, 55(1): Art. 5.

Ball SJ (1981) *Beachside Comprehensive: A Case-study of Secondary Schooling*. Cambridge: Cambridge University Press.

Barker E (1984) *The Making of a Moonie: Choice or Brainwashing?* Oxford: Blackwell Publishers.

Barnes JA (1979) *Who Should Know What: Social Science, Privacy and Ethics*. Harmondsworth: Penguin.

Beach D and Lunneblad J (2011) Ethnographic investigations of issues of race in Scandinavian education research. *Ethnography and Education*, 6(1): 29–43.

Becker HS (1967) Whose side are we on? *Social Problems*, 14(3): 239–47.

Becker HS, Geer B, Hughes EC and Strause AL (1961) *Boys in White*. Chicago: Chicago University Press.

Beer D (2012) Using social media data aggregators to do social research. *Sociological Research Online* 17(3).

Bell C (1969) A note on participant observation. *Sociology*, 3(3): 417–18.

Bell C (1977) Reflections on the Banbury restudy. In: Bell C and Newby H (eds) *Doing Sociological Research*. London: Allen and Unwin, pp. 47–62.

Bell, MM (1994) *Childerley: Nature and Morality in a Country Village*. Chicago: University of Chicago Press.

Benyon H (1985, 2nd edition) *Working for Ford*. Harmondsworth: Penguin.

Berg B (2004) *Qualitative Research Methods for the Social Sciences*. Boston: Pearson.

Blumer H (1954) What is Wrong with Social Theory? *American Sociological Review*, 19(1): 3–10.

Boelen WM (1992) Street corner society: Cornerville revisited. *Journal of Contemporary Ethnography*, 21(1): 11–51.

Bolton A, Pole C and Mizen P (2001) Picture this: Research child workers. *Sociology* 35(2): 501–18.

Bowles S and Gintis H (1976) *Schooling in Capitalist America*. New York: Basic Books.

Brewer J (2000) *Ethnography*. Buckingham: Open University Press.

Brewer J (2012) Sociologists don't debate quibbles. We are tackling the financial crisis head-on. *The Guardian*, 5 June 2012. http://www.theguardian.com/commentisfree/2012/jun/05/response-sociologists-financial-crisis [accessed 24 July 2014].

British Educational Research Association (2011) Ethical guidelines for educational research. http://www.bera.ac.uk/researchers-resources/publications/ethical-guidelines-for-educational-research-2011 [accessed 6 June 2014].

British Sociological Association (2002) Statement of ethical practice. http://www.britsoc.co.uk/media/27107/StatementofEthicalPractice.pdf [accessed 6 June 2014].

Bryant A and Charmaz K (eds) (2007) *The Sage Handbook of Grounded Theory*. London: Sage.

Bryman A (1984) The debate about quantitative and qualitative research: A question of method or epistemology? *British Journal of Sociology*, 35(1): 75–92.

Bryman A (2012) *Social Research Methods*. Oxford: Oxford University Press.

Bryman A and Burgess RG (eds) (2002) *Analysing Qualitative Data*. London: Routledge.

Burgess RG (1982) *Field Research: A Sourcebook and Field Manual*. London: Allen and Unwin.

Burgess RG (1983) *Experiencing Comprehensive Education: A Study of Bishop McGregor School*. London: Taylor & Francis.

Burgess RG (1984) *In the Field*. London: Routledge.

Burgess RG (1988) Conversations with a purpose: The ethnographic interview in educational research. In: Burgess RG (ed.) *Studies in Qualitative Methodology*. London: JAI Press, pp. 137–55.

Burgess RG (1993) Contractors and customers: A research relationship? In: Burgess RG (ed.) *Educational Research and Evaluation: For Policy and Practice*? London: Taylor & Francis, pp. 21–31.

Burgess RG (1994) Scholarship and sponsored research: Contradiction, continuum or complementary activity? In: Halpin D and Troyna B (eds) *Researching Education Policy: Ethical and Methodological Issues*. London: Falmer, pp. 55–71.

Burgess RG, Hockey J and Pole CJ (1992) Becoming a Postgraduate Student: The Organisation of Postgraduate Training. ESRC Final Report. Swindon: ESRC.

Butler D and Charles N (2012) Exaggerated femininity and tortured masculinity: Embodying gender in the horseracing industry. *The Sociological Review*, 60(4): 676–95.

Byrne DS (2011) *Applying Social Science*. Bristol: Policy Press.

Charles N and Crow G (2012) Community re-studies and social change. *The Sociological Review*, 60(3): 399–404.

Charmaz K (2006) *Constructing Grounded Theory: A Practical Guide Through Qualitative Research*. London: Sage.

Charmaz K (2014) *Constructing Grounded Theory*. London: Sage.

Charmaz K and Mitchell RG (2001) Grounded theory in ethnography. In: Atkinson P, Coffey A, Delamont S, Lofland J and Lofland L (eds) *Handbook of Ethnography*. London: Sage, pp. 160–74.

Christensen P and James A (2000) Childhood diversity and commonality: Some methodological insights. In: *Research with Children: Perspectives and Practices*. London: Falmer, pp. 160–78.

Christensen P and James A (2008, 2nd edition) *Research with Children: Perspective and Practices*. London: Falmer Press.

Christensen P, Mikkelsen MR, Nielsen TAS and Harder H (2011) Children, mobility, and space: Using GPS and mobile phone technologies in ethnographic research. *Journal of Mixed Methods Research*, 5(3): 227–46.

Christensen P and Prout A (2002) Working with ethical symmetry in social research with children. *Childhood*, 9(4): 477–97.

Clifton G (2007) *The experience of education of the army child*. PhD Thesis, Oxford Brookes University, UK.

Coffey A (1999) *The Ethnographic Self*. London: Sage.

Coffey A and Atkinson P (1996) *Making Sense of Qualitative Data.* London: Sage.

Cohen RL, Hughes C and Lampard R (2011) The methodological impact of feminism: A troubling issue for Sociology? *Sociology*, 45(4): 570–86.

Congressi L (2006) Four days in a strange place.... *Journal of Health Services Research & Policy*, 11(2): 122–4.

Cooper B, Glaesser J, Gomm R and Hammersley M (2012) *Challenging the Qualitative-Quantitative Divide: Explorations in Case-focused Causal Analysis.* London: Bloomsbury.

Corrigan P (1979) *Schooling the Smash Street Kids.* London: Macmillan.

Corsaro WA and Molinari L (2000) Entering and observing in children's worlds: A reflection on a longitudal ethnography of early education in Italy. In: Christensen P and James A (eds) *Research with Children: Perspectives and Practices.* London: Falmer Press, pp. 179–200.

Cottle TJ (1977) *Private Lives, Public Accounts.* Amherst, MA: University of Massachusetts Press.

Courtney R (2008) *This is England: Class, culture and ethnicity across non-metropolitan spaces.* PhD Thesis, University of Leicester, UK.

Cox G, Watkins C and Winter M (1996) *Game Management in England: Implications for Public Access, the Rural Economy and the Environment.* Cheltenham: Countryside and Community Press.

Craib I (1992) *Modern Social Theory*. Brighton: Harvester Wheatsheaf.

Croll P (1986) *Systematic Classroom Observation.* London: Falmer.

Crossley N (2008) (Net) working out: Social capital in a private health club. *British Journal of Sociology*, 59(3): 475–500.

Crow G and Takeda N (2011) Ray Pahl's sociological career: Fifty years of impact. *Sociological Research Online* 16(3) http://www.socresonline.org.uk/16/3/11.html

Deem R (2002) Talking to manager-academics: Methodological dilemmas and feminist research strategies. *Sociology*, 36(4): 835–55.

Deem R (2014) Working qualitatively, thinking ethnographically: Exploring leadership and management in higher educational organizations. Paper delivered at the Burgess Symposium, University of Leicester, May 2014.

Deem R, Hillyard S and Reed M (2007) *Higher Education and the New Managerialism: The Changing Management of UK Universities.* Oxford: Oxford University Press.

Delamont S (1984) The old girl network: Reflections on the fieldwork at St Luke's. In: Burgess RG (ed.) *The Research Process in Educational Settings: Ten Case Studies.* London: Routledge, pp. 15–35.

Delamont S (2002, 2nd edition) *Fieldwork in Educational Settings: Methods, Pitfalls and Perspectives.* London: Routledge Falmer.

Delamont S (2003) *Feminist Sociology*. London: Sage.

Delamont S (2006) The smell of sweat and rum: Teacher authority in capoeira classes. *Ethnography and Education*, 1(2): 161–75.

Delamont S (2009) The only honest thing: Autoethnography, reflexivity and small crises in fieldwork. *Ethnography and Education*, 4(1): 51–64.

Delamont S, Atkinson P and Pugsley L (2010) The concept smacks of magic: Fighting familiarity today. *Teaching and Teacher Education*, 26(1): 3–10.

Delamont S and Stephens N (2006) Balancing the berimbau. *Qualitative Inquiry*, 12(2): 316–39.

Denzin N (1997) *Interpretive Ethnography: Ethnographic Practices for the 21st Century.* Thousand Oaks, CA: Sage.

Dingwall R (1977) *Aspects of Illness.* New York: St. Martin's Press.

Dingwall R (1980) Ethics and ethnography. *The Sociological Review*, 28(4): 871–91.

Douglas JD (1976) *Investigative Social Research: Individual and Team Field Research.* Beverly Hills, CA: Sage.

Dovemark M (2012) Freedom of choice as repressive tolerance. Paper presented at Oxford Ethnography and Education Conference, Oxford, 10–12 September 2012.

Duneier M (1992) *Slim's Table: Race, Respectability, and Masculinity.* Chicago: University of Chicago Press.

Dunning E, Murphy P and Williams J (1986) Spectator violence at football matches: Towards a sociological explanation. *British Journal of Sociology*, 37(2): 221–44.

Edwards M and Hillyard S (2012) The role of forced serendipity in qualitative research: The ethics of researching rural schools. In: Love K (ed.) *Ethics and Qualitative Research.* Bingley: Emerald.

Elias N (1961) Application for a Grant for Special Research to DSIR, Unpublished manuscript (Teresa Keil Collection), University of Leicester, UK.

Epstein D (1998) 'Are you a girl or a teacher?': The 'Least Adult' role in research about gender and sexuality in a primary school. In: Walford G (ed.) *Doing Research about Education.* London: Falmer, pp. 27–41.

Erikson K (1967) A comment on disguised observation in sociology. *Social Problems*, 14(4): 366–73.

European A (1920) Intellectual America. *The Atlantic Monthly*, 125: 188–99.

Fenge A and Jones K (2012) Gay and pleasant land? Exploring sexuality, ageing and rurality in a multi-method, performative project. *British Journal of Social Work*, 42(2): 300–17.

Fielding N (1981) *The National Front.* London: Routledge.

Finch J (1984) 'It's great to have someone to talk to': The ethics and politics of interviewing women. In: Bell C and Roberts H (eds) *Social Researching: Politics, Problems, Practice.* London: Routledge and Kegan Paul, pp. 70–87.

Fine GA (2009) Goffman turns to me and says, 'Only a schmuck studies his own life'. *Bios Sociologicus: The Erving Goffman Archives*, 1–14. Available at: http://digitalscholarship.unlv.edu/goffman_archives/20

Fonow MM and Cook JA (eds) (1991) *Beyond Methodology: Feminist Scholarship as Lived Research.* Indiana: Indiana University Press.

Forsey MG (2010) Ethnography as participant listening. *Ethnography*, 11(4): 558–72.

Foster J (1990) *Villains: Crime and Community in the Inner City.* London: Routledge.

Frankenberg R (1957) *Village on the Border.* Harmondsworth: Penguin.

Gane N (2012) *Max Weber and Contemporary Capitalism.* Basingstoke: Palgrave.

Garfinkel H (1967) *Studies in Ethnomethodology.* Englewood Cliffs, NJ: Prentice Hall.

Geertz C (1986) [1973] *The Interpretation of Cultures: Selected Essays.* London: Fontana.

Geertz C (1988) *Works and Lives: The Anthropologist as Author.* Stanford: Stanford University Press.

Giddens A (1979) *Central Problems in Social Theory.* Basingstoke: Macmillan.

Giddens A (1984) *The Constitution of Society: Outline of the Theory of Structuration.* London: Wiley.

Giulianotti R (2005) The sociability of sport: Scotland football supporters as interpreted through the sociology of Georg Simmel. *International Review for the Sociology of Sport*, 40(3): 289–306.

Glaser B and Strauss A (1967) *The Discovery of Grounded Theory*. New Brunswick, NJ: Aldine.

Goffman E (1959) *The Presentation of Self in Everyday Life*. Harmondsworth: Penguin.

Goffman E (1963) *Asylums*. Harmondsworth: Penguin.

Goffman E (1968) *Asylums: Essays on the Social Situation of Mental Patients and Other Inmates*. Harmondsworth: Penguin.

Goffman E (1974) *Frame Analysis: An Essay on the Organization of Experience*. Harmondsworth: Penguin.

Goffman E (1983) The interaction order: American Sociological Association, 1982 presidential address. *American Sociological Review*, 48(1): 1–17.

Goffman E (1989) On fieldwork. *Journal of Contemporary Ethnography*, 18(2): 123–32.

Goodwin J and O'Connor H (2005) Engineer, mechanic or carpenter? Boys' transitions to work in the 1960s. *Journal of Education and Work* 18(4): 451–71.

Gouldner A (1973) *For Sociology: Renewal and Critique in Sociology Today*. London: Allen Lane.

Greener I (2011) *Designing Social Science Research: A Guide for the Bewildered*. London: Sage.

Grimshaw A (2001) *The Ethnographer's Eye*. Cambridge: Cambridge University Press.

Halfacree K (2007) Trial by space for a 'radical rural'. *Journal of Rural Studies*, 23(2): 125–41.

Hammers C (2009) An examination of lesbian/queer bathhouse culture and the social organization of (im) personal sex. *Journal of Contemporary Ethnography*, 38(3): 308–35.

Hammersley, M (1990). What's wrong with ethnography? The myth of theoretical description. *Sociology*, 24(4): 597–615.

Hammersley M (1992) *What's Wrong with Ethnography?* London: Routledge.

Hammersley M (2000) *Taking Sides in Social Research*. London: Routledge.

Hammersley M (2008) *Questioning Qualitative Research: Critical Essays*. London: Sage.

Hammersley M (2010a) Research, art, or politics: Which is it to be? A response to Norman Denzin. *International Review of Qualitative Research*, 3(1): 5–9.

Hammersley M (2010b) A historical and comparative note on the relationship between analytic induction and grounded theorising. *Forum: Qualitative Social Research*, 11(2): Art. 4.

Hammersley M (2012a) Am I now, or have I even been, a symbolic interactionist? In: Athens L (ed.) *Studies in Symbolic Interaction. Blue Ribbon Papers: Behind the Professional Mask: The Autobiographies of Leading Symbolic Interactionists, vol. 38*. Bingley: Emerald Group Publishing Limited, pp. 153–74.

Hammersley M (2012b) Qualitative causal analysis. In: Cooper B, Glaesser J, Gomm R and Hammersley M *Challenging the Qualitative-Quantitative Divide: Explorations in Case-focused Causal Analysis*. London: Bloomsbury.

Hammersley M (2013) *What is Qualitative Research? The 'What is?' Research Methods Series*. London: Bloomsbury.

Hammersley M and Atkinson P (2007, 3rd edition) *Ethnography: Principles in Practice*. London: Routledge.

Hammersley M and Cooper B (2012) Analytic induction versus qualitative comparative analysis. In: Cooper B, Glaesser J, Gomm R and Hammersley M *Challenging the Qualitative-Quantitative Divide: Explorations in Case-focused Causal Analysis*. London: Bloomsbury, pp. 129–69.

Hand M (2012) *Ubiquitous Photography*. Cambridge: Polity.

Hand M (2014) From cyberspace to dataverse: Trajectories in digital social research. In: Hand M and Hillyard S (eds) *Big Data? Qualitative Approaches to Digital Research*. Bingley: Emerald.

Harper D (2002) Talking about pictures: A case for photo elicitation. *Visual Studies*, 17(1): 16–26.

Heley J (2010) The new squirearchy and emergent cultures of the new middle classes in rural areas. *Journal of Rural Studies*, 26(4): 321–31.

Heley J (2011) On the potential of being a village boy: An argument for local rural ethnography. *Sociologia Ruralis*, 51(3): 219–37.

Hey V (1997) *The Company She Keeps: An Ethnography of Girls' Friendships*. London: McGraw-Hill International.

Hillyard S (2003) *An exploration of the dialectic between theory and method in ethnography*. PhD Thesis, University of Warwick, UK.

Hillyard SH (2009) Divisions and divisiveness and the social cost of foot and mouth disease: A sociological analysis of FMD in one locality. In: Doring M and Nerlich B (eds) *From Mayhem to Meaning: The Social and Cultural Impact of Foot and Mouth Disease in the UK in 2001*. Manchester: Manchester University Press.

Hillyard S (2010) Livestock of the head: Conceptualising and researching the English rural primary school. Paper presented at the Oxford Ethnography Conference, New College, Oxford, September.

Hillyard S and Bagley C (2013) 'The fieldworker not in the head's office': An empirical exploration of the role of an English rural primary school within its village. *Social & Cultural Geography*, 14(4): 410–27.

Hillyard S and Bagley CA (2014) Community strikes back? Belonging and exclusion in rural English villages in networked times. *International Journal of Inclusive Education*. Published online: 13 October 2014.

Hillyard S and Burridge J (2012) Shotguns and firearms in the UK: A call for a distinctively sociological contribution to the debate. *Sociology*, 46(3): 395–410.

Hobbs D (1988) *Doing the Business: Entrepreneurship, the Working Class and Detectives in the East End of London*. Oxford: Oxford University Press.

Hobbs D, Hadfield P, Lister S and Winlow S (2003) *Bouncers: Violence, Governance and the Night-time Economy*. Oxford: Oxford University Press.

Hockey J (1986) *Squaddies: Portrait of a Subculture*. Exeter: Exeter University Press.

Hogan S and Warren L (2012) Dealing with complexity in research findings: How do older women negotiate and challenge images of ageing? *Journal of Women & Ageing*, 24(4): 329–50.

Holdaway S (1983) *Inside the British Police: A Force at Work*. Oxford: Blackwell.

Hughes C (1991) *Stepparents: Wicked or wonderful? An indepth study of stepparenthood*. Aldershot: Avebury.

Humphreys L (1970) *Tearoom Trade: A Study of Homosexual Encounters in Public Places*. London: Duckworth.

Hunter A (1993) Local knowledge and local power. Notes on the ethnography of local community elites. *Journal of Contemporary Ethnography*, 22(1): 36–58.

Hutchinson E (2014) Researching forums in online ethnography: Practice and ethics. In: Hand M and Hillyard SH (eds) *Big Data? Qualitative Approaches to Digital Data. Studies in Qualitative Methodology, vol. 13*. Bingley: Emerald.

James A (2012) Seeking the analytic imagination: Reflections on the process of interpreting qualitative data. *Qualitative Research*, 13(5): 562–77.

James A and James AL (2008) *Key Concepts in Childhood Studies*. London: Sage.

Janowitz M (ed.) (1966) *W.I. Thomas on Social Organization and Social Personality*. Chicago: University of Chicago Press.

Jeffrey B and Troman G (2004) Time for ethnography. *British Educational Research Journal*, 30(4): 535–48.

Jeffrey R and Woods P (1998) *Testing Teachers: The Effect of School Inspections on Primary Teachers*. London: Falmer.

Keenan M (2012) The politics of telling. In: Love K *Ethics in Social Research, vol. 12*. Bingley: Emerald Group Publishing, pp. 91–110.

Kellehear A (1993) *The Unobtrusive Researcher: A Guide to Methods*. London: Allen and Unwin.

Kelly A and Burrows R (2011) Measuring the value of sociology? Some notes on performative metricization in the contemporary academy. *The Sociological Review*, 59(s2): 130–50.

Kindon S, Pain R and Kesby M (2008) Participatory action research. In: R. Kitchin and N. Thrift (eds) *International Encyclopedia of Human Geography*, 90–95.

Lacey C (1970) *Hightown Grammar: The School as a Social System*. Manchester: Manchester University Press.

Lather P (2001) Postmodernism, post-structuralism and post(critical) ethnography: Of ruins, aporias and angels. In: Atkinson P, Coffey A, Delamont S, Lofland J and Lofland L (eds) *Handbook of Ethnography*. London: Sage.

Lawler S (2013, 2nd edition) *Identity: Sociological Perspectives*. Cambridge: Polity.

Lee RM (2000) *Unobtrusive Methods in Social Research*. Buckingham: Open University Press.

Lister S, Hadfield P, Hobbs D and Winlow S (2001) Accounting for bouncers: Occupational licensing as a mechanism for regulation. *Criminology and Criminal Justice*, 1(4): 363–84.

Lodge D (1984) *Small World*. London: Random House.

Lyon D and Back L (2012) Fishmongers in a global economy: Craft and social relations on a London market. *Sociological Research Online*, 17(2): 23.

Lyon D and Crow G (2012) The challenges and opportunities of re-studying community on Sheppey: Young people's imagined futures. *The Sociological Review*, 60(3): 498–517.

Mac an Ghaill M (1988) *Young, Gifted and Black*. Milton Keynes: Open University Press.

MacLure M (2011) Qualitative inquiry: Where are the ruins? *Qualitative Inquiry*, 17(10): 997–1005.

Madison DS (2011) *Critical Ethnography: Method, Ethics, and Performance*. London: Sage.
Maines D (2001) *The Faultline of Consciousness: A View of Interactionism in Sociology*. New York: Aldine de Gruyter.
Mair M, Watson PG, Elsey C and Smith PV (2012) War-making and sense-making: Some technical reflections on an instance of 'friendly fire'. *The British Journal of Sociology*, 63(1): 75–96.
Malinowski B (1922) *Argonauts of the Western Pacific*. London: Routledge.
Mason J (1996) *Qualitative Research*. London: Sage.
Merton RK (1972) Insiders and outsiders: A chapter on the sociology of knowledge. *American Journal of Sociology*, 78(1): 9–47.
Miles MB and Huberman AM (1994, 2nd edition) *Qualitative Data Analysis: An Expanded Sourcebook*. Thousand Oaks, CA: Sage.
Mills CW (1959) *The Sociological Imagination*. Oxford: Oxford University Press.
Mizen P (2005) 'A little light work?' Children's images of their labour. *Visual Studies*, 20(2): 124–39.
Mizen P, Bolton S and Pole C (1999) School-aged workers. *Work, Employment and Society*, 9(13): 423–38.
Moore R (1977) Becoming a sociologist in Sparkbrook. In: Bell C and Newby H (eds) *Doing Sociological Research*. London: Allen and Unwin.
Morrison M and Galloway S (1996) Researching moving targets: Using diaries to explore supply teachers' lives. In: Lyons ES and Busfield J (eds) *Methodological Imaginations*. Basingstoke: Macmillan.
Neal S and Walters S (2008) Rural be/longing and rural social organizations: Conviviality and community-making in the English countryside. *Sociology*, 42(2): 279–97.
Neuman WL (2011) *Social Research Methods*. London: Pearson Education.
Newby H (1977) *The Deferential Worker: A Study of Farm Workers in East Anglia*. London: Allen Lane.
Newby H (1985) *Green and Pleasant Land? Social Change in Rural England*. London: Wildwood.
Newby H (2008) Reflections on Colin Bell and the past and future of community studies. *International Journal of Social Research Methodology*, 11(2): 93–6.
O'Connell Davidson J (2008) If no means no, does yes mean yes? Consenting to research intimacies. *History of the Human Sciences*, 21(4): 49–67.
O'Connor H and Goodwin J (2004) 'She wants to be like her Mum?'. *Journal of Education and Work*, 17(1): 95–118.
O'Neill M (2012) Ethnomimesis and participatory art. In: Pink S (ed.) *Advances in Visual Methods*. London: Sage.
O'Neill M and Hubbard P (2010) Walking, sensing, belonging: Ethno-mimesis as performative praxis. *Visual Studies*, 25(1): 46–58.
Pahl, R (2008) Hertfordshire commuter villages: from Geography to Sociology. *International Journal of Social Research Methodology* 11(2): 103–7.
Pahl RE (2011) Identities and social change since 1940: The politics of method – by Mike Savage. *The Sociological Review*, 59(1): 165–76.
Palmer C and Thompson K (2010) Everyday risks and professional dilemmas: Fieldwork with alcohol-based (sporting) subcultures. *Qualitative Research* 10(4): 421–40.

Parker A (1996) *Chasing the 'Big-Time': Football apprenticeship in the 1990s.* PhD Thesis, University of Warwick, UK.

Patrick J (1973) *A Glasgow Gang Observed.* London: Methuen.

Payne G (1996) Imagining the community. In: Lyon ES and Busfield J (eds) *Methodological Imaginations.* Basingstoke: Macmillan, pp. 17–33.

Pink S (2008) An urban tour: The sensory sociality of ethnographic. *Ethnography*, 9(2): 175–96.

Pink S (ed.) (2012) *Advances in Visual Methodology*. London, Sage.

Pink S (2013, 3rd edition) *Doing Visual Ethnography*. London: Sage.

Pole C (1990) *Records of Achievement in Further Education and the Youth Training Scheme.* University of Warwick: CEDAR Report.

Pole C (1993) *Assessing and Recording Achievement.* Buckingham: Open University Press.

Pole C (1995) Don't shoot the messenger: A study in the politics and control of funded research. *Evaluation & Research in Education*, 9(3): 135–48.

Pole C (1999) Black teachers giving voice: Choosing and experiencing teaching. *Teacher Development: An International Journal of Teachers' Professional Development*, 3(3): 313–28.

Pole C (2001) Black teachers: Curriculum and career. *Curriculum Journal*, 12(3): 347–64.

Pole C (ed.) (2004) *Seeing is Believing? Approaches to Visual Research. Studies in Qualitative Methodology Volume* 7. Oxford: Elsevier JAI.

Pole C (2007) Researching children and fashion: An embodied ethnography. *Childhood* 14(1): 67–84.

Pole C (2010) How could you possibly know anything about that? Methodological congruence in the conduct of life history research. *New Frontiers in Ethnography.* Bingley: Emerald Group Publishing Limited, pp. 161–76.

Pole C and Burgess RG (eds) (2000) *Cross-cultural Case Study*. Oxford: Elsevier JAI.

Pole C and Lampard R (2002) *Practical Social Investigation: Qualitative and Quantitative Methods in Social Research.* Harlow: Pearson Education.

Pole C, Mizen P and Bolton A (1999) Realising children's agency in research: Partners and participants? *International Journal of Social Research Methodology*, 2(1): 39–54.

Pole C and Morrison M (2003) *Ethnography for Education.* Buckingham: Open University Press.

Polsky N (1967) *Hustlers, Beats and Others.* Chicago: Aldine.

Prus R (1996) *Symbolic Interactionism and Ethnographic Research.* Albany: State University of New York.

Pryce K (1979) *Endless Pressure.* Harmondsworth: Penguin.

Robson C (2002) *Real Word Research.* Oxford: Blackwell.

Rock P (1979) *The Making of Symbolic Interactionism.* London: Macmillan.

Roderick M (2006) *The Work of Professional Football: A Labour of Love?* London: Routledge.

Roderick, M (2014). From identification to dis-identification: case studies of job loss in professional football. *Qualitative Research in Sport, Exercise and Health*, 6(2): 143–60.

Sanders C (2008) *Customizing the Body: The Art and Culture of Tattooing.* Philadelphia: Temple University Press.

Savage M (2010) *Identities and Social Change in Britain since 1940: The Politics of Method.* Oxford: Oxford University Press.

Savage M and Burrows R (2007) The coming crisis of empirical sociology. *Sociology*, 41(5): 885–99.

Savage M and Burrows R (2009) Some further reflections on the coming crisis of empirical sociology. *Sociology*, 43(4): 762–72.

Savage M, Devine F, Cunningham N, Taylor M, Li Y, Hjellbrekke J and Miles A (2013) A new model of social class? Findings from the BBC's Great British Class Survey experiment. *Sociology*, 47(2): 219–50.

Scott S (2004) Researching shyness: A contradiction in terms? *Qualitative Research* 4(1): 91–105.

Scott S (2009) Re-clothing the emperor: The swimming pool as a negotiated order. *Symbolic Interaction*, 32(2): 123–45.

Scott S (2010) How to look good (nearly) naked: The performative regulation of the swimmer's body. *Body and Society*, 16(2): 143–68.

Scott S (2011) Confessions of a shy ethnographer. In: *Society for the Study of Symbolic Interaction* (SSSI) *Annual Conference*, Las Vegas, USA.

Sechrest L (1979) *Unobtrusive Measures Today*. San Francisco, CA: Josey-Bass.

Shaffir W and Stebbins RA (1991) *Experiencing Fieldwork: An Inside View of Qualitative Research*. London: Sage.

Shaw CR (2013) [1930] *The Jack-roller: A Delinquent Boy's Own Story*. Chicago: University of Chicago Press.

Silverman D (2013) What counts as qualitative research? Some cautionary comments. *Qualitative Sociology Review*, 9(2): 48–55.

Skeggs B (2001) Feminist ethnography. In: Atkinson P, Coffey A, Delamont S, Lofland J and Lofland L (eds) *Handbook of Ethnography*. London: Sage, pp. 426–42.

Skeggs B (2011) Plenary on class. In: *British Sociological Association Conference*, London, 2011.

Smith B (2013) Sporting spinal cord injuries, social relations, and rehabilitation narratives: An ethnographic creative non-fiction of becoming disabled through sport. *Sociology of Sport Journal*, 30(2): 132–52.

Smith GJD (2012) *Opening the Black Box: Surveillance in Everyday Life*. London: Routledge.

Smith R (2009) Childhood, agency and youth justice. *Children and Society*, 23(4): 252–64.

Snodgrass J (1983) The Jack-roller: A fifty-year follow-up. *Journal of Contemporary Ethnography* 11(4): 440–60.

Sparkes AC (2007) Embodiment, academics, and the audit culture: A story seeking consideration. *Qualitative Research* 7(4): 521–50.

Sparkes AC (2009) Novel ethnographic representations and the dilemmas of judgement. *Ethnography and Education* 4(3): 301–19.

Sparkes AC, Pérez-Samaniego V and Smith B (2012) Social comparison processes, narrative mapping, and their shaping of the cancer experience: A case study of an elite athlete. *Health: An Interdisciplinary Journal for the Study of Health, Illness and Medicine*, 5(16): 467–88.

Spindler, GD (ed.) (1970) *Being an Anthropologist: Fieldwork in Eleven Cultures*. New York: Holt, Rinehart and Winston.

Stacey M (1960) *Tradition and Change: A Study of Banbury*. Oxford: Oxford University Press.

Stacey M, Batstone E, Bell C and Murcott A (1975) *Power, Persistence and Change: A Second Study of Banbury*. London: Routledge.

Stephens N and Delamont S (2006) Balancing the Berimbau embodied ethnographic understanding. *Qualitative Inquiry*, 12(2): 316–39.

Stephens N and Delamont S (2009) 'They start to get *malicia*': Teaching tacit and technical knowledge. *British Journal of Sociology of Education*, 30: 537–48.

Stephens N and Delamont S (2010) Roda Boa, Roda Boa: Legitimate peripheral participation in diasporic capoeira. *Teaching and Teacher Education* 26(1): 113–19.

Strangleman, T (2004). Ways of (not) seeing work: the visual as a blind spot in WES?. *Work, Employment & Society,* 18(1): 179–92.

Stronach I and MacLure M (1997) *Educational Research Undone: The Postmodern Embrace*. Buckingham: Open University Press.

Strong P (1988) Minor courtesies and macro structures. In: Drew P and Wootton A (eds) *Erving Goffman: Exploring the Interaction Order*. Cambridge: Polity.

Thomas J (1993) *Doing Critical Ethnography*. London: Sage.

Thomas WI and Znaniecki F (1918–20) *The Polish Peasant in Europe and America*. Boston: Richard G Badger, The Gorham Press.

Thrasher F (1927) *The Gang*. Chicago: Chicago University Press.

Thrift N (2005) *Knowing Capitalism*. London: Sage.

Thrift N (2008) *Non-representational Theory: Space, Politics, Affect*. London: Routledge.

Thrift N (2012) The insubstantial pageant: Producing an untoward land. *Cultural Geographies*, 19(2): 141–68.

Travers M (2007) Sentencing in the children's court: An ethnographic perspective. *Youth Justice* 7(1): 21–35.

Travers M (2009) New methods, old problems: A sceptical view of innovation in qualitative research. *Qualitative Research*, 9(2): 161–79.

Trevino J (2003) *Goffman's Legacy.* Lanham, MD: Rowman and Littlefield.

Tummons J (2014) Using software for qualitative data analysis: Research outside paradigmatic boundaries. In: Hand M and Hillyard S (eds) *Big Data? Qualitative Approaches to Digital Research*. Bingley: Emerald.

Uprichard E (2008) Children as 'being and becomings': Children, childhood and temporality. *Children & Society*, 22(4): 303–13.

Uprichard E (2010) Questioning research with children: Discrepancy between theory and practice? *Children and Society*, 24(1): 3–13.

Wacquant L (2003) *Body and Soul: Notebooks of an Apprentice Boxer.* Oxford: Oxford University Press.

Walford G (2004) Finding the limits: Autoethnography and being an Oxford University proctor. *Qualitative Research*, 4(3): 403–17.

Walford G (2009) For ethnography. *Ethnography and Education*, 4(3): 271–82.

Warren L, Gott M and Hogan S (2010) Representing self-representing ageing: Look at me! Images of women & ageing. New Dynamics of Ageing findings: 10. http://www.newdynamics.group.shef.ac.uk/nda-findings-10.html [accessed 24 June 2015].

Watson CW (1999) Introduction. In: Watson C (ed.) *Being There: Fieldwork in Anthropology*. London: Pluto Press, pp. 1–24.

Webb, EJ, Campbell, DT, Schwartz, RD and Sechrest, L (1966) *Unobtrusive Measures: Nonreactive Research in the Social Sciences* (Vol. III). Chicago: Rand McNally.

Weber M (1948) [1919] Science as a vocation. In: Gerth HH and Mills CW (eds) *From Max Weber*. London: Routledge.

Weber M (1949) *Objectivity in Social Science and Social Policy*. New York: Free Press.

Wieder DL (1974) Telling the code. Ethnomethodology. In: Turner R (ed.) *Ethnomethodology: Selected Readings*. Harmondsworth: Penguin Education, pp. 144–72.

Whyte WF (1993) [1943] *Street Corner Society*. Chicago: Chicago University Press.

Wiles R, Crow G and Pain H (2011) Innovation in qualitative research methods: A narrative review. *Qualitative Research*, 11(5): 587–604.

Willis P (1977) *Learning to Labour*. Farnborough: Saxon House.

Willis P and Trondman M (2000) Manifesto for ethnography. *Ethnography* 1(1): 5–16.

Wolcott HF (1994) *Transforming Qualitative Data: Description, Analysis, and Interpretation*. Thousand Oaks, CA: Sage.

Wolcott HF (2005, 2nd edition) *The Art of Fieldwork*. Lanham, MD: AltaMira.

Wolcott HF (2010) *Ethnography Lessons: A Primer*. Walnut Creek, CA: Left Coast Press.

INDEX

Page numbers in italics denote figures

CPSIA information can be obtained
at www.ICGtesting.com
Printed in the USA
JSHW012047020822
28819JS00002B/20

9 780761 959649